Sekhet

Irene Miller

THE ANCHOR PRESS, LTD., TIPTREE, ESSEX.

CONTENTS

CONTENTS

SEKHET

DRAMATIS PERSONÆ

SEKHET: *The Goddess of Ancient Egypt, who presided over Love and its Cruelty.*

HER TOOLS AND HER VICTIMS.

Morris Kenyon.
Leopold Stornway (*his college friend*).
Evarne (*Stornway's daughter*).
Tony Belmont.
Lucinda " Belmont."
Geoffrey Danvers (*a young artist*).
Jack Hardy } (*Geoff's studio friends*).
Frank Pallister
Philadelphia Harbert (*an artist's model*).
Maudie Meridith and her Auntie.
Alexander Punter (*manager of the " Scotia's Bard" Touring Co.*)
Mrs. Punter (*authoress of the play*).
John Montgomery (*a printer*).
Joe Harold (*a commercial traveller*).
Archie (*a horsey youth*).
Harry Douglas (*an ex-prize fighter*).   (*Members of the*
Charles Stuart (*a scene-painter*).   *" Scotia's Bard"*
Jessie Kennedy (*a little pianist*).   *Co.*)
Madame Cheape (*an "actress"*).
Mr. Heathmore (*a real actor*).
Mrs. Burling
Mrs. Sargeant   } (*Landladies*).
Miss Brodie
Mrs. Shiells
Jean Brodie (*a seamstress*).

Many minor characters.

SCENES.

The depth of the country, London, Italy, Paris, Egypt.

SEKHET

CHAPTER I

BORN TO BEAUTY

EVARNE Stornway hurried across the fields towards Heatherington at a speed that deprived her gait of much of that graceful yet somewhat insolent sway that caused it to be alike the butt and the envy of the other youthful females of the neighbourhood. Not an hour since she had first heard beyond a doubt the gentle rustling of the wings of the Angel of Death within the sick-room of her father, and, goaded by cruel anxiety, she was—even against the invalid's will—seeking medical aid.

The rapid walk brought brightness to eyes and cheeks, thereby doing much to restore that subtle air of perfect health and happiness that usually added so much to the girl's beauty. But always was Evarne fair to behold ; her dark eyes, so large and limpid, were expressive and intense ; her lips, alluring in curves and colour, spoke to the " seeing eye " of both kindliness and individuality. Yet she could have dispensed with all the charm given by mental grace, and still riveted attention, for she possessed loveliness of that type, supreme above all others, that is independent of expression—the beauty of grace, symmetry of form, and faultless feature. And for this she had been taught to thank—not chance, not merely heredity, but the determination of her father.

Leopold Stornway had a passionate adoration for

physical beauty, regarding it as almost the first of virtues.
And more, he was proud of the vast importance he placed
on bodily perfection, for was it not a reverence characteristic of classic Greece? There it was—in the records of
the never-to-be-forgotten days of antiquity — that Leo
found all his chief interests. Egypt, Mesopotamia, Rome,
and, above all, Greece—each in turn had been the lands of
his adoption. Pericles and Cæsar, Cyrus and Rameses,
Shalmanesur and Hiram, were the gods of his idolatry.
He knew and cared more concerning the triumphant
fortunes of Semiramis ; the proceedings of Antigone or of
Theseus ; the adventures of Agamemnon or Achilles, of
Hector or the pious Æneas at the Siege of Troy, than he
did of the doings of those who sat in the seats of the mighty
in his own century.

The happiest time of his life had been his three years at
Oxford. Almost immediately on leaving college he married
—simply because she was beautiful as any Greek statue—
a young woman considerably beneath him in station, and
possessed of an unconquerably violent temper. He knew
right well, even during the period of his deepest infatuation,
that he had found no mate for his soul. He was sadly
conscious that that part of his mind—of his spirit—that
he cared for most deeply, never would—never could—
unveil itself to the scrutiny of his chosen life-long companion.

To feed his intellectual affections, he relied on the continuance of his college friendship with the brilliant and
vivacious Morris Kenyon. But herein he was doomed to
disappointment. After a brief spell of vain struggling for
literary recognition in London, Leo settled down, contentedly enough, to obscurity in the depth of the country.
There he spent peaceful days occupied in highly intellectual
yet miserably paid writings. Each year he became more
of a recluse—more out of touch with the times. Morris
Kenyon likewise altered. Plunged into the vortex of town

life, seeing and doing everything, going everywhere, courted and flattered and popular, not only on account of his great wealth but for his more personal attractions— every year he drifted farther from being the Morris of yore. The change in both men was but gradual, and through varying stages of disillusion and disappointment, their ardent friendship was long in dying. But the time came when all ended—even correspondence ceased.

Leo's marriage was more successful. His wife made strenuous efforts to rise to his heights, while his admiration of her stately loveliness never waned. Their first child was a boy, who died in infancy, but ere long little Evarne came as consoler. Leo had wished for a daughter, and had always spoken of the expected baby by the Greek name he had already chosen for her—Evarne.

He had strong theories on pre-natal influence, and put them into practice. He read and discussed with his wife poetry and the noblest prose works. Everywhere she turned her eyes in her home she beheld representations of female beauty—magnificent or placid. On the wall of her bed-chamber was a barbaric, richly-hued painting of a Babylonian slave-market. It showed a group of women decking themselves before entering the Market Square, which could be seen through an opening of the tent. They were of many nationalities, but each in her own way represented physically perfect womanhood.

Near to this hung a contrasting picture—a delicate symphony in blue and gold and snowy white. It was the Catholic's Madonna, with placid lips and large uplifted eyes that told of thoughts beyond this world—chaste, calm and pure.

In the corner of the room by the window stood a large cast of a famous antique nude statue of Venus. So perfect was it—the glorious muscles of the body dimpling so gently, so graciously—that even Leo's unimaginative wife could find and feel something of what is soothing and peace-giving in such beauty. Sometimes of an early morning a narrow beam of light would creep into the darkened room between the drawn curtains and illuminate just this statue. Then the young wife, lying wakeful, would fix her eyes on the form of the Goddess of Beauty, drinking in its divine influence, remembering her husband's assurance that its contemplation would go far towards making the little daughter that was to come likewise strong and beautiful.

And Leo's words proved not untrue—a more lovely baby never saw the light. But Evarne's birth cost the mother her life, and after five years of happy marriage, Leo was once again lonely.

Since the child's upbringing was thus left to her father, with his fads and fancies, it was naturally of a unique nature. Mrs. Jarman—the worthy matron whom he engaged to act as nurse to his child, and cook-housekeeper to himself—was wont to declare, both to her gentleman in person and to the village in general, that she was sure Providence had seen fit to appoint a special angel to guard that blessed motherless mite ; otherwise no mortal woman could possibly have succeeded in rearing it.

Mr. Stornway *would* interfere in what Mrs. Jarman held to be no concern of any man—not even of a father. First of all he had been divided in opinion as to whether the infant should be wrapped in swaddling-clothes in true classical style, or should remain in equally classical nudity. The baby had arrived in the summer-time, so the latter idea prevailed, and to Mrs. Jarman's dismay the little one passed the first few months of its existence clad in very little more than its own silky skin. All the experienced dame's traditional ideas of long robes, binders, shortening-clothes, teething-rings, etc., were swept aside as *modern*. Thus they were unworthy of a Greek reincarnation, named after the fairest of the Nereides, and destined to show an altogether degenerate world what beauty had been in the glorious days of old. With the approaching chill of winter even Mr. Stornway agreed to the little form being warmly clad, but his aversion to modern fashions never could be uprooted.

Thus, though Evarne, as she now hastened to summon the doctor to her father's dying bed, was nigh seventeen, she had never owned a pair of corsets, or worn a dress more tight-fitting than could be managed by shaping the material into the waist by gauging or smocking. Indoors, she invariably cast aside her shoes and stockings. She could carry burdens on her head, could run, jump, and swim with the ease and lightness of a young Amazon. She slept soundly on a bed hard as wood, and had never been indulged to the extent of a pillow in her life. Of her own accord she would never have chosen such a harsh *régime*. But at sixteen she knew but this one mode of existence, and habit rendered it congenial enough

CHAPTER II

A FRIEND IN NEED

D R. CROSSWAYS was at home, and at once set out with the girl for " The Retreat." He was a surly old man, and, moreover, he had a particularly annoying habit—of which no amount of gentle correction could break him—of pronouncing Evarne's name without the final " e," thus compressing it into two syllables instead of three, as it is in the musical tongue of ancient Greece, whence the name was taken. As a rule, the doctor was morose and silent, but on this occasion he had at least one piece of gossip to enlarge upon.

On the previous day he had indulged himself in a holiday on the strength of an invitation from the noble lord who had rented the shooting on a big estate some twenty miles distant. Evidently it had been a proud and happy occasion for the little doctor, and it was with ill-concealed gratification that he rattled off the list of those who had likewise been at this illustrious shooting-party. In it was one name very familiar to Evarne—Morris Kenyon. She had never seen her father's early friend, but Leo often dwelt lovingly upon his college life, and Morris Kenyon had been, apparently, the central figure of those never-to-be-forgotten days.

Dr. Crossways took his departure from " The Retreat " in a state of high dudgeon. Accustomed as he was to being called in to cope with every trivial ailment of the local gentry, his professional pride was outraged by Mr. Stornway's presuming to approach so very near to Death's portals without his steps having been carefully guided down the path thereto by the controlling hand of a disciple of Æsculapius. It was absolutely insulting—it really bordered on Christian Science !

After parting from the irate doctor, Evarne returned to her father's room. He raised his weary eyelids as she entered, and looked at her with a troubled, almost remorseful, expression. He had realised vaguely for some time past that he was soon to seek the society of his dearly beloved heroes of antiquity ; but not until this solemn medical visitation had he seriously considered the practical earthly results of his soul winging its flight to the fields of Asphodel.

When once he should be fairly off upon this interesting journey, his young daughter would be left quite alone in this world of sin and woe. What was to become of her ? He was singularly devoid of relations. A few distant cousins and a poverty-stricken and decrepit uncle comprised his entire stock in that line of goods, while he knew nothing of his wife's common family beyond the fact that she had a number of half-brothers and sisters somewhere in Australia. He had but little money to leave his daughter, and the girl had no training in any means of earning a livelihood. He sighed despondently, as too late he recognised this neglected duty.

Evarne sat down by his side, and tenderly stroked his hand. Ere long out came her little bit of interesting news —Mr. Morris Kenyon was within twenty miles of Heatherington.

At the mention of this familiar name a sudden light flashed into poor Leo's worried eyes. Surely for " auld lang syne " this once dear friend would look after his young daughter until she was able to support herself ? Morris was married to a charming wife—unfortunately now a confirmed invalid. Leo had met the young lady at the time of her wedding, and been favourably impressed.

Surely she would feel for the desolate situation of the young orphan. Filled with this idea, he bade Evarne write, telling of her father's condition, and begging that Morris would spare time to come over to visit him.

The letter was duly posted that night; the answer arrived by return, the day after, Morris himself appeared upon the scene. Leo wished to see his friend alone, so on his arrival he was ushered by Mrs. Jarman direct to the sick-room.

With engaging readiness Morris undertook to watch over the welfare of the dying man's daughter when the time came, and lightly brushed aside the broken thanks. But Leo's gratitude was insistent and touching to witness. He dwelt much upon the otherwise lonely situation of the girl.

" It is such a weight off my mind," he murmured again and again. " I never before realised how I have neglected my duty to the child." And he sighed a deep breath of relief.

" Now, you must see her," he went on, as with a trembling hand he rang a bell that stood by his side. In almost immediate answer to the summons Evarne appeared in the doorway.

Leo had made no mention of his daughter's striking personal beauty. Dutiful, unselfish, intelligent—these, and other eminently desirable mental and moral attributes had he ascribed to her as recommendations in Morris's eyes; but upon the subject of that physical quality that counts for so much more than all the virtues under the sun, the unworldly Leo had been silent. Kenyon had somehow expected to see a stolid, robust, and, to him, altogether uninteresting country damsel, and he with difficulty hid his surprise on beholding the fair vision that answered the summons.

Evarne's manner was touched with timidity, but she was not at all shy. She now stood silent and motionless for a moment, surveying her father's friend with a grave and interested gaze. Then, without waiting for any introduction, she advanced towards him with outstretched hand and a little smile of welcome upon her lips. Kenyon rose, and as he clasped her hand and looked with the eye of a connoisseur more closely into those charming features, he was half-ashamed at the consciousness of a distinct sense of satisfaction in the prospect of playing guardian angel to such a singularly lovely creature.

He left " The Retreat " that evening feeling thoroughly recompensed for the loss of his half-day's shooting, and that just occasionally the fulfilling of the duties demanded by friendship might bring their own reward.

Leo Stornway lingered for more weeks than either he or the doctor had anticipated, but one morning, just at the beginning of the New Year, he was found lying calm, pallid, pulseless. His race was run. Silently and in loneliness the end had come to a silent lonely life.

His desire had been to dispose of his earthly frame in as classical a manner as possible. The notion he would have really revelled in would have been a funeral pyre on the common, with the villagers solemnly running races and engaging in wrestling bouts in honour of his Manes, in true Greek style. This being obviously out of the question, he had set his heart upon the nearest thing possible—ordinary cremation. This urgent desire was found solemnly written on the back of a used envelope.

Hereupon arose trouble for Evarne. The local undertaker, who respectfully yet promptly put in an appearance, was aghast at her intention of arranging for the burning of her father's body. He had no sympathy whatsoever with innovations in his staid and respectable business.

" It's the last thing you will ever be able to do for your dear, dead parent, Miss Evarne," said the dour-looking man. " Give him a solid coffin—it needn't even be oak, we have good lines in elm and ash—but *do* give him a decent coffin, and have him put under the earth like he ought to be ! "

Mrs. Jarman was of opinion that such a departure from conventionality would be absolutely indecent. She also waxed eloquent in another direction.

" I allus thought you loved your poor dead Pa. I could 'ave sworn you wouldn't 'ave 'urt a 'air of his 'ead ! " she repeated again and again, as if Evarne's resolve now disposed of that supposition once and for all.

Dr. Crossways was so sure that had he only been consulted in reasonable time neither cremation nor burial would now be under discussion at all, that he declined to offer the least suggestion of any sort. As to the vicar and the curate, they called together on a visit of combined sympathy and expostulation. Both seemed convinced that a case of cremation must prove a serious inconvenience to the Almighty on the Judgment Day—even if it did not place Him in an absolute dilemma.

Into this general confusion and misery, Morris Kenyon— summoned by Mrs. Jarman—descended with all the *eclat* of the God in the Machine. He arrived at the very moment when the two rival dressmakers of Heatherington, having appeared simultaneously armed with yard measures and black patterns, were quarrelling in stage whispers in the porch.

This weighty matter settled, he proceeded to take all the arrangements into his capable hands. Finally, he sat down to a quiet conversation with the grateful Evarne, the more beautiful for the pallor and distress, concerning her future.

He learnt that her great ambition was to become an artist. She possessed decided talent, combined with an ardent appreciation of the beautiful, but she was absolutely without training, and had evidently no idea of the long years of steady labour—to say nothing of the " filthy lucre "—that must be offered at the shrine of Art by would-be disciples. Looking at Morris, her big eyes filled with a wistful anxiety, she inquired if the little money her father had left could, by the strictest economy, be made to last out until she was able to thus keep herself. If not—and she had evidently come to this conference with her ideas fully formed—could she not learn shorthand and type-writing? Even then she hoped that, by rising early and working at her painting after office hours and on Sundays, she might ultimately earn her living by Art.

Kenyon smiled inwardly at the life she thus proposed for herself. If he knew aught of the world, the sons of Adam would see to it soon enough that this particular daughter of Eve did not spend her days simply and solely divided between banging the keys of a typewriter and daubing sticky colours on a canvas. It was merely his luck that he happened to be first in the field.

To Evarne he appeared kindliness itself. Certainly she could and she should study Art; and this brought him round to a suggestion that he hoped would give her plea-sure. He possessed a delightful villa in balmy Naples, where Mrs. Kenyon was now staying to escape the rigours of the English winter. Evarne must come out and stop awhile with his wife. On the journey through Italy, she should behold all its Art treasures. That alone, he assured her, would form a splendid foundation for her later artistic training.

Despite her sorrows, Evarne's face lit up with a sudden brilliant light of happiness at this altogether delightful prospect, both for the near and distant future. Her brightened expression thanked her guardian more ardently than did her softly-spoken words, and so it was settled.

CHAPTER III

A RICH CASKET FOR A RARE JEWEL

DESPITE the heavy heart with which Evarne bade farewell to her home, the weeks occupied by the protracted journey to Naples became a period in which the light-heartedness of youth gradually conquered sorrow. It was so crowded with interest, novelty, fresh sights and experiences, that every week seemed as a month, and her former monotonous existence faded rapidly into the background. She seemed a different being, living in a strange, new world. It was a world in which Leo had never had a place, so that its progress was in no ways affected by his absence. Evarne mourned her father sincerely ; shed many tears for him in the silence of the night ; and sometimes felt pangs of compunction that novelty and interest should have such powers of overcoming grief. But despite her reluctance to accept their aid, these great forces continued their healing work.

Amid its other charms and novelties, this new life was one totally devoid of the necessity of considering ways and means. The girl's natural tastes were far from simple, and the luxury in which Morris lived and travelled soon seemed not only congenial, but proper and customary.

At Paris, where they stayed some time, she first discovered the subtle delight that lies in the possession of dainty clothes. Her guardian gave her *carte blanche* at both costumiers and milliners, but, through diffidence, she took little advantage of this generosity. Realising this, he visited one of the leading *ateliers*, and gave orders direct to madame herself to lavishly stock Evarne's wardrobe.

Thus the girl found herself clad in garments totally different to any she had ever seen—let alone possessed. She reluctantly consented to try to endure corsets, but very soon gave up the attempt in despair. But madame, far from discouraged, exerted her ingenuity to array the girl's lithe yet well-developed young form to the best advantage without any such fictitious aid, and she succeeded even beyond her expectations.

Never before had Evarne realised the latent possibilities of her own figure. She took unconcealed delight in beholding her reflection in the mirror, and positively revelled in her silk linings, silk petticoats, silk stockings, and other hitherto undreamed-of silken luxuries.

Venice was visited, then Ravenna, Florence, Pisa and Rome. Day after day Morris was untiring in the thought and care he took for his new toy. Evarne, apparently, looked upon his utmost and constant attention as merely part of the accepted routine of the journey, and noted it with the quiet indifference of a spoilt beauty. Yet there was no suggestion of coquetry or affectation about the girl. Her mind, as well as her person, was developing on calm, stately and dignified lines.

She was, in her turn, almost as quietly affectionate and attentive to him as she would have been to her father, but the vainest of men could not have persuaded himself that she made the least effort—open or covert—to at all unduly ingratiate herself into his regard " Kindness in women, not their beauteous looks, shall win my love," sings the wise poet, but Morris had been taught so early and so often how many women are over-eager to be " kind " to a wealthy man, that Evarne's simple ways were attractive by reason of their very novelty. It served as a *sauce piquante*, and before Naples was reached he felt more genuine love for this sweet child than he had deemed that well-worn article—his heart—would ever again have the good luck to experience.

It was not until they were actually in the train bound for Naples that he broke to her the information that the looked-for introduction to Mrs. Kenyon must be postponed for the present.

"A letter from my wife reached me just before we left Rome," he explained. "She is very nervous, and fears Vesuvius is working up for another eruption. She often thinks that—pure fancy, of course! Anyway she has gone on to Taormina, in Sicily. She will return to Naples when she can muster courage."

"How much she travels about," remarked the unsuspecting Evarne.

"Doesn't she!" agreed Morris with a grim little smile, thinking of the invalid to whom the daily journey from bedroom to boudoir was an arduous undertaking.

Then, noting a troubled expression on Evarne's face as she gazed out of the window at the fast-flying landscape, he asked, with a tiny hint of sadness in his voice—

"Am I such dull company for a bright little girl that you look thus solemn at the prospect of a few more tête-à-tête meals?"

He took her hand as he spoke. Evarne had long ago got to the point of finding it pleasant to feel her slender fingers enclosed in his strong magnetic clasp. She smiled a little and shook her head slightly in response to his question, but the fingers he held moved restlessly, as if they half-sought to free themselves.

Evarne's mental upbringing and education had been as unusual and unconventional—to say the least of it—as had been her physical training. She learnt the Greek and English alphabets almost simultaneously, and while other damsels of her years were skimming through novelettes, she had been poring over the eternal and inspiring works of the writers of antiquity. Which form of exclusive mental diet created, on the whole, the most impracticable, the most false, the most mischievous ideas when considered in reference to the stern realities of modern life, it is difficult to say. Infinitely more than the average girl of her age did Evarne know of the possible sins of humanity, of the grim tragedies of history ; infinitely less of that perhaps more useful field of knowledge—the restrictions, petty malignity, wickedness, and cruelly quick suspicions of modern society.

Nevertheless, an instinct told her that there was a vast difference between travelling under the escort of her guardian to join his wife, and in staying with him at his villa without that lady.

" Do you not think Mrs. Kenyon expects us to go on to her at Sicily ? " she suggested in a hesitating voice, divided between her fear of appearing to presume and dictate, and her instinctive shrinking from this new programme.

Morris read the trouble in the girl's mind, and promptly answered in the one and only manner that was calculated to set her thoroughly at ease again.

" When you are comfortably fixed up at Naples I will go on to Taormina and bring back the truant. As to you, my dear, forgive my plain speaking, but it is time you seriously started to study for your future profession. There are excellent Art masters at Naples, and you can draw in the museum there, but in Sicily there is nothing of all this."

As he had foreseen, this business-like view of the proceeding reconciled her to it as nothing else would have done, and it was with a light heart and a smiling face that she first set foot over the threshold of " Mon Bijou."

Morris himself conducted his little guest to the rooms that had been prepared for her occupation. The villa was situated on the heights overlooking the bay, and Evarne, stepping out on to the verandah, stood enthralled by the beauty around. She gazed over the broad expanse of purple sea sparsely dotted with small sails, white and

brown—at the island of Capri, haunted by the memory of
dark mysteries—at the far distant dome of the Italian
heavens that crowned all. Then she let her delighted eyes
wander over the picturesque roof-tops of the town to the
soft yet never-failing canopy of smoke that mingled itself
with billowy white clouds overshadowing the crater of
Vesuvius the volcano.

Then she looked at the gardens of the villa itself. There
she saw paths made of smooth-coloured pebbles arranged
in mosaic designs, winding amid strange and luxurious
trees and shrubs and blossoms ; saw snowy statues gleaming amid the green growth ; saw arbours, set near the
scent of orange-blossom or mimosa ; while a white marble
fountain—an art treasure in itself—gaily tossed upwards
a sparkling jet of water, which fell with a gentle splash
into a deep, carved basin encircled by thick clumps of
flowers.

Overwhelmed by beauty so universal, so lavish, so
abundant, she stood rapt until Morris's patience was
exhausted. When at length she could be persuaded to
pay attention to her apartments she found them, in their
way, to be equally enchanting—equally appealing.

The chief room was very large, and decorated with an
almost florid luxuriance. Everywhere the eye turned
were pictures, statuettes, carved ivories, bowls and vases
and bronzes—each the embodiment of some artistic dream.
Everything was profuse—there were many books, many
mirrors, much gilding, carving, tapestry and embroidery,
while masses of vivid flowers scented the air.

The characteristic feature, however, was the mad riot
and mingling of every glaring hue, blended together into a
bewildering yet exquisite harmony. There was mauve and
deepest violet, gold, blue, and a touch of emerald green.
The walls were rich crimson, with creamy white introduced
into the deep frieze, whereon dancing maidens were moulded
in relief. The whole scheme of colour was daring, brilliant,

defiant ; it suggested life, youth, vitality, pleasure without remorse.

The little bedroom opened out from this.   It was daintily small, all white and pale green, the one striking splash of colour being given by a bowl of pink roses.   Simple, demure, unassuming, it formed a strange contrast to the tropical violence of its neighbour.

As soon as Evarne was quite alone she placed herself in the centre of the brilliant red room, and pivoting round slowly, surveyed every wall—every corner—anew.   It was scarcely three months since she had left the austerity of " The Retreat "—three months in which she had learnt, seen, done and heard more than in all the previous years of her life.   In the dazzling luxury of this room the culminating point of the extraordinary difference between the past and the present seemed to be attained.   Its mad superabundance of wealth and colour, appealing so forcefully to the emotions, bewildered the child.   Everything about it appeared indefinably wrong—almost unnatural— and for a moment the instinctive fear of the unknown gripped her heart.

Suddenly she became apprehensive, afraid of life, of the hidden future and what it held.   She felt very young, very ignorant, very helpless—a stranger not only in a far land, but in a strange world.   If only Mrs. Kenyon had been here to welcome her !   Apparently no one about the place could speak a word of English save Morris himself— and, of course, his valet.   Even with the bright little maid who was to attend on her, she had found she could only converse by signs.   She walked timidly over the thick, yielding carpet and leant against the open window, breathing deeply of the fresh, pure air.   But a little while and her natural courage rallied, the shadow of depression was tossed aside ; she turned back into the room, glanced round it once again with sparkling eyes lit up by admiration, and all unconsciously broke into a snatch of joyous song,

CHAPTER IV

THE WAY OF A MAN WITH A MAID

NO trace of the uneasiness of the afternoon remained, as Evarne—clad in a Parisian triumph, a loosely-falling dinner-gown of fragile black chiffon and lace—took her seat that evening opposite Morris in the cosy little anteroom in which he had ordered meals to be served in preference to the ordinary dining-room. She was bright and smiling and appreciative, as throughout that first evening beneath his own roof he exerted himself particularly to please and entertain her.

Not that this called for much additional effort. Evarne invariably found her guardian's society to be more inspiring and exhilarating than his own champagne. Even in his ordinary converse with this unusual young girl, the whole of his knowledge of men and matters, his wide experience, his original ideas, all his natural wit and brightness ever flowed forth readily and unrestricted. True, this implied not only the teachings of some doctrines more or less heretical, but a certain element of looseness of speech and the recounting of anecdotes and incidents not usually deemed appropriate to the ears of sweet seventeen.

So, albeit the previous delicacy of her every thought unavoidably gave place to something less ethereal, her character developed and matured by leaps and bounds. " Reading maketh a full man, conversation a ready man." The girl's nature—rendered, perhaps, somewhat over-serious by solitude and much deep reading—only needed the mental stimulant of a brilliant and clever man's society,

to grow rapidly bright and alert.   She learnt to find interest
in many a subject hiterto sealed.   From dress to politics—
from hard facts to vague fancies—from logical deducing to
limitless speculating, her mind was daily led over fresh
fields and pastures new, and rejoiced in this wandering.

Morris and Evarne sat up later that night than they had
ever yet done together.   Within these walls Morris alone
held sway, and both felt the subtle influence of this state
of affairs, so opposed to the constant, comparative sur-
veillance of life in hotels.   At length the musical notes of
the clock chimed the hour past midnight, and Evarne
sprang from her low chair, startled by the flight of
time.

Morris went upstairs with her.   Standing on the threshold of her room she touched the knob of the electric
burners, then held out both hands with her usual frankness
to bid him good-night.

He held them for a few seconds with that firm and
affectionate clasp in which she so delighted.   But then,
suddenly transferring both her hands into one of his, he
put the first two fingers of his free hand to his own lips
and immediately pressed them gently upon Evarne's rosy
mouth.

It was at most a mere suggestion of a kiss, yet with a
startled glance she jerked her hands away, stepped back
quickly, instinctively slamming the door, and Morris,
standing outside with a little grimace of amusement on
his countenance, heard the key turn in the lock.

It was apparently a decided rebuke, yet he went downstairs well pleased by the very violence of her reception of
this experimental advance.   Easily enough had he conquered any temptation to kiss the girl as long as there
remained the fear that she might accept his kisses dutifully,
as mere fatherly salutes.   But the light that had darted
into her eloquent eyes at the simple pressure of his fingers
upon those fresh, unsullied lips of hers, satisfied him that

such an idea—had it ever existed—had been got rid of forever.

Evarne flung herself amid the purple cushions of a big
chair and shut her eyes. Ere long one idea evolved itself
from the tangle of confused thought, and placed itself—
clearly and shamelessly—before the bar of her reason, to be
relentlessly judged. Did she indeed owe all that Mr.
Kenyon was doing for her—was giving her—simply to the
fact that she was Leo Stornway's daughter, or were her
own youth—her beauty—her sex—the real forces that
prompted his generous actions?

Scarcely one second for calm deliberation was granted
her. The very process of actually formulating such a
question, brought into conscious existence a knowledge
that was both crushing and exalting—terrifying and delightful. Doubtless it had been forming itself in her heart and
brain for many a long day, but its appearance as a fully-
fledged fact—something that had to be acknowledged and
reckoned with—came with the dazzling sharpness of light-
ning athwart a summer sky.

Whatever might be the nature of her guardian's feelings,
this one fact she knew all too well. Come what might *she*
loved *him*—loved him devotedly—passionately—with all
the ardour of youth and a nature formed for loving. She
realised that if in his eyes she was not the fairest amid
women, she might as well be possessed of no beauty; if
he did not seek and enjoy her society before that of any
other creature alive, she was worthless in her own sight;
if all this divine emotion that had come to her could touch
no answering chord within his breast, life would be as a
weed, worthless, without colour, perfume or sweetness.

To realise so much during a single tick of the clock was
overwhelming! Instinctively concealing her face in the
cushions Evarne found her breathing oppressed, while as
to her heart—it stood quite still for one brief moment,
apparently daunted by the magnitude of the additional

task suddenly imposed upon it. Then loyally rising to the occasion, it continued to beat, but with altogether unusual violence and rapidity, as wishing defiantly to show that it could bear up with a good grace even under this double duty.

Ere long Evarne sat erect again, while then and there her soul soared aloft into vaporous and shining realms of happiness. Yet no white angel would have veiled its face before this sweet maiden's thoughts and ideals in her first love. Not for some time did she so much as remember that Morris was married, and even then she was in no mood to actively regret Mrs. Kenyon's existence.

That lady's rights were so unquestioned ; Evarne would have shrunk with horror at the mere notion that she should ever come to resent the wife as either a rival or a hindrance.

The fact that she believed Morris was a kind, affectionate and faithful husband, was quite consistent with his returning her love—at all events, love as she conceived it and desired it in return. Notwithstanding her classical reading, the girl failed to realise that her passion—youthful, virginal and absolutely spiritual, yet ardent and enthralling—was an emotion absolutely unknown to any male mind.

Long she sat, enchanted by the fair landscapes of this unexplored country across whose borders her feet had newly strayed. When at length she nestled down into her soft, scented bed, still the same soft visions gladdened her mind.

Next morning, after finishing her coffee and roll, she lay back lazily and reflected with the clearer, more rational, thoughts of the early hours of the day, upon the one topic that now appeared of paramount importance.

After a while Bianca, her little maid, entered, and with painstaking effort repeated in English a short message that she had evidently just learnt. " Master wishes come pay his respects to signorina."

Evarne renounced day-dreams and meditations and

arose immediately. Blissfully independent of hair-curlers or any other such artificial accessories, her toilette could be completed with marvellous rapidity. Now, in considerably less than half an hour, she issued from her room fresh and blooming as a spring flower, and all unconsciously greeted Morris with the richest smile she had ever flashed upon him.

He looked bright and *debonnairé* that morning, and it was difficult to realise that he was in fact the contemporary of the girl's father. He seemed so glad to behold her again after the few hours' separation, asked with such evident interest and concern if she had slept well, held her hand for so long and finished by pressing it so warmly between his own, that Evarne blushed slightly for very happiness, as with unerring instinct her heart answered its own question, " He does care—he does—he does ! "

In her previous notions concerning both men and women who had attained to the mature and dignified age of five-and-forty, she had unconsciously taken it for granted that Cupid always observed a due respect for such elderly hearts. True, she was well-informed respecting poor Hera's troubles. Zeus had surely been old—quite old and grey-bearded—yet apparently he could not ever look down from high Olympus, even on business, without his eye falling on some fair damsel who promptly became entitled to a place amid the crowd of rival fair ones who packed that miraculously capacious heart. Nevertheless, despite this seemingly instructive knowledge, it was only as she grew to know Morris that her ideas became revolutionised on the subject of middle-aged men who were not divinities, but merely modern and mortal. Now, her guardian's years, viewed with the eyes of affection, appeared simply as an additional fascination.

After a while he proceeded to consult her regarding their plans for the day. Would she like to go sight-seeing that morning, or rest after the fatigues of yesterday's journey ?

Evarne was still amused at this novel notion, evidently entertained by Morris, that she was a fragile blossom requiring to be carefully tended and cherished. The idea flashed across her : " How different life will be in a year or two when I am all alone in cheap little rooms in London, earning a precarious living by Art."

This led her to recall what her guardian had told her last night concerning the two most celebrated Art masters in Naples.

" They are very different one from another, both in their style of work and their method of teaching," he had said. " I will take you to visit both studios, and you can see if one appeals to you more than the other."

Now she reminded him of this promise.

" I want to oversee the unpacking of my boxes," she said, " and then, if you please, I should like to visit the studios you spoke of. I want to start working in all seriousness almost at once."

" Oh, no hurry ; postpone that ! " was the lazy advice.

But she shook her head with righteous emphasis.

" I don't mean to delay and delay like the foolish virgins in the Bible. You remember that story ? "

" I can't say I remember those particular damsels," rejoined Morris, with a twinkle in his eye ; " but candidly I maintain that *all* virgins are foolish."

" That's a very debatable point ! " retorted Evarne, smiling, yet slightly biting her under-lip. " Seriously, I want to start work at once. Now, let me go and put on my hat, and we will place business before pleasure, like good people."

This time Morris wisely checked the response that rose to his lips.

The rival studios both got visited that day, and the one wherein Evarne was to experience the pangs and delights of the aspiring Art student was duly settled upon. It was really somewhat absurd that a mere beginner, totally untrained in the very rudiments of drawing, should be introduced into such an advanced coterie as that of Florelli's.

As Evarne gazed with admiring yet somewhat saddened eyes at the work of the other students, she felt this herself. To her they all seemed finished artists already ! She could certainly get herself up in a loose overall plentifully besmeared with paint and charcoal, she could allow a curl of hair to escape from its confining bonds, and thus—as far as appearance went—be on an artistic equality with those of her new companions who were of the feminine persuasion. But would she ever be able to work as beautifully as did these young men and women ? She doubted it, and yet, appalling realisation ! these superior young people were not winning fame and fortune. Alack and alas, they were still studying—still knew their work imperfect—were still striving to attain !

The momentary wave of despair was followed by a somewhat frantic impatience to make an immediate start along this far-stretching road that lay before her. She wanted to return at once to " Mon Bijou," to set up a pot or vase and endeavour to make a drawing of it in which the two sides should at least decently resemble one another. It was all very nice and amusing to sketch pretty little faces with huge eyes, tiny mouths and masses of very curly hair ; to cover sheets of notepaper with angels whose big, feathery wings and vapoury bodies conveniently vanished into nothing. But one day in Paris she had tried to make a correct drawing of a dull, unimaginative vase, and her effort had been brought to an abrupt and highly unsatisfactory conclusion by the much-employed indiarubber working a hole in the paper.

That evening, as she and Morris walked in the garden star-gazing, she honestly confided to him her fear that the attaining of artistic excellence would be a longer task than she had at all realised. He did not appear to sink under the shock, but, on the contrary, inquired calmly enough "what that mattered." Hesitatingly, Evarne broached the subject of expense. It was a matter that pressed rather heavily upon her mind.

His answer was unexpected. Half opening his lips as if to speak, he closed them again firmly, looked frowningly into her tremulous, upturned countenance, then suddenly slipping his arm round her waist, drew her closely to him. Her instantaneous impulse was to free herself—not because she wanted to, far from it—but because she knew well enough that such were dull duty's dictates. Still, she hesitated a moment, and thereby lost the strength of mind necessary to maintain strict propriety upon its lofty pedestal. On the contrary, she rested quite impassive, and Morris felt her soft uncorseted waist heave slightly with the deep, quivering breath she drew. Somewhat fiercely clasping her yet closer, in a second his other arm was also around her, and he was straining the flexible young form to his breast with all the abandon of a man who, having reluctantly practised self-control for long, lets himself go at last.

But his very ardour and heedless violence frightened Evarne immediately. Using the whole of her considerable strength she endeavoured to break away from his clasp. "Don't, don't!" she cried in unmistakable earnestness, and besides genuine alarm there was a touch of decided anger in her voice.

As soon as she had freed herself she stood irresolute—motionless and fascinated—yet obviously prepared at any second to dart away. Indeed, unconsciously, prompted by her athletic instincts, she rested, poised with her heels already slightly raised off the earth.

She looked more Greek than ever at that moment; fitted indeed to form part of some legend—

> "Of deities or mortals, or of both;
> In Temple, or the dales of Arcady."

Morris gazing at her with eager, ardent appreciation, yet read a warning that he must venture no farther that night! Trusting and confiding though Evarne might be, she was too serious, too thoughtful, to accept such overtures with childish carelessness.

Her expression gradually clouded, for the unknown Mrs. Kenyon rose in indignant might before her mind's eye! Morris, guessing the nature of some of her thoughts, knew that in dealing with a young woman possessed of such painfully lofty principles, discretion was indeed the better part of valour. Moreover, he was far too genuinely attached to her to wish to cause her undue distress, and, however strong she might be physically, he knew well that where her feelings were concerned, Evarne was in deed a "fragile flower," to be guarded well and treated tenderly.

So he just smiled calmly and reassuringly, and into his eyes came that kindly, indulgent look that always stirred the girl's very heart.

"Come, pretty one," he said, "hold my hand quietly, and go on telling me the troubles about the drawing."

Such a sudden change of manner and topic was quite bewildering; Evarne could not accommodate herself to it all with equal rapidity. There was a considerable pause, while he stood waiting with his hand outstretched. The imprint of very varying emotions passed over the girl's gentle countenance. By the brilliant light of the moon every fleeting expression could be seen, and the look with which she at length laid her hand in his could not have been displeasing even to the chaste goddess whose clear rays rendered it visible.

Somewhat hastily Evarne proceeded to chatter about the studio, but her nerves were overwrought, and her voice sounded strange to her own ears.

"Let us go in," she urged ere long; "I'm cold."

'Cold now, perhaps," murmured Morris softly, "but, if

I mistake not, magnificently capable of burning with the most divine of all fires."

She made no answer. He could not be sure that she had heard, or if she had, that she understood. Neither was he at all sure that the time had even yet come when it was really desirable that she should hear and understand

CHAPTER V

THE WILES OF THE FOWLER

WITHIN a week of taking up her residence at " Mon Bijou," Evarne started her career at Florelli's. She proved very painstaking, and earnest—so much so as to cause considerable surprise to the other students, who had judged, from the luxury of her attire and appointments, that she was a mere *dilettante*.

She was far and away the most elementary pupil in the studio, and truth to tell did not find it particularly interesting to sit alone hour after hour in a corner, covering reams of Michallet, and using up boxes of charcoal in repeated struggles to depict gigantic plaster replicas of detached features from Michael Angelo's " David," or innumerable casts of torsos, of arms and legs, hands and feet, in all sizes and attitudes—painfully suggestive of amputations.

For stimulus and encouragement she would peep into the two rooms where the more advanced students were working from life, in one room from the costume model, in the other from the nude. The mental atmosphere of these rooms was so full of energy and enthusiasm that she would return with fresh ardour to her limbs and features.

Not that she was able to devote all her time to the services of the exigent Muses, nor, alas! could this pursuit arouse the keenest, most engrossing thoughts and energies of which her nature was capable. Interest in this, as in everything else in the wide universe, showed pallid and feeble before the overwhelming and concentrated interest of her love for Morris Kenyon. There was something almost tragic in such a domination. Barely seventeen, her heart and mind should have been still too youthful, too immature, to conceive and sustain such force of emotion.

Morris had many friends in Naples, and both visited and entertained considerably. Evarne, both by reason of her studies and her recent loss, could be prevailed upon to take very little part in any fêtes. Still, she started to learn Italian, and was soon able to express her will to Bianca in all simple matters, and to amuse Morris by her courageous, laughable efforts.

She fancied herself a perfect little diplomatist, and was blissfully unaware that her affection for him was very soon betrayed to his experienced eye by her every look—every word—every action. Under the circumstances, silence on the momentous topic so uppermost in both minds was naturally not maintained for long.

One night as she sat on a footstool at his feet, spoiling her eyesight by delicate fancy work, not speaking much, but at intervals contentedly humming a little song, a sudden impatience at further waste of time took possession of him.

"Evarne," he said abruptly, and as the girl in all unconsciousness stayed her needle and looked up inquiringly, he bent forward, and without any warning pressed his lips to hers. Then, shaken from his habitual calm, he placed his hands heavily upon her shoulders and gazed intently into her eyes, his expression telling yet more than his actions.

She remained motionless as if hypnotised, her face still uplifted. "Evarne, sweetest little Evarne!" he murmured after a pause, in accents tender and caressing. At the sound of his voice she dropped her head slowly lower and yet lower, until it finally rested upon his knee. Still she spoke nothing.

Slipping his arms around her, he forcibly drew her up until her head was pillowed upon his breast. Then he kissed her again and again, kissed her brow, her hair, her cheeks, her mouth.

" Darling, are you happy ? " he breathed at length into her ear.

Upon this the girl released herself from his hold, and kneeling erect by his side, looked with wide-open, excited, somewhat horrified eyes straight into his. It was no highly-wrought sentiment either of love or indignation that fell from her lips. Simply, yet emphatically, she cried—

" Oh, we mustn't ! we mustn't ! We were both forgetting your wife ! "

Morris was rather proud of his versatility, and cultivated the art of being all things to all women. The last lady on whom he had temporarily bestowed his affections had, like Evarne, been tactless and inconsiderate enough to invoke the memory of the happily absent one at a critical moment. To Evarne's predecessor he had lightly remarked, " Oh ! hang my wife, Birdie. She doesn't count." Birdie had giggled, called him a " naughty man," and there had been an end to that topic.

To have addressed any such flippant answer to Evarne and her clamouring conscience would have meant the end of all things. Morris unhesitatingly took the one and only course that would serve his turn now. He adopted the plan of apparent perfect frankness, not only regarding the legal partner of his joys and woes, but concerning much else that he had hiterto kept hidden.

With many a sign of great mental struggle, now flashing forth eloquent glances, now veiling his eyes from her clear, searching gaze, he made confession of his deception concerning Mrs. Kenyon's promised presence at " Mon Bijou." He waxed alternately ardent and pathetic as he discoursed upon the love he bore Evarne and all that it meant to him, vowing that it was the intensity of his affection alone that had prompted him to his falsehood. He abused himself so unsparingly, that half-unconsciously she was moved to utter a pleading little cry of pity and expostulation.

Thereupon he went on to explain in touching terms that he was but a lonely, desolate man, rapidly becoming weary of life, embittered and miserable, until her charm, her sweet goodness, aroused him, awoke affection and brought fresh zest into his existence—and so on, and so on.

" My wife, well, she was a nicely-brought-up, rather silly girl, pretty enough once and good-natured too, but now soured and aged by permanent, incurable illness. There is no bond of any kind between us. We have not a thought in common. There are no children ; she can never be either companion or wife to me. Frail though she is, she has a marvellous vitality, a wondrous clinging to life. Such unhappy existences—a curse to themselves and others, —are always prolonged. Think of it, dearest, think what it means to a man to be practically tied to a corpse, cut off from all the joy of living."

Then he soared to lofty heights of moralising, told her— or at least implied—that all his hopes of heaven rested upon her gentle influence and affection. " I may seem to others but a hard, somewhat cynical man of the world, yet I have got here "—and in true dramatic style he struck his breast over the supposed region of a presumably panting heart—" I have got here a longing for a true woman's disinterested, faithful affection, such as many a sentimental stringer together of rhymes has never experienced. Evarne, care for me a little ; love me, darling. Let me love you. It means everything to me."

All this sentiment quite overcame his sweet-natured listener. Morris had made a studied though carefully veiled appeal, either by his looks or his words, direct to her most generous instincts. If much of it was mere acting— exaggerated and artificial—his passionate desire to gain her love was real enough. It was no reproach to frank, unsuspicious, inexperienced Evarne—already blinded by affection—that she could see only the evident sincerity that inspired all this bombast.

A flood of tender pity and sympathy swelled in her breast; all resentment at his deception, all hesitation and restraint, were swept away. If the assurance of her deep love, her utter trust, did in very truth mean happiness to him, it should be his. Rising to her feet impulsively, she pressed his head with almost fierce force against her bosom, murmuring, " I do love you, my dear one. Indeed, I do love you." Then she bent over, and almost reverently pressed a long kiss upon his brow.

So far, so good, and in mutual love confessed Evarne's ideal was attained! It was rather incomprehensible that she could for one minute have supposed that "finis" would be written in Morris's masculine conception of the old, old story, at a similar point to where it appeared in the poetical version that had been evolved from out her imagination. Yet when, in the course of a very short time, the inevitable discovery was made that he had never entertained the notion of loving her as an "inspiration to a noble life," nor as a "kindred soul," nor as his "good angel," but merely as a man always loves a woman, and that he sought a return of affection in kind, it came as a stunning revelation.

At first Morris had not been at all sure but that she would endeavour to shake the dust of "Mon Bijou" from her feet without delay. In fact, he always declared that, probably inspired by the vicinity of Capri, she had given him to understand that he was on a moral level with the defunct Tiberius. But for her own part her first recollections that were at all clear and distinct were very different.

In all moments of mental disturbance her first desire was for solitude, and in this crisis, bidding Morris not to follow her, she sped wildly out into the dark garden.

There, leaning for support against the pillar of a statue, and gazing up at the serene masses of white clouds and the tinted halo encircling the moon, breathing in the perfume of the earth and its green growth, while a gentle breath of sea-breezes played with her heavy hair, she gradually regained calmness.

Her Greek studies had taught her much—so much that she had believed there was but little left for her to learn. Yet to us all is life an untold tale—strange, unique, unguessed. What wisdom of sage, what sensual raptures of pagan poet, had ever prompted her to anticipate the exaltation, the triumph, that awoke at the realisation that she too had her share in the resistless power of womanhood? She felt plunged into full harmony with nature—felt herself knit to the great heart of woman all the world over by the sentient cords of sex-sympathy.

Carried out of herself she flung back her head and gave utterance to emotion by lifting up her voice in song—just full rich notes that rolled forth unconsidered, all unhampered by words—a spontaneous outpouring of glorification and the joy of victory. Pressing both hands hard upon her bosom she felt the force with which it rose and fell beneath her deep breathing, and strangely delighted, the girl laughed triumphantly with the notes of her song.

A sudden step near by startled her into abrupt shamefaced silence: Morris stood by her side. He had been seeking her in the garden and had traced her by this wild song that broke the stillness of the night. Unrestricted displays of feeling were entirely new to Evarne, her previous uneventful routine having given scant cause for much excitement of any sort. Now she felt keen abashment at her extraordinary show of emotion, and was almost humiliated to realise that she was not alone.

"I told you not to follow me. I don't want you," she said quickly and decidedly.

For a moment Morris was startled ; then he understood the change that was beginning to take place in her mind. No longer was she a simple child addressing her guardian and benefactor, but a woman growing conscious of her own power. Of course she would be whimsical, capricious, alternately authoritative and submissive, wilful and yielding, like the rest of the darlings.

" I meant to obey," he answered with ready meekness, " but can you blame the impotence of mortal man's resolution when the siren calls ? "

Sudden anger flashed over Evarne at this vague suggestion that she had fled from him only to draw him to her side again by her voice.

" I'm not a siren, and I don't say one thing and mean another, though I know you find it difficult to believe that of any woman," she replied curtly, and with head erect walked back through the French window into the brightly-lit room. Once safely out of sight, she darted rapidly upstairs to the safety of her own room.

In a minute or two she heard her name called softly through the door, then the pleading whisper—

" Evarne, I can have no rest unless I know you are not angry with me."

She was silent for a moment, but the delay was brief. No resentment could endure before the music of that dear voice. She guessed right well that a locked door between them was all-sufficient for Morris to endure, so answered him generously, as her heart prompted—

" Rest, then ; rest happily now and ever."

Within the peaceful sanctuary of her delicate green and white bedroom, the chief amid her more normal thoughts and feelings resumed their sway. Foremost came that imperative demand for self-approbation—that pride in self—that made her ever the slave of what she held to be honourable. The spirit of righteousness sprang up alert, quick to wage war against the mere suggestion that under any provocation—any excuse of overwhelming stress of love—she should permit herself to be stained by dishonour.

Strong and self-confident, the girl at last sank to sleep. But her slumber was light, and early next morning she was awake and thoughtful. She acknowledged being glad to have experienced the sensations of last night—glad to have been granted that period of exaltation, and to have revelled in it to the full. It had made all life seem more understandable and interesting—yet it had brought about no wondrous change of personality ! Evarne still remained herself ; still good and conscientious and new to the ways of love ; a young philosopher, and therefore indulgent to the natural frailties of mankind. She esteemed Morris not one whit the less for having shown himself but human ; yet—realising that he could not make her his wife—her conscience and her wishes united in the resolution that love 'twixt him and herself must ever remain a thing ethereal—a poem—a fair dream—a sweet sentiment blossoming only in the soul.

She went to Florelli's as usual, but her studies occupied a very secondary place in her thoughts. All she meant to say to Morris—all he might perhaps answer—all the beautiful sentiments she had to express and which she was sure must appeal so irresistibly to him—all the lofty ideals of her soul that she was going to impart to his—obtruded themselves between her mind and her drawing.

As she dressed for dinner that evening an unexpected shyness crept over her, and it was with quite an effort that she went downstairs. But all imagined difficulties and embarrassments faded like snow before the sunlight of his eyes. Her own danced for joy at being in his presence again, yet there was a touch of stiffness and formality in her demeanour that was new.

Morris listened more or less patiently to her dear little sermons, and with difficulty resisted stopping her pretty lips with kisses. But she was very much on her dignity

that night, so assuring her that she was nothing more
than a sweet, refreshing baby, he merely delivered a
sermon on his own account, with a very different text.

That night the influence of the day's high meditation
rendered her proof against his sophistries, but as time
passed their steady reiteration began to make headway.
Morris unswervingly bent all his powers to gain control
of the situation. The sport amused him. He had nothing
to distract his attention, and the prize was so well worth
the winning that time and trouble were as nothing. He
attempted no sudden decisive *coup*, feeling greater confidence in the weapons of gentle argument and persuasion,
patience and a discreet mingling of ardour and forbearance.

CHAPTER VI

A SOUL'S BATTLE

EVARNE grew steadily more troubled—more unhappy —more shaken in her once firm convictions.
Up to the present, save in a few unconsidered
trifles, she had always obeyed the dictates of her
conscience. Now this prop failed her ; indeed, she seemed
to have two opposing consciences, each struggling for
supremacy.

While one inward voice would desperately recall the
existence of Mrs. Kenyon, the other would reply by scornfully declaring that it was but selfishness, cowardice,
calculating prudence and cold lack of trust, that clutched
hold of the vision of the distant invalid whose finger bore
the only wedding ring that Morris could give, and that
these contemptible qualities used the wife but as a moral
shield behind which to conceal their own mean, hideous
forms. There was no breaking up of a previously happy
home involved, no ruthless destroying of another woman's
peace of mind ; while beyond a doubt she was depriving
the man she professed to love—and to whom she owed
everything—of the only return she could make for all his
kindness and devoted affection.

Obviously this spiritual civil war could not forever
consist of drawn battles between the rival forces. Ere
long even her own self-respect—the chief bulwark of the
defending army—trembling beneath resistless attacks,
was on the verge of capitulation. True, she might have
fled from " Mon Bijou," but convinced of Morris's engrossing love, she could not do this without likening herself

to the snake of the fable, who, warmed back to life in its rescuer's bosom, then turned and stung him.

But unless she thus left Morris desolate, and cast herself helpless and penniless upon the world, she was forced to continue to accept everything—mere food and raiment, let alone luxury—at his hands, and above all to receive daily and hourly that care and devotion that can only be repaid in coin of the same nature. He so obviously delighted in giving; was she, for her part, empty of all sense of gratitude, of all generosity?

Almost she began to deem herself something to be despised, and self-reproaches bordering upon remorse caused the bread of charity to taste bitter in her mouth. At times every sentiment that is most ennobling seemed ranged amongst the forces that bade her let love pay its debt. This veering of the tide of battle was not very visible, even to the man's watchful and experienced eye. His patience was getting exhausted. He had been fully prepared to wait, but with the passing of time, the light in which Warren Hastings regarded the questionable acquirement of his much-discussed Indian fortune became applicable to Morris Kenyon's state of mind concerning his dealings with Evarne. He began to feel " surprised at his own moderation."

Therefore, on coming up quietly behind her one afternoon as she sat sketching in the garden, he overheard with some satisfaction the words she was softly singing as she worked. It was the beginning of Emerson's little poem—

> " Give all to love;
> Obey thy heart;
> Friends, kindred, days,
> Estate, good-fame,
> Plans, credit, and the Muse,
> Nothing refuse."

When a fair maiden beguiles her solitude by dwelling tunefully upon such sentiments, it may reasonably be supposed that they are not altogether uncongenial to her mind.

He announced his presence by covering her eyes with his hands, and lightly dropping a kiss on the top of her head. When she had laughingly shaken herself free he lay down on the grass at her feet, and, plucking a flower, commenced to pull it to pieces.

"You need not have sung that song to the birds," he declared, after a protracted survey of her fair face. "They need no such promptings, sweetest. They do obey their hearts."

"I suppose it is only meant for selfish human beings, then," she answered somewhat plaintively. Then, moved to a sudden impatience at her burden of doubts, she threw her drawing-book on the ground, crying, "But how very futile to speak of birds. There is no comparison. What concern have they with 'good-fame,' or with any other splendid responsibilities? We human beings have got souls—or—or something of that sort, that we must consider, haven't we?"

"You think so!" and the man's tone was mocking.

"And so do you," came the quick retort. "You remember that picture we looked at the other day? You yourself said it had no soul in it."

"That's altogether different. The sort of soul I meant is the gift of the Muses. Come, my Greek girl, have you forgotten what you yourself told me about your precious Socrates and his views on the necessity of 'divine madness' in creative work? Now I, in my turn, assure you that the brightest amid the Nine never bestows souls on those who refuse submission to Venus. Those who will not bend the knee at that shrine remain forever sane—but uninspired! You see, I know more of the classics than you give me credit for."

"Don't you believe that I love you, that you tell me this? Oh, Morris, Morris dear, do understand!"

"Little darling, it is you who do not understand. Your love for me is but that of a sweet child; you know nothing

yet of that irresistible force that dominates the life of the
world. The soul, as you like to call it, that you already
possess, is sleeping. It has slept long enough, Evarne ;
you must not be afraid of its awakening."

The girl shook her head.

" How little you know me, it seems. I could never
care for you more than I do already. I'm sure—oh,
you can't tell—but I'm sure I bear already the very
fullest extent of love that my nature is capable of ever
producing."

" Your believing that only proves the finite capacities
of the powers of imagination ! You see, you cannot even
realise that there may be—and I assure you there are—
possibilities of emotion lying dormant within your mind
more powerful than you can even conceive of at present.
Only those who can, and who will, shake themselves free
from all hampering limitations ever become truly great
in any direction. It is quite useless to hope that the
' divine madness ' of the Muses may be given to you, unless
you are already possessed of courage to seize on true freedom, for that is the only soil in which anything worth
having can ever take root, thrive and grow."

" I don't quite understand," she murmured nervously,
reluctant to believe.

" In refusing to accept the full companionship of the man
who loves you, Evarne, and whom you love in return, you
are simply enslaving your emotions, enchaining them, and
hopelessly preventing their perfect development. The
technique of your chosen Art you will doubtless gain by
time and perseverance, but you are scornfully neglecting
to bring to fruition a far more subtle source of power—
the rich ripeness of soul that alone can appeal to humanity's
soul—the flame that can set blazing the fire that lies at
the heart of the race of man."

Evarne again parted her lips as if to speak, but without
hesitation Morris went on with his homily.

" Whether you set forth to create pictures or books or music, you cannot possibly give more to the children of your brain than is to be found within your own innermost self. Only by having known the most intense, the loftiest, the deepest, in the whole range of emotional experience will you be enabled to put knowledge into your work, and without that, what worth has any work of Art ? Believe me, ignorance cannot possibly ring true—truth alone can live and enthral.

" Now, believe me or not, as you like, Evarne, but I assure you that because of all this, love is the one and only teacher that can really evolve a great artist. Forgive me for thus assailing you on all sides, my sweet iceberg, but your happiness and success are very dear to me. I simply cannot bear to see you thus blindly and ignorantly opposing the unfolding of the bright flower of your genius. As I started by saying, your soul is still sleeping, and it will slumber on until you can become reconciled to letting love awaken it."

A protracted silence followed these last words. Evarne continued to gaze at Morris with the rapt expression she always wore when he was pouring fresh thoughts into her mind. This suggestion of a triple alliance between illicit love, the possession of a soul, and success in Art, possessed all the charms and the startling qualities of novelty.

" You are trying to make me think selfishly," she murmured at last, " but you must never believe that my own progress is of more consequence to me than —— " She looked at him in silence again, and her eyes and her thoughts grew full of tenderness. Clasping her hands together, she went on, " And oh ! if it were, I'm sure, oh ! so sure, that the love I feel for you already is—is—— "

" It is not of the sort that counts."

" But Socrates says that pure love—— "

Morris interrupted her. He felt that this troublesome antique philosopher must be resolutely suppressed once and for all.

" I cannot claim as intimate an acquaintance with the
opinions of that gentleman as you possess, little sage ;
nevertheless, I'll be bound that he supports my opinion.
I can't definitely remember, mark you ; I am only sure on
general principles that no one who taught your pretty,
sentimental rubbish—forgive me, sweetheart—could have
contrived to get himself accepted for so long.   You look—
or rather we will seek together—and I'll warrant that I
find and show you confirmation of my words."

        .   .   .   .

That night Evarne retired considerably earlier than
usual, but unable to sleep, and soon utterly weary of the
darkness and her own tangled thoughts, she resolved to
follow Morris's advice of the afternoon.   She would delve
once more into that master-mind that they had both
invoked as upholding their contrary ideals.

Flashing on the light, she went into the red room, and
returned with her arms filled with the six big volumes of
Plato.   Tumbling them all on the table by her side she
slipped into bed again, and reclining comfortably amid her
soft, faintly-perfumed pillows, drew a volume at random
from the pile, then hesitated a moment before opening it.

She had perfect confidence that in these works of Plato
no sentiments would be found of the nature that Morris
sought.

" My dear one is unwise, after holding up fame and
success as a bribe, to send me to read this—which is my
Bible—and which teaches that happiness lies only in the
pursuit of wisdom, of virtue, of all that is good," was her
thought, as she lazily laid open the pages.   Little did she
deem that her bewildering doubts and difficulties were at
length to be definitely solved.

It is hard to avoid the terrible belief that there exists a
malign omnipotent Spirit at enmity with the race of man ;
an evil Power untiringly concentrated on watching for and
contriving opportunities to work dire mischief—to create

miseries of all kinds—to impose agony of mind and body upon all that has life. Not without some show of reason have there ever been secret sects of devil-worshippers, who recognise the existence of, and seek to propitiate, this force so hostile to humanity, this merciless Something that works with superhuman ingenuity to aid and bring to fruition that which is of itself—evil—to conquer, to destroy, to render impotent all that which is of a contrary nature ; or more terrible still, to bend such to its own purposes, employing all that is best and noblest and sweetest in life and human nature as tools wherewith to work destruction.

Within a few minutes of opening the Oracle, Evarne was sitting erect, all her sleepy indifference and listlessness gone. Throughout all the time of her mental stress she had not appealed to these familiar works. What more could a further study of Socrates do than intensify her desire to remain his faithful disciple ? She had deemed it quite useless to look for special guidance as to which of the two opposing courses open to her really led to the acquisition of true wisdom, virtue, and spiritual beauty. That she should now open directly at one of those strangely rare definite statements concerning right and wrong, was a coincidence so extraordinary that it is difficult to believe that a controlling intelligence had not arranged this apparent chance.

She re-read the sentence upon which her eye had fallen, vaguely wondering how she could ever have forgotten its doctrine. It was a portion of the " Phædrus," and referred to that eternal topic, love, or rather to a certain imitation of the glorious reality. This semblance was characterised as " being mingled with mortal prudence, and dispensing mortal and niggardly gifts," and its dire result was " to generate in the soul an illiberality which is praised by the multitude as virtue, but which will cause it to be tossed about the earth and beneath the earth for nine thousand years, devoid of intelligence."

Naturally, it was not a belief in the threatened aftermath of harbouring this " illiberality " that appalled her. It was the sudden revelation that the inspired Socrates—far from upholding and approving her present discreet line of conduct—would have condemned her for " illiberality praised by the multitude as virtue," as unhesitatingly as she was now willing to confess that she herself held it in contempt ! After the first moment's shock she found comfort in the reflection that the opinion at which she had arrived independently, albeit slowly and reluctantly, found confirmation in the words of this great teacher.

Something outside herself now seemed to take possession of her body, and to control her deeds. Immediate action became imperative. Instinctively, almost mechanically, she sprang out of bed, flung her white silk dressing-gown around her, and sped barefooted along the corridor and up the little flight of stairs that led to Morris's rooms.

There was still a light showing under the door ; quite steadfastly and without hesitation she turned the handle, and when it refused to yield she rattled it violently. Hearing a quick step inside she felt the blood surge to her head, but no suggestion of faltering or regret came to trouble her finally settled conviction. This seemingly wild impulse—being in reality the climax of long reflection—was far from being a transient ebullition of feeling. It was rooted in her will ; and Evarne's will, once fairly turned in any direction, was impervious to conflicting influences.

In the unnaturally exalted state to which her highly-strung nervous system had now lifted her, it would have seemed a mere nothing to have walked into an arena of wild beasts for the sake of the man she loved—easy to have flung herself upon swords to give him happiness—yea, she would unhesitatingly have followed him to hell itself had he beckoned. Are those amid mankind who never knew the " madness " of Eros to be pitied or envied ?

CHAPTER VII

ROSES AND RAPTURES

IN a time of fair summer, amid varied scenes of beauty, the next phase of Evarne's life glided past—vivid, brilliantly happy—as devoid of apprehension or sense of finality as is the dream of a lotus-eater. As the spring advanced, and Naples became over-sultry for those reared in northern climes, Morris took her to cooler regions. Together they wandered through Switzerland and the Austrian Tyrol, and only with the approach of the winter season were they again in residence at " Mon Bijou."

With the ensuing spring, Morris's restless spirit once more asserted itself, and the summer saw them in London. There he held a social position which led him into circles where no man can introduce a woman who occupies the position Evarne now held. But he saw that plenty of diversions and gaieties of one kind and another came her way. She was still interested in her Art, and, happy in love given and returned, she wasted no sighs over those society gatherings from which she was forever strictly tabooed.

Morris studied appearances to the extent of paying an occasional brief visit to Mrs. Kenyon at their country home ; in the autumn, too, he sometimes left Evarne to her own devices in the flat wherein she was mistress, while he joined shooting parties at various country houses. But at the first breath of winter he was quite ready to be coaxed back to the girl's little Paradise on earth, " Mon Bijou."

On their settling down once more at Naples, she was again

seen at Florelli's, bent on making up for lost time. Her
artistic studies had been of necessity but intermittent.
In Morris she beheld her paramount duty ; he had been as
ardent and jealous as any young lover, lamenting and
grudging every minute that Art took her from his service.
He laughed at the persistence with which she continued to
snatch stray hours for drawing. Her future was his care
now, he insisted. He hated to think of those soft, brown
eyes squandering their beams upon inanimate objects.
Why did she want to waste any of the precious hours of
her glorious youth shut up in a crowded, overheated studio,
that stank of paint and turpentine and microbes and
humanity ?

But Evarne had not entirely abandoned the study of
Philosophy for that of Love. She told him, with fascinating seriousness, that in order to maintain the mental
balance that was described as " Happiness," it was necessary to both cultivate and provide an outlet for the intellectual faculties, as well as for those impulses that were
revelling with such joyous abandon amid " the roses and
raptures of vice."

Thus she was sadly disappointed when, within a fortnight
of settling down once more seriously to work, Morris
announced that he was going to Paris for a week or two,
and of course expected her to accompany him.

She had just arrived at one of those stages, so delightful
to pass through in any study, when a distinct advance in
power is felt. The close of each day's efforts left her with
the exhilarating feeling of having surpassed herself—of
having successfully overstepped her previous highest limit.
To abandon her work at this crisis was the last thing she
desired.

" Morris, dearest," she pouted in sudden protest, " why
do we wander about so very much ? It is so delightful
here."

" But I must go to Paris now. I have business."

" I thought you never had to do anything you didn't want to ? Anyway, dearie, couldn't you live without me for a fortnight ? I know how it will be ! If you have got me with you we shall end up by roaming all through the winter, but if I am here at ' Mon Bijou,' waiting for you— why, then, you will return quickly."

Morris protested, but in the end Evarne for once took her own way. It was quite unusual for her not imme- diately and unhesitatingly to set aside her own wishes should they chance to conflict with those of her lover ; on the other hand, Morris always duly consulted her respecting the plans and arrangements of their mutual life, and had never realised how entirely it was his will alone that controlled their movements. Now his vanity was wounded—not so much that she should question his ar- rangements, as that the form the opposition took should actually imply her willingness to bear a separation. It was something fresh and strange in his wide experience, and—to his way of thinking—far from flattering ! What he always expected was the necessity of soothing jealous fears and apprehensions arising from periods of absence of his own making.

Thus he went off with a feeling of displeasure against Evarne that was new. He did not comprehend that it was the very knowledge of the strength of her own affection that enabled her to see him leave the arc of her personal magnetism and influence without feeling any anxiety. In London she had been forced to spend days alone while he was in the company of others—women, high-born, beautiful, no doubt—yet she had never feared for his loyalty. Sweet, blind trust !

.   .   .   .   .   .

Shortly after his return from Paris, Morris showed that he had no intention of spending the whole of the winter and spring at Naples, as he had done during the two previous years.

"I've got a bright idea," he announced one evening. "Let us spend the winter in Egypt, voyaging up the Nile with a party of our gayest, jolliest pals. What say you, Evarne? I know of a dahabeah, built for private use, that has lost its income, I suppose, for now it's willing to let itself out on hire. I wrote concerning it, and here's the answer, together with any number of photographs, both of its personal appearance and its internal regions."

He passed over a pile of papers, which the girl studied with keen interest. Morris, Naples and the studio was a triple combination that it had seemed impossible to improve upon ; nevertheless, Morris, Egypt and a gay, bright party formed a decidedly alluring prospect if an alternate programme for the winter months was not to be avoided.

"Now, whom would you like to invite? We must resign ourselves beforehand to the idea that it will probably be the grand finale of our acquaintance with all whom we honour by our choice. The best of friends invariably quarrel on long voyages."

"You and I will set them such an example that concord and harmony will reign supreme, won't we? *Absit omen.*"

"I really think we may defy Fate on that point, little sweetheart. Now, to business! We can have eight besides our charming selves. Let's ask the Varesios—see what they gain by being able to speak English. Then there are those rowdy Philmers from London—that's four. Then Giuseppe—he'll keep us lively too ; he's like a jolly English boy, isn't he? Not too overwhelmingly polite. Then there's Tom Talling—we must have some more women, mustn't we?"

"I think equal numbers are best."

"Oh, wise young judge! Well, look here, we can transport Talling to heaven as well as Egypt if we like to give him permission to invite that little French girl he's so mad over —Justine Feronnier, she's called. She's a quiet, demure little minx, with curious, flaxen hair. She looks down the side of her nose all the time, as if she had just come out of a convent school. I'm sure you can't dislike her, and I should be glad to do Tom a good turn. Do you mind ? "

" Not a bit. Who else ? "

" Um-m-m, who ? Good gracious, I was forgetting Tony Belmont."

" The man you were with so much in Paris last month ? "

" That's it. He must come, and we will tell him to bring Lucinda."

" Is Lucinda another little minx, like Tom's friend ? "

" Well, she chooses to describe herself as Mrs. Belmont, and it wouldn't be kind to show undue curiosity concerning the date and place of the wedding ceremony. We've settled upon one too many, haven't we ? But Guiseppe is well accustomed to being tucked in as a sort of makeweight, so I declare this parliament prorogued."

" Tell me, what is the dahabeah called ? "

" ' The Waterfowl ' at present, but that's only fit for a houseboat on the Thames. I shall rechristen her ' Evarne the Beautiful,' " and Morris smiled indulgently.

But the girl shook her head, declaring with a touch of coquettish self-confidence that she could not consent to such a name being chosen. One Evarne the Beautiful was quite enough to occupy all his thoughts.

" Then, Lady Vanity, you must exercise your own ingenuity," he answered, and after a moment's solemn hesitation over the rival merits of " The River Queen " and " The Radiant Isis," Evarne decided on the latter name as more appropriate to a craft destined to breast the waters of Old Nile.

Each desired guest accepted the invitation with flattering alacrity, and ere long " The Radiant Isis " was fairly off upon her voyage up the great river of the land of the Pharaohs.

CHAPTER VIII

LUCINDA BELMONT

ALL the guests were quite well known to their young hostess with the exception of Mdlle. Feronnier and Tony and Lucinda Belmont. As Morris had said, there was little, so far as the average observer could discern, either to like or to dislike in the quiet, flaxen-haired, little French girl. Lucinda Belmont, on the contrary, possessed a distinct and striking personality. Erect in carriage, and bearing herself with an air of unassailable self-confidence—with a full bust, and a waist so disproportionately tiny that Evarne surveyed it with mingled scorn and wonder—she was unmistakably what is popularly meant by " a fine woman." Her big eyes, fringed by long, black lashes, were the tiniest bit protruding, whereby they were enabled to roll up and down and round about in wondrous glances, languishing or flashing, according to the requirements of the occasion. Her features were ordinary, yet her vivacity, her animation, together with her carefully chosen costumes, her elaborate coiffure, and the brilliance given by a most discreet and effective use of paint and powder, transformed her into a woman who excited appreciative attention from most men.

Despite her now considerable store of worldly wisdom, Evarne had not got rid of a somewhat unwise confidence in humanity. Tennyson tells how Vivian was able to see evil of one sort or another in the most noble of characters through the simple method of " imputing her own vileness " to the thoughts, the deeds, the motives of others. In the same manner did Evarne instinctively credit everyone

with her own loyalty and honour. Assuredly Justine
Feronnier and Lucinda were both unusually striking
representatives of the female sex as far as appearance
went. But the French girl was understood to belong to
Tom Talling, and Lucinda—politely described as Mrs.
Belmont—had the legitimate owner of that surname in
attendance upon her, so Evarne experienced no unpleasant
anxiety in beholding the attractive flaxen demureness of
the one, or the flashing brunette brilliance of the other.

.　　.　　.　　.　　.　　.　　.

The long days devoted to the uneventful journey of
" The Radiant Isis " through the flat reaches of the lower
Nile were relieved from monotony by the spirit of mirth
that possessed all aboard. Morris had indeed chosen his
companions with discrimination, if frivolity and constant
laughter were what he sought.

Of course each individual was provided with that hall-
mark of the traveller in the East, a hand-camera, and the
results of the snap-shots of these amateur photographers
caused many a shriek of laughter. Morris, Guiseppe and
Signor Varesio had all brought their foils. But neither
Italian had much chance against Morris, who was quite
a champion in this art, to which he owed much of that
slim, youthful-looking figure that was his pride. Then
there were games, dances, visits from Arab entertainers,
fantasias by the crew—all serving to make time pass
delightfully.

Yet, slowly but surely, unhappiness crept in. The
whole trouble had root in the resolute transference of
Tony Belmont's ardent attentions from Lucinda to the
altogether unappreciative Evarne. She found him always
by her side, even when it must have been obvious to
the meanest intelligence that she and Morris were more
than contented alone. At first she bore his society with
outward patience, but soon there came an irritated dislike to this destroyer of so many pleasant *tête-à-têtes*

between herself and the man who still ruled her entire
heart.

Besides, there was the deserted, disconsolate, sulky
Lucinda to worry about, and since neither Evarne's
snubs nor hints, or even actual commands, could drive
Tony back to his neglected privileges, it became obviously
Morris's duty as host to do his best to prevent the forsaken one from feeling too overwhelmingly lonely. So it
came gradually to pass, to Evarne's dismay, that Morris
spent most of his time by Mrs. Belmont.

The girl felt herself so helpless; in the privacy of
their cabin Morris always answered her loving complaints
so gently and affectionately, deploring the fact but insist-
ing on its necessity and its temporary nature, that she
sought at first to be trustful and comforted. But the
time came when she could no longer refuse to see that
her lover was, in sooth, fully satisfied with the present
state of affairs, and desired no other.

Then the days grew full of anguish to the girl. Justine
alone noticed aught amiss, and showed a desire to advise
as how best to cope with the situation. But Evarne
could not bring herself to actually acknowledge that here
she was suddenly plunged into a vulgar struggle with
another woman—and one so coarse, ignorant and inferior
to herself—for the possession of a man.

Instead, all that her youthful wisdom prompted was
to strive to arouse jealous doubts and fears in Morris's
breast. So, for a weary, dreary day or two she was
bewilderingly responsive to Tony's dull talk and banal
and often over-bold compliments. But all she gained, as
her laugh rang out gay and bright enough to rivet attention, was an indulgent smile from Morris, and the irritating remark from Lucinda—

" How splendidly you two do get on together! And
I'll warrant all your little jokes are secret, so that Mr.
Kenyon and I must be resigned to be left out in the cold."

CHAPTER IX

HOW EGYPT WAS RUINED FOR EVARNE

AT length the dahabeah drew up by the wharf of Luxor. From the beginning of the cruise the arrival at this world-famed spot had been eagerly anticipated, and on the very first morning the travellers gaily mounted donkeys and set forth on the short journey to the ruined Temples of Karnak. The spirited animals that they rode—so very different from the poor little European drudges that go by the same name—covered the ground with celerity, the dusky donkey-boys running hard behind, keeping up with difficulty, yet shouting and flourishing their sticks, to urge on any of the fiery mounts that showed signs of a failing lack of ambition to be foremost in the race.

On arriving at Karnak, loud was the expression of amazement at the extent of country over which was spread the ruins of this vast collection of temples, with their halls, their courts, their huge entrances, their obelisks, columns and statues.

" I believe really it would be quite possible that one should lose one's self hopelessly amid all these ruins," declared little Justine, her pale face still flushed from the fun of the amusing gallop.

The only dismal countenance in the party was that of Hassan, their dragoman. This gorgeous and most self-satisfied personage was always rather inclined to sulk when expeditions were in progress. He then looked upon his lot as that of a much injured individual. Morris

knew Egypt well, and his interesting talks on the topic
had made the old history and religion intensely attractive to Evarne before and during the voyage. He now
very rightly considered himself a far more interesting
cicerone than the verbosely ignorant Arab. He therefore
restricted Hassan to the mere business details, while he
himself undertook the task of conducting his guests, of
enlightening their ignorance and training their taste.

As time passed and the day grew in heat, luncheon
became the next item on the programme, and at this
point Hassan, coming into a portion of his kingdom again,
brightened perceptibly. He carefully spread out the
dainty meal in the shadow cast by a great wall, whereon
sculptured pictorial records of the war-triumphs of a
Pharaoh dead for thousands of years still preserved his
royal memory green to posterity. Then, seating the
company, the dragoman waited upon them with satisfied
importance.

After all had recruited their strength for the afternoon's
further exploration, Morris suggested that they should
mount the sandy slope and stone steps that led to the
summit of the pylon—the great gate that formed the
entrance to the whole of the ruins. The view thus obtained
was wonderful, he assured them ; the sun was not too
hot to defy the shelter provided by veils and parasols,
while any cool breezes that might chance to be wandering
around would be more easily found at a height. Thus
encouraged, everyone started with such energy up the
long, severe slope, that within a very few minutes a halt
had to be called, while all stood and panted breathlessly.

" More haste, less speed," declared Morris. " Now,
Mrs. Belmont, you and I will play tortoise to their hare,
and we will just see who gets to the top first." And,
proffering his arm as a support to Lucinda, he encouraged
her to persevere.

Tony, who had been sitting cross-legged on the sand,

sprang to his feet, and with a sweeping bow offered Evarne a similar attention. She accepted it with a smile, and in due course the summit was attained.

Certainly it was worth the trouble. In the background, against the vividly blue sweep of lofty skies, appeared the sharp and clearly-defined outline of the arid, rose-tinted hills, concealed amid whose rocky recesses lay the tombs of the Pharaohs of bygone days. In the mid-distance the wide Nile—here dignified and placid, untroubled by dams, reservoirs or cataracts—flowed calmly and gently, cool even to behold.

Between the water and the temple the eye roved over pastures, carefully cultivated, often of a most vivid emerald, broken by clusters of lofty, feathery palm-trees. In the fields and on the pale dusty roads were Arabs, their many-hued garments adding to the rich brightness of the scene, yet without rendering it at all *voyante*. Over all was the glamour of a dancing haze of golden sunlight.

Near to the pylon, the Old and the New appeared in close conjunction. To the left lay a temple, ruinous yet still massive, and another pylon, far older than the Christian religion, but still almost uninjured by its vast weight of years. Nearer still stretched a wide avenue bordered on either hand by rows of huge ram-headed sphinxes.

To the right of these great works of times long past, lay a tiny poverty-stricken Arab village. It stood in the midst of a thin grove of palms, and was then encircled by an irregular wall of mud bricks. The small houses, also of dried mud, had, for the most part, been erected by their provident builders around the trunks of palm-trees, which helped support the huts, and gave some degree of shelter from the fiery rays of the broiling summer sun. The flat roofs were covered with piles of sugar-cane, amid which played naked brown babies and small ragged children. The terrifying half-savage dogs that defended the village and all its belongings during the hours of night, now basked peacefully in the mid-day warmth, or strolled around the top of the encircling wall.

The summit of the pylon itself, though fairly wide, was rough and steep. Its height was great, and the extensive view accentuated the feeling of loftiness. But Evarne's few years of " softness " and luxury had not sufficed to entirely undo the effects of her early training. The sensation of height had small effect upon her well-trained nerves, and when she wished to gaze particularly into one special little courtyard within the village, she walked boldly to the farther end and edge of the pylon.

As the party had neared the top their ears had been greeted by the sound of numerous voices uplifted in unison ; on gaining this point of vantage the source of these cries could be seen.

Evidently death had visited the village that day, for the courtyard of one of the largest of the small houses was filled with women wailing and lamenting, while little knots of females were approaching with all speed from the entire countryside. Clad in their shapeless and voluminous black robes, with trailing ends leaving clouds of dust in their wake, their heads veiled, their faces hidden in the yashmak, they formed a strange, weird spectacle as they advanced, all uttering concerted cries of mourning that grew louder as they neared the village in which the dead man lay. The European witnesses of this phase of native life were convinced that only the departure to another world of one of the male half of humanity would have sufficed to create such a stir in the surrounding district.

A band of mourners reached their goal. Their arrival was the signal for the already assembled women of the village to wax yet more demonstrative in their display of anguish. The long shuddering moans, the shrill piercing cries, grew louder and more insistent, while dozens of lean brown arms were raised in despairing appeal to heaven, then descended with force upon head or face, and others of the mourners tore frantically at the garments over their breasts.

" It's just as it is drawn on the ancient monuments, the very same ; they haven't changed a bit in all these thousands of years," cried Evarne. She was far more thrilled by this illustration of the realism of Egyptian art and of this justification for that romantic term—The Unchanging East—than moved to sorrow by the conventional mourning of the many wailers.

Evidently the news had spread widely. From all directions black figures bore down upon the village, sometimes in groups of six or eight, sometimes in bodies of thirty or more. Each one on her arrival passed into the low hut wherein the corpse lay, then came out after a minute or so to add her quota to the increasing lamentation for the dead. This business of mourning was clearly still the prerogative of the female sex. No men took any share in it—indeed, the only two existing in the whole place, as far as could be seen, were squatting calmly in a neighbouring yard, unconcernedly holding and milking a buffalo.

Evarne looked round for Morris. He stood just at the top of the slope, Lucinda still clinging to his arm.

" Come along to where I am, Morris," the girl called out to him. " You can see everything much better from here."

He made a movement as if to follow her suggestion, but Lucinda said something in a low voice, whereupon he replied—

" Mrs. Belmont feels too giddy either to walk or to be left alone ; but don't you bother about us, my dear. We can really witness all the fun of the fair quite nicely."

" That chap may have died of fever or smallpox, or goodness knows what," remarked Tony's voice by her ear. " With all these women trotting in to have a last stare at the old boy—why, it's enough to infect the neighbourhood, isn't it ? "

To Evarne the Jealous the health of the whole country-side was as nothing at that moment compared to the fact that when she had directly called upon her lover to join her, Lucinda should have had the assurance to promptly whisper a suggestion that he should remain where he was, and that the wish of her rival should have sufficed to keep Morris from her side.

She turned to Tony.

"Take my smelling-salts over to Mrs. Belmont," she said, opening her hand-bag and producing the little crystal bottle with its jewelled stopper. "Stay by her and look after her if she feels bad, won't you, so that Mr. Kenyon may come here where it is easier to see?"

But a different remedy for overcoming the lady's attack of nausea had already been prescribed. Supported by Morris's arm she had commenced to descend from the height.

Evarne instinctively uttered a little exclamation.

"Let 'em go," suggested Tony. "We don't want to go down yet, do we, Miss Stornway?"

Evarne glanced around at the remainder of her companions. Tom and Justine were seated close together on a stone by her side, apparently as rooted to the spot as ever Theseus and Pitheous could have been; the others were grouped near at hand, all staring downwards with the keenest interest.

Evarne was obliged to agree. Nature had been very neglectful in not imbuing her with the art of scheming and contriving events to suit her own purposes. True, she had now a daily object-lesson in the manœuvres of the adept Lucinda, and without being conscious thereof, her education in this direction was in progress. However, she was still in the very early stages, and could devise no method on the spur of the moment for preventing this hateful division of the party.

She shook her head and pursed up her mouth discontentedly.

" It's very evident that no one else wishes to descend yet awhile," she acknowledged. " Just ask Mr. Kenyon, then, where we shall find him when we do return to earth."

Tony left her side, and as rapidly came back.

" It's arranged that we are to have tea at four o'clock on the same spot where we lunched. Kenyon says let's meet there at that hour, and all wander about anywhere we choose for the rest of the afternoon. If there's anything particular we want to see again, Hassan knows the way about. That's all right, isn't it ? "

She nodded, but dared not trust herself to speak.

" Aren't we tired of this diversion ? " cried Guiseppe, joining them a couple of minutes later, his bright spirit having no inclination to dwell long on aught connected with death.

" The others are not, but that is no reason why you should remain," she answered rather eagerly. " Anyone who does not want another hour at least up here is to go with Mr. Kenyon. Hurry up ! "

She experienced a certain malicious delight in the idea that she had thus counteracted Lucinda's trick, but her self-congratulation was but short-lived. Guiseppe promptly returned to her side.

" Kenyon says Mrs. Belmont's head is too bad to stand my noisy chatter," he explained. " Noisy chatter, d'you hear, Tony, old boy ? My noisy chatter, forsooth ! That to me, the most timid, retiring violet of the whole lot of you," and he set to work to prove his words by causing the very echoes to ring with his clear musical laughter.

Evarne clenched her hands, and a ferment of emotions tore her breast. Of course she had known all along that Morris was perfectly capable of procuring *solitude à deux* in the face of any difficulties if such were his wish. Now this proved it ! It was his will, not his ingenuity, that had failed, when subduing Tony's attentions to herself had been the problem.

CHAPTER X

THE SHRINE OF SEKHET

AT the hour appointed for tea they all headed their course towards the site chosen for meals, and there, already seated on the rugs, comfortably leaning against the wall, were Lucinda and her escort.

"Where have you been?" shouted Guiseppe. "You don't know what we've just been learning, ignorant ones that you are. The columns in the great hall are three thousand five hundred feet high, and——"

"No, no! three thousand five hundred years old," he was corrected.

"Oh, I retire crushed."

"You need a cup of tea to revive your failing mental powers. So do we all." And ere long the spirit-stove boiled away merrily and the general desire was gratified.

"You have indeed missed an interesting sight this afternoon," declared Signora Varesio.

"My unfortunate giddiness!" sighed Lucinda plaintively.

"What have you seen to compensate for it?"

"Oh, we have been over to a little temple—most interesting. But I was fated to receive shocks this afternoon. In it there is——"

"Don't tell," interposed Morris. "After tea we will take them all over and let them make the discovery for themselves. It will delight you, Evarne, I'm certain."

As he spoke he looked across at the girl with that tender

smile that always penetrated to her very heart. It could do much even now to heal that dull ache that would make itself felt despite her belief in his repeated assurances of the fixity of his affection towards her sweet self, and her consequent faith that the affair with Lucinda was a mere temporary flirtation. She tried hard to be reasonable, and so long as she could think that Morris's earnest and serious love was still hers, and that the attraction any other woman might have for him was merely temporary, she felt that—although a degree of anxiety and apprehension was inevitable—she ought to be able to look down from the superior heights of constancy and make allowances for that dancing butterfly—a man's fancy.

Still, this course of diplomacy—laid down by that most successful of royal mistresses, Madame de Pompadour—is difficult and painful indeed when the heart-happiness of the resident on the superior heights depends wholly upon the vagaries of the butterfly. Moreover, Evarne's poor little vanity was receiving a series of severe blows. For so long she had been accustomed to being first and foremost in Morris's regard—to seeing the society of all other women set aside, if at all possible, for her own. Now, despite her combination of trust and philosophy, this new state of affairs was a protracted anguish. She was resolutely brave under it—perhaps too much so to be quite pleasing or flattering to Morris. Even the deep-rooted hatred she bore Lucinda was almost entirely hidden.

When the slight meal was ended and the moment came for once more setting forth, Mrs. Belmont arose with a childishly pretty air of happy importance. " Now I must be dragoman," she declared, and proceeded to lead the way amid the ruined masses of stone and fallen columns. But she was soon fain to confess that she could not remember the track, and called upon Morris for aid.

Smiling, he took the lead. Poor Evarne ! Life seemed to have become a series of heart-squeezings. Her keen

eye noted the smile that was flashed upon Lucinda, and
it appeared to her to be every whit as indulgent and
kindly—almost as caressing—as that which had hitherto
been reserved for herself alone.

It was necessary to cover quite a long distance over a
plain besprinkled not only with fallen stones, but with a
long spiky growth that rendered progress difficult.

" It is well worth this walk," declared Morris, joining
her after a while, " for what we are going to see is the
most perfectly-preserved temple in the whole of Karnak.
It is very small, but one gets from it a better idea of what
these buildings must have looked like in their palmy days
than the larger ruins can show."

" Talking about ' perfectly preserved,' why didn't the
old 'Gyps pickle their ' corpsies ' instead of bothering to
stuff them ? " demanded Tony.

" Don't be nasty," retorted Evarne curtly ; and a few
minutes later the goal was reached.

" Now, go in one by one," suggested Morris, " and
ladies, be prepared for a shock."

Despite this warning, Evarne could hardly suppress a
little cry as she, in her turn, entered alone into the inner
sanctuary of the tiny temple. Its walls were completely
decorated with richly coloured representations of weird
deities and worshipping mortals. There was no window,
but the rays of the sinking sun filtered in through a small
opening in the roof. The chamber was dim and gloomy,
but the one square beam of light was arranged to fall
with concentrated force upon a solitary upstanding statue
in polished black basalt. It depicted a slender woman's
form, surmounted by a cat's head. So perfect was it in
every detail, so realistic, so full of quiet animation, that
for a moment Evarne had believed herself to be in the
presence of something living and dreadful.

Almost immediately, of course, she realised her mistake,
and knew it for what it was—a representation of the

ancient Egyptian goddess Sekhet. Already that day the girl had stood in the middle of an open field—once the site of a great temple, of which the ruins lay all about —and gazed around the extensive circle of large, gleaming, black marble statues of Sekhet that now alone remained to hint at the departed grandeur of this vanished temple.

Evarne's brown eyes had grown graver, and all-unconsciously she had sighed deeply as she stood amidst those numerous Sekhets seated beneath the clear blue sky. They had struck strange awe to her heart, these symbolic counterfeits of the goddess who presided over the most powerful—the most eternal—forces in heaven and earth, Sekhet—goddess both of Love and of Cruelty ! Ah, they were a subtle people, those ancient Egyptians, skilful in reading the heart of humanity, fearless of the truth, defiant in stripping the gloss from life !

The light laughter and exclamations of her companions had jarred upon Evarne's ear. She felt weighed down with an unreasoning reverence. These solemn figures in the great ruined hall of the temple had seemed instinct with a supernatural power. Battered by the passing of much time, discredited for centuries as representing a great divinity—objects but of curiosity and wonder to this age—they had yet appealed to her as invested with the calm complacency of conscious power. Serenely they sat, confidently awaiting at least the individual recognition and homage of mankind. Strangely did they convey the idea that theirs was the triumphant knowledge that, for so long as human hearts can pulsate, for so long, too, Sekhet—the personification of Love and Lust, and the suffering both bring—shall find her throne, her shrine, her arena.

This figure that Evarne now stood before was not seated. Somewhat over life-size it stood, stiffly erect, one foot advanced, the symbol of Life held in its grasp. It was raised above the sand of the floor on a low pedestal. Evarne stood motionless, gazing upwards. The battered figures in the open had been impressive, but this one—uninjured, and with the artificial advantage of its surroundings—was more than that! It was terrible, awe-inspiring, with its inhuman head, the menacing feline features bearing so clearly the impress of unpitying and vindictive cruelty, malignant spite, merciless joy in the inflicting and witnessing of the direst agonies that can rack tortured brain or flesh or spirit.

Evarne had been the last to enter, and as she rejoined her companions outside, the party commenced to retrace its steps. Unperceived, she left them and returned to the temple. She had something to say to Sekhet.

Alone she stood, facing the goddess—the lifeless marble into which the hand of an artist, long since pulseless, had wrought this unhallowed expression with such marvellous realism that it was difficult to remember that no knowledge, no power, no fearsome intelligence, lay behind those gleaming eyes, that low animal brow. Evarne stood motionless, gazing intently up at the brutal face, trying to forget her own individuality and all that was modern. It had been a little prayer that was in her heart as she hastened back, but now she shook her head slowly as the conception of the innate and unalterable cruelty of Sekhet impressed itself with yet greater force upon her mind. This was a goddess who surely had ever been more inclined to fulfil curses than to answer prayers.

As she commenced her half-whispered appeal she recalled some of the titles under which this cat-headed image had been invoked—doubtless many a time and oft—in the dim and distant past. "Oh, Queen of the Goddesses! Oh, Crusher of Hearts! If you can hear me and still wield power, let just tribulation fall on all those who set forth to steal a love that is not free for them—a love to which they have no right—a love that is another's! May success but open the gates of sorrow; may that which

they desired and schemed to gain crush the heart, even
in its triumph, down to the very dust! Deal out stern
justice, untempered by all mercy, to the false, the scornful,
the treacherous, the hypocritical, to those who are unscrupulous and base in thy service, and who cast aside all
honour when in pursuit of that which thou dost offer!"

Then she stood silent awhile, still gazing with fixed
eyes at the impassive countenance before her, monstrous,
yet so strangely human. She had not originally designed
to send forth such a plea into the universe, but it had
arisen spontaneously from the depth of her soul, and she
would not have recalled one word.

Then she turned, and slowly, with strange reluctance
proceeded to quit this dim sanctuary. Still her mind was
not relieved. Impulsively she hastened back and stood
close under the grim black statue.

"Sekhet," she whispered softly and rapidly, " help me—
help me always. Whatever be the price of your aid I will
pay it ungrudgingly. Watch over me ; be ever near me.
I cannot live without love. I do not shrink from its
suffering. Sekhet, at all costs, I am thy worshipper. Do
not forsake me. Do not forsake me ever."

At the throat of her gown were fastened a couple of
crimson roses. They drooped now after the long day,
yet were still rich in perfume. These she unclasped and
laid on the yellow sand at the base of the statue. Then,
with a final glance around the little chamber—once well
accustomed to the sound of prayer, now but the relic of a
dead religion—she hurried away.

CHAPTER XI

A LOSING STRIFE

EVARNE radiated with delight and relief when this Nile cruise came to an end. She could not avoid the mortifying conviction that she had proved herself very childish and incompetent in having allowed a state of affairs so painful—let alone dangerous to herself and her future—to have come to pass, and to continue. Lucinda, ignorant as a kitten on Egyptology and all kindred subjects, had been wont to wax enthusiastic over what she appeared to consider Evarne's quite superhuman fund of knowledge and marvellous intelligence, as contrasted with her own much-lamented but unconquerable silliness. Yet the girl guessed shrewdly that had the situations been reversed, the frivolous, empty-headed Lucinda, so given to harping on the topic of her own incompetence, would have proved an infinitely more resourceful and successful tactician.

Delightful indeed was it to see the last of the Belmonts—both so objectionable in their respective ways—and when she found herself once again alone with Morris at " Mon Bijou," she was gay and light-hearted as any child in her renewed happiness. Florelli's studio saw her not. She devoted her whole time to Morris, as bright, appreciative and amusing a little comrade as man could wish.

But, alack and alas! this sojourn in the oasis of contentment was destined to be but brief. One morning, not long after their return, as they sat at breakfast on the verandah, Bianca entered with the post. No letters ever came for Evarne save bills, which she always passed straight over to Morris ; but this time her name appeared on the face of a delicate pink envelope. On the back were the initials " L. B.," intertwined into a large and involved gold monogram.

The whole thing was highly perfumed, and its recipient sniffed with exaggerated disdain even before she had opened the envelope and mastered its contents. When she had done that she looked up in genuine indignation as she murmured, " The impertinence of the woman ! "

Morris, who had been watching her, now reached over for the letter, and likewise perused the " impertinence." It apparently did not strike him in the same light, for, as he laid it down, a meditative grunt of approval accompanied the action.

" I think we will accept," he said.

" Oh no, no—impossible ! " was Evarne's instantaneous and startled response.

The letter that had created such emphatic difference of opinion ran as follows :—

" DEAREST EVARNE (for so I always think of you),— Absence makes the heart grow fonder, so they say, and I find it true that it wasn't until the radiant time on ' The Radiant Isis ' was over that I realised how very attached I'd become to you, dear. I do hope we shall mature our friendship begun under such delightful auspices, so I am writing to ask you if you will become my guest in Paris for some weeks. Do come, dear ; I am so looking forward to seeing you again.

" I'm well aware when I ask this that Mr. Kenyon is the fair Evarne's devoted shadow, and I mustn't dare to enjoy the sweet charm of the rose without its accompanying thorn (of course that is quite between ourselves, dear) ; but Tony is writing to him, for he has promised (dear fellow !) to take Mr. Kenyon off on long masculine jaunts (and we won't inquire too deeply where they go, will we, dear ?) while you and I are enjoying the Paris shops and other feminine frivolities in one another's society to our heart's content.

"I am looking forward to a most enjoyable time, darling Evarne.

" Your affectionate friend,

" LUCINDA BELMONT.

"P.S.—We shall be both getting our new season's ' rigs-out,' shan't we ? I know of such a heavenly place for hats."

"Oh, indeed, I don't want to go ! I should hate it. I can't bear either Mr. or Mrs. Belmont," cried Evarne, after a silence long enough to show only too plainly that Morris was not going to readily yield to her desires in the matter.

On the contrary, he proceeded to argue. At her age she ought not to seek to bury herself in the solitude of studios or a villa remote from the centres of civilisation. She owed it to herself to be seen and admired. She must go more amongst people, and the companionship of a good-natured, clever woman of the world—such as was Mrs. Belmont—would be of vast benefit to her in every way.

The girl retorted that she had no objection to the centres of civilisation as such, nor to meeting as many of Morris's friends as he wished, but that she would not visit Mrs. Belmont, with whom she had not a taste or a thought in common ; who was, in fact, a person entirely and absolutely hateful in her eyes.

Her voice quite quivered with apprehensive distress, but when Morris proceeded to speak on Lucinda's behalf, lauding her tact and worldly knowledge, Evarne rose in indignant wrath.

If those were the qualities that were characteristic of Mrs. Belmont, then, for her part, she hoped never to become tainted by their possession. " But," she declared, " without being either as tactful, or as wise, or as experienced as that middle-aged designing creature, I'm not quite the abject fool she seems to take me for. She need not think that her sickening show of affection towards me has ever deceived me one jot. I put up with it and her in Egypt because I couldn't help myself, but I'm not going to her house, and you can write and tell her so, for I shan't even answer her hateful, hypocritical letter ; so there ! "

Having delivered herself of this ultimatum, she flung her serviette on the table and swept away, heedlessly dragging over her chair with the train of her morning gown. Morris gazed in amazement at her empty place.

It was the first serious clash of wills that had ever risen between the girl and her lover. The dispute was ardent and protracted, but very soon it became evident that both her coaxing and her resolutions were equally vain when opposed to his wishes. While ostentatiously leaving her perfect freedom of choice for herself, he was going to Paris !

So, with the utmost reluctance and a considerable sense of humiliation, Evarne submitted as gracefully as might be. She could not bring herself to so far cherish her dignity as to remain haughtily alone at " Mon Bijou," knowing Morris to be once more within the range of the wiles and allurements of a clever and unscrupulous *demi-mondaine*. Although she believed that, up to the present, she still retained her sway upon his affections, his own teachings led her not to place too confiding a reliance upon the Joseph-like qualities of the most devoted of lovers.

Never before had she bade adieu to her beautiful brilliant room with such a heavy heart. She stood in the doorway, gazing longingly around, imprinting every corner, every contrast of colour, freshly upon her memory. How happy she had been at " Mon Bijou " ! How dear it all was to her !

Both common-sense and diplomacy prompted her to greet Lucinda with smiling, albeit somewhat stiff, cordiality, and she effectively concealed her scorn when her hostess, gushingly embracing her, put her face close up to hers and made a hasty little smacking sound into the air, first on one side, then on the other—Lucinda's only conception of how to kiss another woman.

Morris had given Evarne a cheque-book, and opened a generous account for her at his bank, and for the first few days the programme promised in the invitation was carried out to the letter. He and Tony did, in fact, derive whatever satisfaction and benefit was to be gained from one another's society, while their female belongings amused themselves together by shopping and such-like diversions. The girl could not but acknowledge that Lucinda's vivacity and bright flow of talk were far from unamusing, yet to recognise the efficiency of the weapons of one whom she felt to be her remorseless foe did not at all ease her mind or soften her reciprocal feelings of enmity.

Very soon the foreseen change came to pass.

" It's absolutely stupid to have nice men on hand if one is to see nothing of them. One might just as well be a miserable Egyptian woman right away," announced Lucinda, and none could contradict her words. " It's too mean of me to bore dear Evarne by keeping her all to my dull self," was her next statement. And so the divided expeditions of the party ceased, and then it was not long ere the old miserable state of affairs that had ruined the cruise of " The Radiant Isis " was again in full swing.

But even this was not enough. Next came the suggestion that *tête-à-tête* expeditions were, after all, better. Lucinda was sure that, as Evarne was so clever, and an artist too, she, of course, must want to go round the galleries and see the statues and such-like things. Lucinda herself was so very silly she couldn't appreciate old masters one bit. Then she got such dreadful headaches in the close atmosphere. It must be lovely to be strong just like a man, as dear Evarne was, but for her part she got utterly exhausted in half an hour. Really, she must reluctantly relinquish these delightful expeditions to dear Tony. Tony had quite gone off his head lately; he had actually taken to trying to improve his mind. She couldn't imagine why! As if dear Tony wasn't quite clever enough as it was for a silly, frivolous little woman like herself, who only cared for chiffons. Perhaps it was the beneficial result of Evarne's society on board " The Radiant Isis." She only wished she was half as clever as dear Evarne; cultivated women acquired such a good influence over men —so much more powerful and lasting than silly, frivolous creatures like herself could ever hope to gain.

Evarne hated her! Hated her for her gibes, her scarce-concealed mockery, and, above all, she loathed her for the sarcastic flattery and never-failing show of affection under which thin veil she sought to cover her intention of stealing the girl's rich lover, if she could encompass that act. It was a method that made retort difficult; and, moreover, Evarne was under the disadvantage of still retaining her over-sensitive self-respect. It was revolting to her to openly admit that she was engaged in a vulgar struggle with another woman—and a woman so far beneath herself— for the possession of a man.

Now she said simply and frankly that her interest in museums had always depended entirely upon Morris's society, and that without him such things did not appeal to her much. But, far from pleased by this statement, he frowned darkly, spoke of neglected opportunities, and discourtesy to her host. Finally he acknowledged that— relying upon her being otherwise pleasantly occupied—he had arranged to take Mrs. Belmont for some expeditions in a certain swift motor-car that only accommodated two. Thus, short of creating a scene, the girl found herself faced by the alternatives of remaining alone in the flat, obviously sulking, or endeavouring to cover her defeat by accepting Tony's eager escort and pretending to enjoy visiting the antiquities and art treasures in the Louvre.

She had already implored Morris to leave Paris, but he had turned a deaf ear to her appeal. Now, although she managed to smile at Tony and to declare, gaily enough, her willingness to further encourage him in improving his mind together with her own, she was torn by agony of spirit at this new proof of her beloved's rapidly maturing infatuation for her rival.

Nevertheless, it all had the advantage of preventing the final blow from falling as a bolt from the blue. Nor was the hour far off.

CHAPTER XII

SEKHET, CRUSHER OF HEARTS

ONE morning, weary and depressed after a wakeful night, her determination had faltered at the very moment of setting out on an expedition with Tony as sole escort. With her foot actually on the step of the carriage she had suddenly informed him, somewhat curtly, that he really must amuse himself that day, returning and shutting herself in her room, deaf to all expostulations.

Tony, decidedly chagrined, had loitered for a while in the lonely flat—teased the dog—flirted with one of the maid-servants—and had finally taken his departure.

Evarne sat on in solitude, alternately striving to read a novel and freely permitting her tortured imagination to dwell on the vision of Morris and Lucinda being whirled happily together through the fresh country lanes.

A few hours later, hearing a footstep and the sound of the opening front door, and wishing now to make peace with Tony before the others returned and troubled her with " whys " and " wherefores," she went to the drawing-room, prepared to be very sweet and amiable. But the footsteps had not been those of her host. It was the motoring couple who had returned thus early.

Lucinda, vivacious as usual, had already removed her hat and veil, and was drawing off her long gloves. She worked industriously at the fingers of one hand until she had drawn a loose end of the white kid forward over each finger-tip then suddenly called upon Morris.

"I'm impatient. I can't tear these things off. You had better come to the rescue."

Gathering up the already loose ends between his thumb and finger, Morris took hold of her other hand also, and suddenly jerked both her arms forcibly over his shoulders. As she unavoidably fell forward on his breast he encircled her waist and kissed the laughing face so near to his own.

"There's none like you, you damned little witch," he declared.

Evarne had not desired to be an eavesdropper, and had no thought of concealing her presence now. She still held in her hand the book she had been reading, and, with a sharp indrawing of her breath, announced her presence by violently flinging the volume to the ground with a loud bang.

Seeing her, Lucinda uttered a scream and fled. Morris remained without moving, gazing at the girl with the utmost nonchalance.

"You've precipitated matters, Evarne," he said calmly.

Her first outburst of anger was directed against Lucinda.

"There's nothing in all this world that is more utterly despicable and hateful and detestable, more altogether vile, than to pretend a friendship for a woman in order to get chances to steal her lover!" she cried, with sufficient energy to suggest that she was directing her opinion through the closed door that Lucinda had banged after her in her hurried flight.

"All's fair in love and war," retorted Morris.

"That's a lie," was the startlingly frank answer.

"Is it? Then what about you and Tony?"

"Tony Belmont? Be careful, Morris! What about us? That creature, seeing something more to her taste in you, has flung her cast-off lover at my head. He has played into her hands readily enough, and you have stood by and seen it being done. How dare you then ask such a question?"

"Well, you may choose to look at it in that light, but

the fact remains unaltered and undeniable that Tony practically deserted Lucinda from the time he first saw you, and you didn't care one jot what suffering it caused that poor little woman."

" Poor defenceless little darling ! "

The words were spoken with bitter sarcasm, while the fiery indignation already surging within the girl's breast increased tenfold beneath this amazing accusation—this unscrupulous falsifying of the truth. There was a moment's silence, then her words rang out with passionate force—

" Oh, the arch hypocrisy ! Liars, both of you—abject liars—trying to make excuses for your own foul treachery ! It's sickening ! I shan't stay another night—no, not another hour—beneath her roof."

" It is Tony's roof, and you had better remain."

" I won't, I won't ! How can you even suggest such a thing ? I can't breathe the same air that she does. It's poisonous—contaminated ! "

" Gently, gently ; you'll be overheard."

" Rubbish ! I don't care ! I won't be gentle. What do you mean by defending her ? What is she to you ? "

And the verbal refusal to be gentle was confirmed by a violent blow on the table.

Morris, albeit decidedly surprised, answered with un-ruffled suavity. He was quite willing to make allowances for this natural anger and show of indignation ; at the same time the wondrous patience the girl had exhibited hitherto had given him little cause to anticipate the tem-pestuous quality of her aroused wrath.

" Is your philosophy all culled from antique authors, sweet student ? Have you never found time to peep into Darwin and assimilate the doctrine of the Survival of the Fittest ? "

" What's that to do——— ? " she cried in bewilderment,

not seeing at first any connection between her question and this answer. Yet even as she spoke came a sudden mental illumination of his meaning.

"Morris, you can't mean to say you really do prefer that vulgar, coarse-minded, spiteful, abandoned creature to—to—— Oh Heaven!"

She brushed her hair roughly back from her forehead, and stared at him fixedly, her big eyes still full of incredulity. Then she uttered a brief laugh of mingled bitterness and disdain.

"But there! From a man's point of view, I suppose the Fittest always and only implies the Newest. Despicable wretches, the whole lot of you."

Morris, amused at this sweeping statement, smiled as he answered—

"But it's a little weakness that is no ways confined to mere man. It isn't only to us that constancy spells boredom. It's all very well for middle-aged women, who feel their power of pleasing on the wane, to cling like limpets. We expect it, and it's one reason why wise men avoid 'em. It always means beastly rows in the long run. But, thank goodness, at your time of life, my child, variety is charming, even to the fair sex."

The latter portion of these sentiments fell unheeded —practically unheard. All the girl's thoughts and senses were concentrated upon her own agony of spirit. Fully grasping now, for the very first time, that Morris's defection was serious and deliberate, all indignation and resentment were swamped by a wave of wild grief and horror before which all else broke down. When she could speak it was only in disjointed sentences, in a voice that quivered under stress of emotion and struggled with choking sobs.

"Oh, oh! Can I only bore you now by loving you? You can't mean that. Not really and truly. I can't have lost your love so utterly. What have I ever done?

Oh, Morris, what have I done ?   I've never altered to you, and I never would.   I would always be faithful to you—always.   Is it a curse to have a faithful heart ?   I can't stop caring for you, because you tell me to ; how—how can I ?   Are you really altogether tired of me ?   I knew men did get tired, easily, cruelly easily, but somehow——— Perhaps if I'd been different ?   Oh, I did try !   I did, always !   I did !   But there, I've been so utterly miserable lately, it's better really to know the truth straight out at once.   Tell me the truth, Morris."

" But you know it, my dear."

" Tell me, tell me ! "

" Now what is the good of upsetting yourself like this ? Come, come ! "

" You're going to give that—that woman—my place ! Oh ! you'll be sorry.   She's only selfish and mercenary. She doesn't love you, and I do.   You—you don't care for that, though.   Oh, how can you ? "

Morris was feeling awkwardly uncomfortable.   He took a flower from a vase, and put it in his buttonhole before he spoke.

" I'm perfectly aware," he confessed at length, " that in the abstract Lucinda is neither so handsome, so brilliant, nor so really delightful as you are, but still—still—— " He paused.   " There, I'm not worth bothering about, so dry your eyes."

By a powerful effort of self-command she managed to regain some degree of composure, and to steady her voice. Quite quietly she repeated his words, " not worth bothering about," then, after an interval, " Ah, me ! "

The tender yearning tone in which this little exclamation came was fraught with significance.   After another moment's thought she approached quite close to him, and rested the tips of her fingers upon his chest.

" I'm afraid you *are* worth bothering about, my dear," she went on, making a rather pitiful little attempt to hide her sick anxiety by pretending to smile. Then, after a somewhat protracted pause, she spoke again.

"I—I—there, why should I be ashamed to say it again, even now? I love you still—oh, so much! I'm sure I shall always love you. I can't help it. We can't arrange our feelings so that they shall always be convenient and suitable. It was never really right that we should care for one another at all, because—because of your wife, and I would never—no never—have taken her place if you had even so much as hinted that you might one day come to look upon it as something merely temporary; something that could be lightly set aside as soon as you met another woman whom you—liked a bit.

"No, don't speak, Morris! I haven't done yet. You know full well that though I loved you, oh! so dearly, I never wanted to lead any other than what I thought was a perfectly honourable life. You know you didn't win me easily, in spite of everything being in your favour. You told me that because you had made a mistake in your marriage you were lonely and unhappy, and that, though you couldn't make me really your wife, our union should be as lasting and sacred as any legal bond. It was to be your true marriage. You're not treating me fairly now, dear, you're not really. You ought to feel really more tied to me by honour and loyalty than you would do even if I were indeed your wife, and had not lost my good name for your sake. I've never been troublesome and jealous, you can't say that, and when you found you were getting—well, seriously attached to another woman, it's not a bit unreasonable of me to think you ought to have avoided seeing her again. You owed it to me to be true always—you did, indeed. You knew I was not like Mrs. Belmont, who treats these ties so lightly. Come away now, darling —come away from Paris. She can't really have won your heart yet—only your fancy, only your passing fancy, Morris. You would soon forget her. Come away with me, and we will be so happy together again, and honest and upright and without any cause to be ashamed, either of us. Do come, darling—do, do."

Her arms were tightly clasped around his neck, and her wistful, eager face—the piteous brown eyes moist and beseeching—were close to his. But beauty that has palled no longer possesses power. Sentimental appeals to honour and loyalty were very troublesome ; while the reference to an imaginary link that was to be held binding upon him for evermore was merely vexing.

" You're a good, sweet little soul," he said, rather testily, unclasping her arms—" no one knows that better than I do—and I should have supposed, therefore, that you would be the last to suggest that we should continue our life together without mutual love. On the contrary, a woman of your moral excellence ought not to be willing to consent to such a proceeding. And, what's more, you mustn't blame me, you know. Remember your own wise words, ' We can't arrange our feelings, our affections, according to what would be, perhaps, the most conducive to a quiet life.' We may all be but the sport of the gods, but let's go on strike against taking part in any tragedies for the entertainment of the higher powers. Let's insist on being merely comedians. We will say good-bye smilingly, and thus snap our fingers at Fate."

Evarne twisted her hands together helplessly. She had much to say, so much, but further speech was beyond her power.

Her throat swelled, she bit the inside of her lower lip pitilessly to stay its quivering, but was scarcely conscious of the tears that poured down her cheeks unheeded. After a minute's futile struggle to retain some show of self-command, she moved away a step or two, sank into an arm-chair, buried her face in the cushions, and sobbed without restraint.

A tumultuous medley of wild impassioned ideas surged

within her brain, incomplete thoughts, disconnected and rapidly cast aside. But, amid them all, were none urging calm submission, dignified resignation. On the contrary, all alike were directed on evolving some method of warding off this unendurable blow—or, at least, since it had fallen, of nullifying its effects.

The thing seemed so incredible, unreal, impossible, the end of all life. She resolutely declined to admit that there was nothing whatsoever to be done ; she could not consent to allow all hope to leave her. And yet—yet—immovable and grim, the bedrock underlying these wild surgings of despised and deserted love, was the conviction that her richest store of eloquence, the whole of her most intense and protracted efforts, would prove powerless to alter the inevitable. Distracted, tortured, she gasped between her sobs—

" I shall kill myself."

Morris was just in the act of stealing softly from the room. Looking rather foolish, he turned sharply, and crossed over to her side.

" Tut, tut ! You don't know what you're saying now, you're talking wildly," he declared soothingly. " You really mustn't take things so to heart. You'll make yourself quite ill. Go and lie down quietly, and I'll send Bianca in to you with a cup of tea."

" You think I don't know what I'm saying, but I know that I'm not saying half I feel," she declared truthfully enough. Then, after a moment's further reflection, her momentary composure again gave way. " Oh, how could you make me love you, only to treat me like this ? It was cruel, brutal ! How can I bear it ? "

Morris patted her shoulder encouragingly, but remained silent. He had been through a few tempestuous scenes ere this, and knowing that a man did not shine on such occasions, was resigned to looking and feeling foolish while it lasted, devoting his efforts chiefly to getting the *mauvais quart d'heure* over as quietly as possible. For this, his one theory lay in the proverb, " Least said, soonest mended."

Evarne put out her hand and pushed him away.

" Don't do that—don't ! You know you hate me now."

Again Morris smiled ; women always went to such extremes.

" Bless you, not a bit of it ! Why, I hope we are going to part the best of friends," was his lightly spoken disavowal of this accusation.

" To part ! " murmured Evarne, after him, monotonously—" to part ! "

Then suddenly an inward voice seemed to commence repeating over and over again, " There is nothing so dead as a dead love. There is nothing so dead as a dead love. Nothing so dead, nothing, nothing ! " It was maddening. The unhesitating certainty—the calm conviction animating the phrase—brought final despair. In it she heard a call, inspired by the wisdom of ages, the outcome of the most bitter experience of long generations of mankind ; a call to abandon efforts that were predestined to be sterile. It was as if she were abruptly faced by the inscription that Dante read over the gateways of hell. Sitting erect, she lifted her voice in lamentation.

" Oh, Morris, darling, you can't change so utterly. You're the same man. I'm still the same woman. How many times did you swear you would love me always and ever—always and ever—and now I'm only just twenty ! " she wailed, catching at his arm and pressing her cheek to his coat-sleeve, while her sobs grew louder and more convulsive.

Morris, already wearied, felt a tiny twinge of compunction, and was thereupon easily moved to anger by her impassioned weeping.

" For goodness' sake, Evarne, do let us have an end to this ridiculous scene," he said roughly, shaking himself free from her despairing hold. " Do recognise the fact that not all the pleading in the world will have any effect on me. If you don't pull yourself together you'll have hysterics in a moment, and I've no patience with hysterical women."

The action, the cruel words themselves, and the tone in which they were uttered, combined to goad the girl to sudden wrath. She sprang to her feet, and without a moment's hesitation frantically struck him on the chest with her clenched fist.

"Don't think I shall ask anything of you now—no, not so much as your patience," she cried. "I don't intend to plead with any man for his love, least of all with you— don't think it! I never want to see you again, never! Go to Mrs. Belmont—go and make her your mistress."

Morris allowed himself to be thoroughly angered by the blow.

"Thanks for the permission," he said curtly; "but it happens to be quite unnecessary, as we have not waited for it."

He now anticipated being deluged beneath a torrent of words, but though her lips parted, Evarne stood quite speechless, only blinking her eyes a little, as if bewildered and dazed. Then she slowly retreated backwards across the room step by step, until she was brought to a standstill by reaching the china cabinet. Leaning against it, she turned her head from side to side for a minute or two, then, producing a flimsy, ineffectual little handkerchief, proceeded, with strange, unlooked-for composure, to wipe her eyes and tear-stained cheeks.

"So now you see you may just as well be sensible and resigned, eh?" suggested Morris, with forced carelessness.

Evarne made no sign of having heard, but continued her touching little occupation. The protracted silence became embarrassing. Morris was haunted by the fear that this apparently delightful calm must be but ominous and deceptive.

"I'll make different arrangements by to-morrow," he continued at length, in a business-like tone. "I can understand you don't care to be in the same place. I ought not to have allowed it. I apologise."

Still silence. He was just about to speak again, when Evarne announced in tones of quiet conviction, seemingly to herself, "I must get away from this house at once— at once!" and walked towards the door as if about to suit the action to the words without any delay.

But Morris hurried over to prevent the fulfilment of this impulse.

"Believe me," he assured her, retaining his grasp of the door-handle, "there is some one who would rather that all the rest of us should slip over the fourth dimension than have you undertake the *rôle* of vanishing lady. Darwin applies all round, remember, and to Tony's way of thinking you are the fittest in all the world."

A dangerous gleam darted into the girl's eyes, and she stamped her foot passionately.

"How dare you offer me such an insult? Haven't you done enough yet to make yourself hateful to me? Have you no shame whatsoever? Be silent, I tell you— be silent!"

He made a gesture of despair.

"Of all the unreasonable people! Now, why should listening to a simple statement of facts cause you to get into such a temper?"

"Why?—why, indeed! You can't see; oh dear no, it's quite beyond your comprehension, isn't it? Learn this, then: though you have made me a more degraded creature than I ever before realised, you haven't killed all my soul, neither shall you."

"Souls at this moment! Good gracious, my dear girl, I only wish I had made you a bit more practical. But there, I fear you're utterly incorrigible. Poor old Tony mayn't be quite your ideal knight, but do try to realise that while sugar-icing forms a charming coating for a cake, the cake is just as sustaining without it. Are you positively so blinded by silly sentimentality as to be really incapable of seeing any cause for congratulation in the lucky chance that has led him to take a fancy to you? A good-hearted fellow with plenty of money. What more can you want?"

Anger had found small place in the girl's breast while she was being made to realise the dread truth that her lover was finally weary of her and of her affection; nor had even lasting indignation awoken until he taunted her with the display of bitter grief that this very knowledge had evoked. When he thus persisted in what she could but deem the last of insults—this determination to regard her only as a light toy, to be tossed from one man to another— then the capacity for wild wrath that she derived from her violent low-born mother, and a long line of fiery-tempered maternal ancestors, showed itself in all its power.

Up to the present her own personal gentleness of spirit, aided by the trend of her education, and the affection by which she had always been encircled, had sufficed to keep even the girl herself in ignorance of the capacity that lay dormant in her blood for feeling and displaying wild fury. Now, in circumstances provocative of wrath such as had never yet occurred in the whole range of her limited experience, she became entirely her mother's daughter.

"If ever again I touch a farthing of such money may I fall down dead!" she cried wildly. "That's my only answer. Oh! It's the devil gives money to men of your stamp, so that you may with more certainty work out your own damnation."

"Do not be melodramatic," implored Morris, giving each word its full value to render it more impressive, while he shook his head, and screwed up his face in superior disdain. "Of course——"

"I don't want—I refuse, absolutely refuse to hear

anything more you've got to say ; so you may as well hold your tongue," interrupted Evarne fiercely.   "Get out of the way ; stand aside from the door ; let me get out of this room."

But Morris did not move.

" Not so, you're far too excited.   There's no knowing what you might do."

He made a great mistake in preventing her from finding the solitude she instinctively sought.   His words and presence were unendurably exasperating at this juncture.

She sat down on a couch, and tapped the floor impatiently with the toe of her velvet slipper.

Morris tried again.

" If you could only persuade yourself to look at the matter clearly——" But he broke off abruptly.   Evarne had merely raised her head and looked at him, but that was all-sufficient.   " It's evidently no use talking sense to anyone so beside herself as you are now," he concluded lamely.

" No use, so let me pass."

She sprang to her feet, and came close to him.   Her face was flushed, while her eyes seemed to fairly blaze with passion ; every breath she drew was distinctly audible. It really spoke something for Morris's strength of mind that he stood his ground.

" Not until you're calmer," he insisted.

Her lips set themselves into a firm line, and for a moment she appeared to be contemplating the employment of physical force to gain her will, but apparently she thought better of it, for, quite suddenly sweeping over to the opposite side of the room, she turned her back on Morris and leant both elbows on the mantelpiece.

" You know that Tony——" he recommenced, somewhat unwisely ; then changed his sentence : " If you would but believe that I am only considering your best advantage——"

" Believe you ?—never again   Liar ! Abject liar ! "

Morris was thoroughly aroused.

" Now, look here, what do you suppose it matters to me what you do now ? " he demanded fiercely. " I could more than discharge all my obligations to you by a final cheque, and I don't want any further show of ingratitude if I give you also the benefit of my advice. I tell you, a young woman of your personal charms needs not only money but a protector. However, please yourself."

Evarne turned sharply, and again broke in upon him before the words were well out of his mouth.

" Do you want to drive me mad ? " she shouted. " I hate you, I loathe you, I despise you ! Oh, if some one would only protect me now from you, you coward ! "

The veins stood up on the man's temples.

" It's difficult to see why you persist in going on like a fool, and trying to deceive me. I'm perfectly convinced that, whatever the price demanded you will no more be found living without luxuries in the future than you have in the past, so why indulge in these absurd airs and graces of outraged virtue ? "

For a moment everything whirled before Evarne's eyes ; then, incapable of remaining without action, she commenced to pace up and down the room. A little table on which stood photograph frames, a vase of lilac, and various similar knick-knacks, stood in her path. Without a moment's hesitation she flung it aside, scattering the dainty ornaments in all directions.

" It's foolish to be angry with you," said Morris, suddenly calming himself. " You are clearly not responsible for what you do or say. You must go to your room and lie down. Do you hear ? I insist. It would serve you right if I did leave you to your own devices entirely, but you are so young and silly that for your father's sake I'm going to see your future settled somehow, whether you say ' thank you ' or not. Now come."

" Don't you dare to touch me ! " screamed the girl.

" You've no right now to interfere with my life, and you shan't do it. How dare you speak of my father, when you've so brutally betrayed his trust ? You've lied, and tricked, and ruined me. I suppose you can't help being so ignoble and contemptible that loyalty and faith are only objects of derision to you ; but that you should be willing—anxious—to pass me on to a despicable rake— not so vile as yourself, but still vile—that I shall never forget and never forgive, and, if I can help it, God likewise shall never forgive."

" What a ridiculous position to take up ! Do you really expect to be ever anything more than one upon a string of beads ? You knew you hadn't been otherwise with me, and you never will be now with any other man —so you may as well make up your mind to it, and think yourself lucky if——"

The girl, distracted and infuriated, waited for no more. Snatching up a silver statuette she hurled it with all her force at her betrayer's head. Then for a time she knew nothing ; all was a blank—devoid of memory—of thought —of consciousness of action. Quite suddenly she seemed to regain her senses—to awake to find herself alone—the carpet covered with fragments of broken glass, streams of water, disordered flowers, books, scattered ornaments, while she herself was throwing madly, fiercely, everything on which she could lay hands, smash against the closed door by which Morris had been standing.

CHAPTER XIII

OUT OF THE GILDED CAGE

INSTANTLY subdued by amazement, she stared aghast at the surrounding destruction. At the dread realisation that she was beholding the work of her own hands, a shrinking horror—a terrible fear of herself—filled her breast. Why, in very sooth, this looked like the doings of a madwoman, and she had known nothing of what she was about. What could it portend? Trembling violently, she leant against the wall, scarcely able to stand, her hands pressing her cheeks, her eyes dilated and glancing around as if in apprehension.

How blessed just at that moment would have been the care of her mother—or, indeed, of any tender woman. But she was quite alone—or worse than that, surrounded only by those who had reduced her to this state, and by servants filled with curiosity.

After an interval of quietness the door was cautiously opened a trifle, a head was popped in and rapidly withdrawn. Evarne had not time to notice to whom it belonged, but she immediately regained sufficient strength to walk across the room. She could not endure to be thus made into a spectacle, neither could she longer gaze upon this dire material destruction that typified, only too cruelly, the fate that had befallen her love, her happiness and her future.

As she opened the door and appeared on the threshold, there was a general sense of rustling, of rapid footsteps, of stifled exclamations in the corridor and the surrounding rooms, as various figures hastened to efface themselves. But the girl, heeding nothing, made directly for her own apartment and securely locked herself therein.

Then, after a moment's reflection on what had passed that hour, she again collapsed beneath alternate transports of anger and heart-tearing grief. Now she would be sweeping wildly to and fro, with clenched fists and hurried strides, her body swaying and shaking as she walked ; next, exhausted, flinging herself upon bed or floor, torn with sobs, drowned by tears, only to spring to her feet again as stress of anguish goaded her to action.

Her feelings towards Morris were variable as the wind. At times the memory of his brutal insults, his treachery and faithlessness, were uppermost in her thoughts ; then she felt for him only the most intense and passionate hatred, bitterly grudging every hour of happiness to which she had contributed in the past ; praying wildly that the future might hold for him agony of spirit equal to that into which he had so ruthlessly plunged her. Then, again, a flood of her old devotion would rise above all else. " Morris, Morris, come back to me ! Oh, my darling, my darling, how can I live without you ? " was her sobbing appeal ; but there was none to answer.

For the most part she sorrowed in silence. She was aware that whispered conversations were in progress outside her door, and more than once the handle was turned cautiously. Later in the afternoon, Bianca, who was genuinely attached to her beautiful young mistress, ventured to tap again and again, at the same time imploring, in a tremulous voice, to be allowed to do something—anything. But Evarne turned a deaf ear to all.

Time passed, and the first violence of her emotion burned itself out. Then she became conscious that she felt sick and ill, and that her head ached to distraction. Letting down her thick black hair, she threw herself once again upon her tumbled bed, and made a first serious and

protracted effort to remain absolutely quiet and calm.
Long she lay there, staring at vacancy, sighing piteously
at intervals, until as the evening twilight crept into the
room, the lids drooped over the wild eyes and the exhausted
girl sank into slumber.

When she awoke, it was night. The room was shrouded
in darkness, and perfect silence reigned. As recollection
returned she despairingly pressed her hands to her head,
but firmly forbade any further lapse from self-control.
The determination she had arrived at during the weary
time she had lain passive before falling asleep was now to
be put into action. When the traitors who were beneath
that roof awoke in the morning, they should find their
victim gone. She shrank from again meeting either of
the Belmonts; Morris it was better she should not see.
One of the trains that left Paris in the grey of the morning
should bear her away—far beyond the reach of these, her
enemies.

Her thoughts turned towards London. She was not
exactly a feminine Dick Whittington; at the same time
the great metropolis certainly seemed to offer the greatest
hope for one who had her own way to make.

Flashing on the light, she looked at her watch. It was a
quarter-past three. She rose up, and drawing the curtains
over the windows, set about packing the few things it was
imperative she should take. At first she seemed to possess
neither bag nor box of a suitable size, and, gazing helplessly
around the room, realised how weak and nervous, and, above
all, how curiously dull and stupid, she was feeling. With
an impatient effort she pulled herself together, and concentrated all her wits upon this question of a box. Finally,
she thought of her dressing-bag. By removing most of
the fittings she was able to crush into it all she had sorted
out to pack.

Then, slipping off the embroidered muslin morning-gown
she still wore, she sought for her plainest and most service-

able outdoor costume. Evarne's taste in dress in no ways
inclined to simplicity. She gloried in frills and furbelows,
dainty details, falling lace and fashionably cut skirts.
Even her tailor-built gowns were not really severe. The
fact that a brown face-cloth was made with a short skirt
prompted her choice. It was elaborately stitched and
strapped, but demure in tone, its only contrasting colour
being a touch of delicate rose-pink—chosen by Morris
himself to match the exquisite tint of her cheeks.

She took no ornaments, but drew from a corner in her
jewel-box a small enamel watch, the last gift of her father.
With a stifled sigh she wound it up, and, shaking it a little
to make it recommence its long-abandoned duties, pinned
it on her dress, while she laid the yet tinier bejewelled toy
that had superseded it back into the case.

She would scornfully leave behind every ornament that
had belonged to brighter days ; Morris would find them
all and perhaps be a bit sorry ! But money she must have,
and she looked anxiously into her purse. It contained but
a couple of napoleons and some silver. There were four
more gold pieces in her desk ; her velvet bag with the
turquoises contained only two. The embroidered bag,
bought to match her latest green costume, contributed
three, while a few stray francs lay on the dressing-table.
She gathered them all into her lap and counted them.
Only a little over twelve napoleons altogether. It was
alarmingly little, but it would have to suffice. This done,
she again studied the hour. It was not yet four. She had
no idea when the earliest train set out, but felt convinced
that it could not start so matutinally.

It was nearly sixteen hours since she had last tasted
food, but she was not at all conscious of hunger. She was
in a strangely numbed state of mind. Beyond an impatience to be once fairly off, she seemed unable to care
for aught else. Nothing mattered ! Nothing ever could
matter now ! Still, the sight of a plate of fruit reminded

her of her long fast, and she half-peeled a banana, but even as she raised it to her lips, a sudden repugnance at the idea of eating anything further beneath this roof, caused her to put it down untasted.

Ready even to her hat and gloves, she sank into an arm-chair to wait an hour or so before venturing forth. Not until she sat there, gazing with half-unseeing eyes around the delicate room, did she begin to grasp the full significance of the complete change that had so suddenly taken place in her circumstances.

Not only was her path in life to lie apart from Morris Kenyon's for evermore, but she was abruptly and un-expectedly plunged into the direst poverty. She had no hope, even remotely, of a reconciliation with her one-time lover, but she felt curiously calm and indifferent now. Then, although she knew well enough that poverty, with all its shifts, deprivations and unpleasantnesses would be hateful to her—she could not feel really concerned at the prospect. Nothing mattered—nothing ever could matter again ! Everything was finished !

She was without the least idea of what she could possibly do to earn an honest livelihood. As far as went that capacity, she was every whit as ill-placed as when her father died. True, she had been studying art, more or less seriously, for the last three years, but no one knew better than herself how futile would be any attempt to earn money by this means.

What then ? The effort to think was painful. What had come over her ? Somehow she seemed incapable of even remembering trades or professions, to see if she could not manage to fulfil the necessary qualifications.

What did other young women do ? Oh ! of course, they were governesses, or children's nurses, or companions to invalids or old ladies, or—or—that sort of thing ! But posts such as these surely required some capacity, and above all, a good reputation. She was, then, in truth, worse off than when she had first left Heatherington with Morris, so confident, so full of hopes for the future.

What were girls allowed to do without their miserable past existences being scrutinised ? How about telephone girls and those who served in shops of one sort and another, those who were attendants in restaurants ? Those who—who—well ! She couldn't think of anything else just then ; but there was clearly quite a choice of honest ways of grubbing up a livelihood—if one must live at all ! Without exception, all appeared absolutely hateful. Viewed in anticipation, it seemed as if she might as well be dead at once, as devote all the days of one week to earning just enough to keep herself alive the next week, so that she might work through that, in order to be able to live the next seven days, and so on, and so on, with cheap clothes, poor food, scarce and low-class diversions, until old age overtook her—and then—what ?

She passed through a moment of positive fear and repulsion, and instinctively her thoughts turned to Tony. After all, was she not rushing into a battle in which she must fall conquered. She could please men—that she knew well—but could she do anything else in life ? She was so accustomed to wealth and ease and comfort now. What could she do without it ? Would the time ever come when she would despairingly view this hour, when she wilfully abandoned what certainly appeared the flowery track through life, with its luxury, elegance, leisure for higher pursuits, its surroundings of grace and beauty that she appreciated so fully, and that only money—ill-gotten or otherwise—can procure ?

But the pride and purity of the spirit forbade any real faltering in her resolve. Thousands of other girls lived—contentedly enough she hoped and supposed—upon the market value of their poor little capacities. Upon what grounds was she to be held different ? Young and strong,

why should not she work as well as others ? She felt she
ought to be ashamed of herself.

She shut her eyes so that she should no longer see
the tempting wealth and elegance she was abandoning.
Coloured spirals seemed to whirl in the darkness, and the
ensuing giddiness reminded her of her smelling-salts.
She slipped the bottle into her hand-bag, then resolved
not to sit down again, but to go. She had never before
taken a railway journey alone, and must allow ample time
for contingencies. It was getting on for five o'clock.
The time was ripe.

She crept from her room, and very softly, with many a
pause to listen, proceeded to unfasten all hindering chains
and locks. But no sound was heard within the sleeping
flat, and undisturbed she gained the outer air.

Morris lay wrapped in slumber, all unconscious that the
child he had received at her dying father's hands, innocent
and wholly dependent on his honour, was now stealing
forth homeless into the chill morning, broken-hearted, with
a sullied story, and but a few pounds between herself and
utter destitution. Nor, had he known, would it have
caused him any serious pangs of remorse. The pride of
spirit, the refinement of sentiment, that forbade her to take
away any of the valuable gifts he had lavished upon her,
was totally beyond his comprehension. He could see that
it was a pretty enough conceit in theory, perchance, but
such a piece of high-faluting foolishness put into practice
was, to his mind, quite sufficient to deprive her of the
sympathy of all rational beings. In some peculiar manner
the fact that any immediate pecuniary difficulties would
be entirely of her own making, was in his mind all-sufficient
to absolve him from entire blame in the whole affair.

It was a quarter to six when Evarne arrived at the Gare
St. Lazare, and learned that the first train for Dieppe
started in five minutes. Hurrying to the booking-office,
she ordered a first single, then contradicted herself, asking

for a second-class ticket. It was so difficult to have to remember to economise.

The slow train, stopping at every station, took six hours to cover the ground, but Evarne felt no impatience. The steamer did not leave until half-past one, and until then one place was as satisfactory as any other. Indeed, it was even restful to sit quietly in a corner, and not have to force her numbed brain to think and plan.

About nine o'clock the train stopped at a station, where she bought a cup of coffee and a roll. As she sipped and nibbled she reflected that at a corresponding hour on the previous morning she had eaten just such another little *premier déjeuner*. How remote then appeared the prospect of her very next similar meal being taken thus—parted from Morris for ever, dazed and broken-hearted, bound in solitude and fear for another land. " After all, life ought to be somewhat interesting, for it is certainly unexpected," she thought, with a grim, mirthless little smile.

The Channel being on its best behaviour, she escaped the additional trials of illness, but none the less, on arriving at Newhaven, she felt incapable of further effort, and resolved to put up there for the night. The day being Sunday made a good excuse for this feebleness. It really would be most undesirable to arrive in London on the Sabbath evening. She turned with relief into the nearest hotel, and went straight to bed.

She slept ; she lay awake ; she trembled beneath evil dreams ; she shed tears again. The long weary night passed somehow, but left her haggard-eyed and unrefreshed. A maid brought breakfast to her bedside, but Evarne turned with repugnance from the stolid bacon and overdone poached eggs, and it was after a mere pretence of a meal that she arose, paid her bill, and took her seat in the Victoria train.

CHAPTER XIV

HELPING HANDS

IT was a fresh and beautiful morning when she arrived in London town. The sun shone, the sparrows chirruped merrily, violets and mimosa were displayed at the street-corners; English spring was at its best. Evarne changed the remainder of her French gold at the station, and then wandered out of its main entrance —aimlessly—ignorant of where to go—which way to turn.

In the station yard she narrowly escaped being run over by the numerous 'buses that were constantly either entering or leaving. Her first impulse was to mount one of these and let it take her where it would, but condemning this as a foolish fancy, she crossed the road, and commenced to wander down the street directly facing the station. But the wide grandeur of Victoria Street was oppressive. She was anxious to find the cheaper parts of London, and get settled in a moderate-priced hotel or boarding-house without delay. This feeling of absolute homelessness was dreadful.

She was passing an attractive-looking refreshment-shop. It was now about twenty to twelve, and at noon she was accustomed to her first serious meal. She became aware that she was sinking for lack of food, and entering, ordered something to eat

The neighbouring establishment was devoted to the sale of religious pictures, crucifixes and other church requisites, but taking advantage of the great width of the pavement, the enterprising proprietor had placed outside his window some tressels and a board, which was now covered with numerous second-hand books, under the protection of a small boy.

As Evarne ate her meal she distracted her thoughts by watching a girl who was seemingly proposing to purchase a volume, for she was bestowing upon them a protracted study. First one was picked up and glanced into, then another, but Evarne soon saw that it was not the printed wisdom that was filling her mind. Every few seconds her eyes cast anxious glances in the direction of the station, and ere long she abandoned even the pretence of book-gazing, and stood there, frankly waiting and watching for somebody.

She had obviously made her toilette with great care and attention to detail. She wore a long coat and a white hat with a black feather drooping over towards her shoulder. She had on spotless white kid gloves and smart shoes, and a little bunch of blossoms was fastened at her throat by a small pearl brooch. Noticing all this, Evarne guessed at once what it was that kept this girl loitering about thus long, gazing so earnestly towards the station. " She is in love—I can see plainly. Little fool ! It will only bring her misery," was the verdict of this young cynic, for suddenly the far-distant temple at Karnak had risen again in her memory ; she could see the cruel eye, the set lips, of the Egyptian goddess of Love—of Sekhet—in her implacable silent power.

At length Evarne felt compelled to take her departure. But to where ? Who could advise her ? She studied the countenance of the damsel by whom she had been waited upon. It was not unpretty, but oh ! so sadly shallow and unsympathetic. No kindly aid would be forthcoming from that quarter. Silently she quitted the shop.

Not far from the door stood the girl who had already attracted her attention. She certainly did not look as if she could be much acquainted with the shifts of poverty, but he did look as if she could be kind and willing to be helpful. Yielding this time to an impulse, Evarne approached, and without preamble asked where one could obtain cheap lodgings in London.

To her relief the girl with the plume did not evince the least surprise. She appeared to consider it quite natural to be asked such a question by a daintily-clad stranger, and calmly proceeded to consider the matter.

"How cheap do you mean?" she inquired. "There are a great many boarding-houses in Bloomsbury—near the British Museum, you know—where you would be made quite comfortable for two pounds a week, or even less. Still, there are much cheaper ways of living than that, if you prefer."

Evarne decided that Fate had guided her to one who was, seemingly, an authority on precisely the class of knowledge she was seeking. Two pounds a week was certainly very moderate, but when one is possessed of less than eight pounds in the world—no, that was beyond her means. She could not allow her whole fortune to be dissipated on a month's riotous living!

"Please tell me about the cheaper ways. How—do you happen to know where girls live who can only spare one pound a week?"

"Well, it chiefly depends on the girl. Some hire cubicles in clubs, or homes, or places of that sort, and get most of their meals out. But it's not nice—they treat you as if you were a child—I've never known any one with any 'go' in them who liked it. Shall I tell you what I should do myself?"

"Yes, please do."

"I should go to the stage-door of this music-hall just here"—and she carelessly waved her hand in the direction of the edifice she mentioned. "Then ask the doorkeeper for some addresses, and he will tell you where the artistes stay when they are engaged at the hall."

Here she broke off, and took a short step sideways in order to see between the people passing to and fro, but in a minute turned her attention again to Evarne.

" You can get a room and attendance for ten shillings a week, or thereabouts, and arrange what you'll eat according to the state of the exchequer. I've done that myself, so I know it isn't half-bad. You do your own marketing, you understand, and the landlady does the cooking."

Somewhat surprised at this confidence, Evarne thanked her gratefully.

" Am I not fortunate in having ventured to ask you ? " she said in her sweetest voice. " I should never have dreamed of such a nice way on my own account."

The girl with the plume seemed pleased, and accompanied her the few steps to the corner of the side-street in which the stage-entrance of the music-hall was to be found ; there they parted, and Evarne proceeded on her exploring expedition alone. Sure enough, she soon beheld a very narrow, red folding-door, over which " Stage Door " appeared enticingly in white letters. The flaps were already slightly ajar, and, pushing them wider open, she peered inside the sacred portals.

There was a commissionaire's box sure enough, but no official of any description to grace it. Nothing daunted, Evarne climbed a winding flight of stairs that was just ahead. This ended in a big, square landing, on to which opened several doors. All were closed but one, which, standing wide open, exposed to view a row of washing-basins on a high table, a portion of uncarpeted floor on which lay a jester's cap and a stuffed dog, a huge truss of hay propped up in a corner, together with a couple of guns, and a chair covered with a pile of garments.

Since, save for these rooms, the landing was a blank alley, Evarne was about to descend when a step was heard, and a very young man appeared in the open doorway.

Partly with a view to accounting for her trespassing, the girl explained : " I want to find the hall-porter."

The youth's response was far from useful.

" Well, he isn't here now, and I don't know where he is, or when he will be back."

The idea came to Evarne that possibly this stranger might serve as well as the porter.

" I wanted to ask if he could tell me of any nice lodgings about here," she said.

The youth at once waxed quite enthusiastic.

" Well, I can jolly well tell you that ! We are staying at the only decent place in the neighbourhood. We go there about four times a year, and we wouldn't go to anybody else than Mrs. Burling, not for toffee. When are you coming in ? "

" I want a room at once."

" Well, I can't say what she's got vacant. We've got— let me see—a sitting-room, and one, two, three bedrooms."

" Would you mind telling me what you pay for that ? "

" Well, we're charged a pound a week for our lot, and that's inclusive, coals and light and everything. I'll give you the address. You can't better it, I'll take my oath."

He scribbled an address, and Evarne again sought the outer air. At the corner of the street was the girl with the plume, still waiting, who inquired after her success.

Evarne showed her the slip of paper.

" It's the Vauxhall Bridge Road. Is that near by ? " she asked.

" Oh yes ; just cross over and go straight ahead, past that clock."

But to get across this crowded thoroughfare was an undertaking that Evarne, with her shaken nerves, was scarcely capable of managing. Again and again she set out only to return, startled and alarmed, to the pavement. Undue timidity was so new to her that her pretty brow deepened into wrinkles. It was dreadful that stress of mental suffering should have reduced her to this foolishly weak and incapable condition of mind and body.

The girl with the plume once more came to the rescue. " You're not used to London, I can see. I'll take you across And now I'll just show you the right road," she continued, when they had reached the opposite pavement in safety.

" I do hope," declared Evarne slyly, " that nobody specially interesting will happen to come along over there while you are being so kind as to see after me."

Her companion looked for a moment as if she had suddenly discovered herself to be in the society of a clair-voyante. Then she answered lightly enough— " It doesn't matter much if she does."

But Evarne was not to be deceived by the feminine pronoun.

In a couple of minutes the girl with the plume stopped. " Good-bye," she said, holding out her hand, " and good luck."

Evarne was sorry to have to say farewell. She clasped the hand that was offered her.

" Good-bye," she said roguishly, " and I do hope that then he—um—I mean she——"

The girl with the plume interrupted her by a little laugh of amusement. Evarne laughed too, and thus they parted.

It was just a stray meeting—a momentary friendship never to be renewed—but it put Evarne in a new frame of mind. Whether it was owing to the meal, or to having so far forgotten her own woes as to indulge in the fun of bantering another girl, or whether it was to the practical kindness and help she had received in finding a *pied-à-terre*, she knew not ; but certainly she walked down Vauxhill Bridge Road with a considerably brighter ex-pression than heretofore.

The number found, her knock was answered by Mrs.

Burling in person.   Evarne inquired after accommodation and terms.

"Are you a pro, miss?" inquired Mrs. Burling.

"A pro?"

"I mean, are you on the stage yourself?   But there, I can see you ain't."

The girl acknowledged it.

"Does that matter?"

"Not a bit; come in, my dear."

Evarne entered, and trying to close her nostrils against the smell of onions that was wafted along the passage, followed Mrs. Burling into a sitting-room.   This apartment was overcrowded by a suite of shiny black furniture, and decorated lavishly with antimacassars, and objects of one description and another under glass cases.   The girl thought it hideous, and almost unbearable to have to live amid such surroundings.

"Take a seat, miss.   I've only got a ' combined ' vacant now, but next week——"

"I don't want to pay much," confessed Evarne frankly. "How much is the ' combined,' and may I see it?"

She hadn't the least idea of what a " combined " might happen to be, but was not going to desplay her ignorance twice within the first three minutes.

Mrs. Burling led the way up a couple of steep flights of stairs, into a smallish room that she herself probably thought charmingly harmonious and attractive.   Its walls were covered with a dull yellowish paper whereon was a design of pink poppies as big as one's head, with ramping green leaves of a size to correspond.   There were two cupboards painted white, but picked out with green, while the threadbare carpet was likewise of a verdant hue.   By the window was a writing-table, covered with an ink-stained emerald cloth, and the wicker arm-chair that stood before it tried to render itself cosy and enticing by means of a couple of thin cushions—both green, sure enough, but

scarcely a happy combination of the shades of that colour
to be reposing cheek by jowl. In the corner stood a
spotlessly white fluffy-looking bed ; there was a wardrobe
with a disfiguring mirror for the door ; a washing-stand—
with china pink and green—altogether it was complete
enough, but oh !—Evarne's artistic soul shuddered.

However, she had made up her mind that the poor must
be easily pleased, and on learning that she could become
mistress of this domain for ten shillings weekly, inclusive,
she accepted the position without demur.

" 'Ave you got any more luggage at the station ? "
inquired the landlady, " because my Tommy's got a
'and-cart that he can bring it along in."

Evarne said that the bag she had left in the hall downstairs was all she owned in that direction.

" It's my custom to ask for part of the rent in advance,
miss," promptly announced Mrs. Burling.

Without comment, Evarne meekly opened her purse
and produced half-a-sovereign.

" Send up my bag, please," she said, and in another five
minutes found herself alone with all her worldly possessions
in her first independent home in London. Her new life
had indeed started.

CHAPTER XV

THE PROBLEM OF EXISTENCE

BY the time darkness fell solitude had become un-endurable. She did not know a single person in London whom she could visit, so resolved to go forth into the open streets. Even to see strangers passing and repassing would be better than the companion-ship of her own haunting memories.

She wandered around aimlessly, half-confused and some-what entertained by her first contact with busy London after nightfall. She had soon strolled down Victoria Street, and crossed Westminster Bridge, and was amid the activity of the populous and poor south side of the Thames.

After a while, the sight of a noisy flaring street-market in full swing, reminded her that she must make some purchases if she wanted dinner on the morrow. Accord-ingly—after commencing operations by buying a capacious wicker marketing-basket, in emulation of the busy pur-chasers who were evidently experienced housewives—she set about considering her next day's *menu*.

Despite her quiet demeanour, she attracted a great deal of notice. Many heads were turned to gaze after her ; nudgings and whisperings heralded her approach. She disliked this attention, and unaware that her face, apart from its arresting beauty, still bore traces of the emotional anguish she had so recently passed through, put it all down to her attire. She could not fail to see that her costume—albeit the simplest in her late wardrobe—was of an entirely different stamp to that worn by her surrounding sister-women, and resolved on the morrow to get a really cheap skirt and blouse for such occasions. That night, the purchase of food required all her thought.

All went off well, save at the butcher's. There she considered she made a fool of herself! Although it was Monday night, each shop of this description was surrounded by a crowd of carnivorous humanity. " Buy, buy, buy ! " the salesman was shouting encouragingly. " Here's a lovely little joint. Walk up and look—no call to buy. Prime beef. Buy, buy, buy ! Walk up, people, walk up ! "

At length Evarne followed this advice, and did " walk up." The counter outside the shop consisted of a series of divisions marked by numbers ranging from four to ten, and each containing a mass of smallish portions of meat.

Those in number ten partition looked less dried and utterly repulsive than the rest, so, deciding on a tiny piece, the girl daintily touched it with the tip of her finger and inquired its price.

" Tenpence," shouted the noisy butcher, darting away to attend to another customer.

Evarne considered that was far too dear for such a wee portion. She wasn't going to be cheated because she was nicely dressed ; she just wouldn't have that piece ! Settling upon a thin chop, she once again made business-like inquiries concerning its price. Strange ! This was even smaller than her first choice, yet it was tenpence likewise.

This was really puzzling. Ah ! Perhaps it was tenpence a piece, regardless of size. It didn't seem likely, but if so, she would see that she got her money's worth, and lifting up the largest portion of all she once more succeeded in attracting the butcher's attention.

" How much is this bit, then ? " she inquired.

The unkind butcher man actually got rude. " Lor' love

yer, can't yer 'ear me a-telling yer it's *tenpence*, and ain't
it printed plain enough ? "

Evarne was affronted by this unaccustomed disrespect.

" I'll take this piece, then," she announced with the air of
a duchess, whereupon the man, in no ways abashed,
promptly flung it out of sight under a row of hanging joints,
into the interior of the shop.

Evarne remained stationary.

" Walk inside, miss," cried the man, as the crowd jostled,
and others claimed his attention.

The girl obeyed. In its turn her choice was put on the
scales.

" Thirteen ounces, sevenpence-halfpenny," cried the
weigher, wrapping it up with all speed in a bit of newspaper
and handing it over.

Only then did it dawn on Evarne that this universal
price of tenpence meant nothing more nor less than tenpence a pound, and thus the mystery was explained !
Until recently she would have laughed merrily over such
an incident, but now all life was the colour of tragedy.
She saw in this absurd little incident only an allegory of her
all-round practical ignorance, her incapacity, her sordid
position, and the general misery and humiliation of her
probable future. She returned home weary and dejected,
and that night likewise soaked her pillow with tears.

She breakfasted in bed, then dressed and went out to
get a newspaper to study the list of situations vacant.
Buying two or three she inquired the way to the nearest
public gardens. The policeman directed her to Hyde Park,
and ere long she was seated facing the Row, idly watching
the equestrians as they cantered past.

How cheerful, how light-hearted, they all seemed !

People on foot, even though richly clad, often looked
discontented and ill-natured. Those driving in the finest
of motors, or the most splendid of carriages, with prancing
horses and all outward tokens of luxury, might appear

dreadfully bored with existence; but one and all who were mounted upon these well-groomed steeds on this fresh spring morning appeared to radiate health and happiness as they passed.

It was scarcely a kind Fate that brought Evarne to this spot, with the very papers in her hand in which she hoped to find the printed announcement of some quiet little corner in the labour market into which she might creep to earn mere bread and cheese. She looked with eyes that were frankly envious upon the riders. How unfair it seemed that some people should have so much money and others none at all unless they either slaved or sinned.

Had she been plunged into poverty with Morris still true—still loving her—she could have faced the turn of Fortune's wheel with a stout heart and a cheery smile. But the stroke that had been dealt to her affections seemed to have crushed her very spirit.

Nor had she any, save her own moral resources, upon which to lean for support. This would have seemed a period when the glorious and elevating influence of Socrates should have had power to lift her into lofty realms of philosophical resignation. But for the greatest of her griefs, the most gnawing, the most unendurable, the teacher was worse than useless. Scant comfort does he give to those whose love is unhappy. On the contrary, his words, his ideas, as they had been interpreted by Evarne, merely served to gall the wound, and she dared not dwell upon them.

She did not open her papers, but sat watching the passing throng. She smiled as two little girls came galloping by at full speed. They rode astride, and a groom led the pony of the youngest by a leading-rein. The hats of both tiny maidens had blown back, their flying curls rose and fell, their faces were flushed bright pink with excitement and delight. Next a young woman rode past at a walking pace. By her side was a man. She too looked radiantly happy, but it was not the exhilaration of exercise that had brought that glad light into her eyes. Evarne looked after them sympathetically. Although her own story had ended in destruction and misery, she still found a pair of earnest young lovers the most interesting—the most attractive—sight in the world.

Numbers of elderly rotund gentlemen trotted along. For them the morning ride was but a doctor's prescription —still, they took it with a cheerful countenance—this delightful recipe! Then passed two women, both evidently over fifty; they still possessed elegant and slender figures, shown off by immaculate habits. They were mounted on magnificent horses—lithe, powerful, big— horses fit to carry heavy men, and to whom the weight of these slight women must have been a mere nothing. Evarne imagined that these two riders were wealthy maiden sisters —the great ladies of some country district—who came to London just for the season. She fancied they had lived side by side in state and dignity from infancy upwards, and that there had never been a hero in the story of either of their lives.

Immediately after them came a golden-haired damsel— gay, *débonnaire*, handsome—but marred by an irrefutable touch of vulgarity. Her find form and shady morals had gone to make her a prosperous career! Her life had never been without a hero. Next came a youthful and highborn mother, cantering easily, looking down with smiling care and pride upon the gallant little son and heir who rode so manfully beside her on a shaggy white pony. Ah! there was life, happiness, health, wealth, love— everything! But she must waste no more time. Moving to a less prominent seat she opened her papers.

Doubtless if Evarne had been an artistic genius she would have declined to abandon entirely the pursuit of art. As it was, knowing her own incompetence, she at once hopelessly renounced all ideas of art as a profession.

What then offered itself ?   If she had happened to possess
a knowledge of shorthand there were many openings, but
then she didn't happen to, so that was no use !   A smart
girl about eighteen was wanted to assist in a grill-room and
make herself generally useful.   A stifling grill-room !
Horrible !   Some bakers required a young lady as book-
keeper and to assist in shop.   Arithmetic had never been
her strong point.   A barmaid was wanted.   Heaven for-
bid !   Another lady was required to push the boot trade.
" Pushing " anything was also not her strong point.

The " C's " were all cashiers and clerks.   Arithmetic
and shorthand again.   Useless !   Oh, there was also a
demand for cooks.   Well, she could boil eggs and potatoes,
and make toast, but that was hardly sufficient.   Drapery
establishments required ladies for various departments.
That was decidedly the most promising so far.   She would
write to some of these.   Dressmakers wanted hands,
assistants, improvers and apprentices.   Oh dear, dear !
Several hotels wanted mangeresses or housekeepers, and
an infirmary required a female lunatic attendant.   It was
terribly disheartening work.   Lady canvassers—that again
required the gift of being pushing.   Laundry-managers—
mantle-machinists—milliners—servants.   There ended the
choice.   Appalling !

However, she proceeded to answer a few of the advertisements, when the idea came to consult Mrs. Burling.   The
landlady was a practical working-woman, and therefore
perhaps the very best possible adviser.

So Evarne to a certain extent became confidential.
What did Mrs. Burling think was the easiest way of earning
a livelihood for a girl who had not been taught any profession, and who, owing to deaths and unexpected losses,
found herself obliged to earn money right away ?

Without a moment's hesitation, Mrs. Burling suggested
the stage.   This was not unnatural, considering that the
worthy matron spent her days waiting hand and foot upon

plain, commonplace women and inane men, who, by that means, contrived to lead leisured lives. That was the one and only trade, business or profession she knew of that seemed to call for neither brains, industry, previous preparation, nor—in her opinion—any particular talent or qualification whatsoever.

"I do assure you, miss," she went on, "I've 'ad ladies and gents 'ere earning good money, who would 'ave been in the work'ouse if they wasn't in the profession."

Evarne considered. She was blankly ignorant of everything connected with life behind the scenes. True, she had met several so-called "actresses" in the society of Morris's friends, but these ladies never seemed to be acting, so she could not consider that they represented the genuine article. She had a vague idea—gleaned from she scarce knew where—that the men of the dramatic world were all vulgar and vain and familiar and inclined to drink, unless, on the other hand, they were popular, fascinating and romantic; while the women were jealous, rather rowdy, and overdressed, until those upper ranks were reached wherein they figured on picture postcards, when they were models of every public and domestic virtue. Still, to the girl's imagination, a stage life certainly seemed far more bearable than the vision of herself measuring out lace and ribbon from morn to eve; or serving round grilled chops; or fighting with lunatics.

"I really think I shall try that," she announced at length; "but I'm dreadfully ignorant about how to get a post. Does one go to the theatres, or write to the leading actors, or the managers, or what?"

"There's all sorts of ways," declared Mrs. Burling. "For one thing, you must 'ave a good photo of yourself to send round. What 'ave you got?"

Evarne confessed that she had nothing.

"Then you must 'ave one took, and 'ave sticky-backs made from it."

" Sticky-backs ? "

" Yes, fifty a shilling. Don't you know 'em ? I've got some stuck in my visitors' book. I'll get it, and let you see."

She returned in due course and presented the volume.

" I've got a message for you," she went on. " I jist mentioned to the ladies and gents in the sitting-room, when I went in to git the book, what I wanted it for, and when they 'eard you'd never bin on the stage and was thinking of starting, they sent up an invite that if you'd take supper with 'em when they return from the 'all this evening, they'd be very 'appy to give you some advice."

" Oh, that is kind of them," declared Evarne with alacrity. " Will you tell them I'll be very pleased to accept ? "

Mrs. Burling took her departure, and the girl amused herself by studying the visitors' book. Clearly, no praise of the worthy landlady was deemed too exaggerated, and quite often tactful self-advertisements had been un-blushingly inserted by the writers. Evarne studied the method by which it was achieved, with a view to future use. Thus " Wally Wentworth, Mrs. Wally Wentworth and Miss Arundale Sutherland, on highly successful return visit with sketch, ' The Perils of the Dark,' stopped here, and found complete satisfaction with both cooking and accommodation." Very ingenious !

Another, a gentleman whose jolly countenance was preserved to future ages through the medium of a " sticky-back," declared—

" Owing to being braced up by Mother Burling's high-class cookery, sang ' Cats a-walking on the tiles ' and ' Lazy Lily's Lullaby ' as never before ! Brought down the house ! "

" The Giggling Coon Girls " were also full of praises of Mrs. Burling, but did not forget to add that at the music hall they were " encored nightly."

Evarne was quite carried away by the childish self-complacency, the light-hearted tone of gaiety that pervaded this book, and began to wax quite enthusiastic over the idea of going on the stage herself. Perhaps she would be a great success, and become famous, and earn any amount of money. Then Morris, of course, would hear of her triumphs, and then—— But she stayed these fairy visions with a stern hand as soon as Morris appeared in them. The pain grew too cruel. Nothing could ever undo the past.

She wondered if she could act well. She had never had any ambition in that direction, and so had never tried, not even as an amateur. But surely anyone could learn to undertake small parts quite easily. She did not expect to be called upon to play "Juliet" or "Pauline Deschapelles" immediately.

The hours passed. She found an old novelette in a drawer, and occupied her time in reading the rubbish, until a scream of laughter, the bang of a door and a general sense of uproar, proclaimed that the "sketch party" had returned from its evening labours. A few minutes later a tap came on the door, and in response to the injunction to "Come in," a tall, slender girl, with faint traces of "make-up" still clinging around her eyes, appeared on the threshold.

"We've come back, Miss Stornway," she announced in a friendly manner, "and I've come up to bring you down to have a bit of supper with us as arranged."

Willingly enough Evarne went downstairs. The meal was laid in readiness in the sitting-room, where two men and a buxom middle-aged female, all lounging around waiting for the first course to appear, seemed to fill the already overfurnished place to repletion.

The girl who had run up to conduct the guest downstairs now undertook the task of effecting a general introduction.

"This is Mr. Hal Cuthbert, the manager of our 'Fun in the Hayfield' sketch company," she commenced, indicating the elder of the two men. "This is Mrs. Hal Cuthbert." The lady in question bowed so deliberately and graciously that Evarne felt constrained to solemnly return the formal salutation. "This is Mr. Bertie Anderson." Here the girl exchanged smiles with her acquaintance at the hall. "My name is Margaret Macclesfield, and you are Miss Stornway, so now we all know one another."

Everyone hereupon started to speak at once, but Mrs. Burling appearing with a dish of soused mackerel, all subsided for a moment, took their seats, and the little meal commenced.

Very soon Evarne arrived at the conclusion that if this party was typical of theatrical ladies and gentlemen, she had been vastly mistaken in her estimate of such. They were evidently not unlike ordinary human beings, only rather jollier. They were very lively, very light-hearted, easily amused at not remarkably brilliant witticisms, whether the product of their own genius or that of their companions. They were, moreover, exceedingly frank and open, telling her all about themselves, their whole history and that of their respective families. They waxed enthusiastic on their past dramatic successes and their future hopes—future fears they seemed not to possess. Altogether Evarne quite forgot herself, and enjoyed the chatter after her period of involuntary solitude. It was not until the meal was over, and tobacco fumes filled the air, that the subject of her future on the stage was mooted.

But this little band of professionals was far less sanguine and encouraging than Mrs. Burling had been.

Mr. Hal Cuthbert opened the debate.

"It's a dreadfully overcrowded profession you are thinking of embarking on, Miss Stornway, and unless you have influence or money, even talent has a hard fight."

"I have no influence, and very little money, and I

don't really know that I've got any special talent," declared
this applicant for stage honours, making no attempt to
conceal the true state of affairs."

Mr. Cuthbert shook his head portentously.

"That is not a very hopeful prospect," he declared.
"Haven't you got a voice? There's a piano yonder.
Let's hear what you can do."

Evarne in her turn shook her head. "I'm afraid I
can't sing," she said regretfully. "I've never had my
voice trained at all."

A momentary silence seized the party.

"Perhaps you can dance?" suggested Margaret Macclesfield, hopefully.

"Only ordinary ballroom dances."

"That's no go," and a silence still more melancholy,
more profound, held sway.

"There's no place for you on the halls, then. Perhaps
you'd do all right in legitimate drama. Can you recite
something?"

"I'm alfraid I don't know anything dramatic," Evarne
was obliged to confess, her cheeks growing pinker. "I
don't know much poetry at all, and what I have learnt
from time to time are only pretty little bits that have
taken my fancy."

"Dear me——" Mr. Cuthbert was recommencing,
when his wife broke in——

"Don't you do it, my dear. It's a dreadful profession
for them as haven't got the gifts. It's a grinding, killing
business. I'd as soon see a girl of mine in her grave."

"The old lady isn't far wrong," agreed Mr. Cuthbert.
"You take my advice, Miss Stornway, and try something
else."

"But," declared Evarne despairingly, "whatever I
tried it would be just the same. I——I'm not properly
qualified for anything. It's not my fault, but there it is!
I didn't think of the stage when I found I'd got to earn

my own living, but now it has been suggested to me I feel sure I stand a better chance of earning money quickly that way than any other."

" You've got a real beautiful face, if you don't mind my being personal," said Margaret. " Perhaps you might get a thinking part, right enough—or there's pantomime. You're tall, aren't you? If you've got good legs and a fine figure—— What's your waist ? "

Yet once again Evarne was compelled to shake her head apologetically.

" I'm afraid—— " she started, then stopped abruptly. However, frankness seemed to prevail here, so she continued after an imperceptible pause. " I don't think I've got what you mean by a fine figure. I need very careful and special dressing to look really nice. You see, I don't wear corsets, and so—— "

" My dear ! " interrupted both ladies simultaneously, " how can you manage without ? "

" Well, I was brought up to it," explained the girl hastily.

" I should feel as if I'd got no backbone."

" I couldn't keep up. I should flop."

" But you can wear some now if you like."

" That's exactly what I can't do. I tried once, quite seriously, and it made me ill—really ill—and I don't suppose it gets any easier to change one's habits as one gets older."

Mrs. Cuthbert flourished her hands despairingly.

" It's no go, my dear. Put the idea of the stage out of your head at once. No voice, no talents, no experience, no money, and no waist ! "

A general cry of expostulation greeted this rather cruel résumé of poor Evarne's deficiencies.

" You've got a lovely face anyway, my dear," said Mr. Hal, " and you look to have a nice figure, whether you have really or not, if I may say as much. I think the old lady's advice is good, but you mustn't let your feelings be hurt."

"That's all right," declared the girl stoutly. "It's only too good of you to trouble about me at all, and you mustn't think me either vain or ungrateful if I say that I am still resolved to try my luck. I believe I could act, and I've never yet found my personal appearance a disadvantage to me; I expect that, even without corsets, I can manage to look as well as the average girl. I must start to earn money at once, that's sadly certain. I've been thinking over every other means, and none of them seem suitable, so if you would end up your kindness by giving me some hints as to how to get work on the stage at once I shall be infinitely obliged."

Their good-nature in no way disturbed by their unanimous judgment being thus flouted, they gave her advice as best they could. Like Mrs. Burling, they declared it was imperative she should have some photos of herself to send round. Then she must go to agents, and answer advertisements in the theatrical papers, and—well, really it was hard to say, engagements came somehow—if any of them got a chance they would certainly put in a word for her.

For this she was duly grateful, and a little later the party broke up.

CHAPTER XVI

EVARNE'S FIRST ENGAGEMENT

NEXT morning, accompanied by the two younger of her new acquaintances, Evarne sallied forth in search of a photographer's.

Carefully they studied various photographic show-cases of modest pretensions. She was reluctant to spend any of her limited capital in so seemingly frivolous a manner, and was anxious to expend as small a sum as possible on this preliminary. But here it was clearly possible to be "penny wise, pound foolish," and she recoiled at the prospect of being made to look anything like the self-conscious, staring, pictured females that the really low-priced artists of the camera set forth as attractive products of their prowess—the specimens best calculated to tickle the vanity of the passers-by and draw them into the toils of the producer of such representations.

At length they discovered one whose masterpieces seemed less terrible than those of his rivals. Margaret undertook the *rôle* of spokesman.

"Only one copy of each position is required," she said, "but they must be delivered without delay, as the young lady is on the stage, and needs them immediately for professional purposes," and she went on to bargain about reduced prices.

After the operator's shutter had made its significant click two or three times, the party wended their way to the Strand, and Evarne had her name duly inscribed upon several agents' books. In some cases this privilege cost money, and she returned home horrified by the rapidity with which funds melted. True, Bertie Anderson had " stood " both girls their luncheon, but despite this, the day's output had been something alarming.

Everyone in the house continued to concern themselves over her welfare. Indeed, from the first hour of her arrival in London she had met with nothing but good-will. Herein Heaven watched over her, for this general kindliness on the part of mankind at large was the best possible balm for her scorned and wounded affections. True, no care from others could really touch the injury inflicted by " the one," but it all served to help melt the ice that seemed gathered around her breast.

Her acquaintance with the merry, good-natured " Fun in the Hayfield " people proved a veritable salvation. Left to herself for any appreciable period, she weakly sank into a state of brooding despair, but save for the evening of the " photographer-hunting " day, she was in their society for practically the whole of the remainder of the week.

Mr. Cuthbert had offered to pass her into the music hall that night, but she declined the offer. She was tired, and shrank from the anticipated noise and glare. But once alone she regretted her decision. Memories of the past crowded thick upon her, with their train of regrets, hot indignation, bitter sorrow, and the thousand and one tearing passions that rendered thought unendurable. Solitude was—for the present at least—but a state of torture to be avoided at all costs. Distraction, company, variety was no longer a matter of choice, but an absolute necessity. She had vainly endeavoured to find relief from the agony of thought by mingling with the passing crowds. Despairing, she returned home and to bed, but her brain had worked itself into a tumult during the long evening hours, and no sleep came. Long she lay awake, weeping, hating, yearning and lamenting.

" You look paler than ever, Evarne, my dear ! What-ever have you been doing to yourself ? " cried Margaret, who came up to present her with some chocolates from a box that some admiring "chap" had sent round to the stage door. She was in high feather over the little gift.

"People think we get so many flowers given us we haven't vases to put them in, and so many pairs of gloves we haven't hands enough to wear them, and so many sweeties we haven't digestions enough to tackle them all, let alone cheques and presents of jewellery about once a week!" she exclaimed; "but I assure you that's a jolly big mistake, as you'll find out, dear. Come on, tuck in to chocs and take some of this row. They've got pinky cream, and you'll have to put some colour on from the outside, if you can't manage to provide it somehow from the inside," and she laughed gaily.

"I do hate to be alone," explained Evarne, brightening visibly at the effect of this chatter. "I—I've had great trouble lately, and when I'm by myself—well—I think!"

Margaret was full of sympathy.

"Poor dear, don't 'think' then, don't be alone. I know what we will do. I'm going to order Mrs. Burling to serve your meals along with ours, and we will see if we can't cheer you up among us."

"I should like that," cried Evarne, jumping at the idea. Thus until the following Sunday, when these kind friends moved on to play their "sketch" in a hall right out of London, she was scarcely left alone for an hour. Every night she went with Mrs. Cuthbert and Margaret to their dressing-room, where she assisted in arraying them, and was instructed in the many mysteries of "making-up." She learnt many things—the knack of melting cosmetic in a teaspoon and applying it to the eyelashes with a hairpin —how to fluff out her hair by combing it the wrong way— how to transform a skin of common lard into glorified face-grease, sweetly smelling of essence of bergamot—and a dozen other little tricks of the trade.

Either Margaret or Bertie accompanied her on her daily visits to the agents, and on Thursday morning—albeit she

had as yet no " sticky-backs "—they helped her study the
new number of the *Stage*. Her experienced friends warned
her that the approach of summer was not a favourable
time to find " a shop."

Nevertheless there seemed to Evarne a goodly and various
demand in the " Wanted " column. There were openings
for pretty attractive chorus girls, soubrettes, a good responsible lady, a powerful leading lady, a pathetic old lady, a
show lady, an emotional juvenile lady, and a dashing heavy
lady ; and if one couldn't place one's self under any of these
descriptions, then one could modestly seek to be a " cham-
bermaid." Also there were sweeping invitations for whole
companies to " write in." Accordingly Evarne " wrote
in "—spent 1s. 3d. on stamps—then waited.

At the end of the week she was forced to part from her
kind friends. She assured them that for their sakes she
would henceforward and forever cherish an affectionate
regard for the whole of the theatrical fraternity. Faithful
promises of correspondence were exchanged, and then the
girl found herself thrown upon her own society.

Mrs. Burling had already let her sitting-room for the
coming week, but the two men who now occupied it—low
comedians—appeared to fastidious Evarne as very low
specimens of humanity likewise. So, when one of them—
encountering her on the front doorstep—showed a tendency
to be affable, she received the poor fellow's effort most coolly.

However, her time was now fully occupied. She mar-
keted daily, haunted the theatrical agents, read poetry
aloud in her best dramatic style in the privacy of her room,
and occasionally expended a shilling on the gallery of some
theatre to study acting and find out how it was done.

By the time the next theatrical paper appeared, she was
the owner of fifty small replicas of the most attractive of her
new photographs, and she desperately set to work to answer
almost every advertisement—likely and unlikely. Alack
and alas, not a single response crowned her efforts !

Then she nearly sank into utter despondency. Whatever was to be done? No work forthcoming, and her little hoard of money melting away like snow in a thaw. Why, it was enough to test the fortitude of the bravest! She was almost in despair by the time she had been in London two weeks, and was still as far from being a wage-earner as when she first arrived.

So the reaction was correspondingly great, when a day or two later she beheld a letter for herself with a Scotch postmark and addressed in a strange handwriting. Mrs. Burling—sympathetically excited—had hurried upstairs with the precious missive and proceeded to wipe some imaginary dust from a vase, while her young lodger tore open the envelope.

The notepaper was headed " Caledonia's Bard Co.," and beneath this was printed a few puffs of the aforesaid concern, which—if one went by its own account—carried a full cast of the most talented artistes, rich and handsome costumes, realistic scenery, etc.

The written address given was Sauchiehall Street, Glasgow, and the letter stated that the manager of " Caledonia's Bard " offered " the small yet effective part " of " Bess " in that production to Miss Stornway, at the remuneration of twenty-one shillings weekly. Miss Stornway was to provide her own costumes, which, however, were of the simplest description, and should she be still at liberty to accept the offer, a gentleman would call upon her to deliver into her hands a railway ticket to Glasgow. The communication was signed " P. Punter."

Its recipient beamed.

" I've got an offer, really! " she exclaimed. " Would you like to see it ? " With these words she handed the letter over to Mrs. Burling, who perused it slowly from start to finish, then sniffed.

" A guinea a week, find your own dresses, and go to Glasgow ! 'Tain't up to much, to my way o' thinking, miss

And 'e don't tell you when the tour opens, nor where it ends up, nor no idea of 'ow long it's going to last, nor nothing about it."

Evarne had not noticed these deficiencies, and now did not heed them.

"Never mind! It's an engagement, and that's everything," she cried gleefully. "I shall hurry up and accept before someone else does;" and seizing pen and paper she wrote her reply.

At all events "P. Punter" appeared a prompt and business-like individual. By return of post came a couple of pencil sketches and instructions concerning the costumes she was to provide for herself. There was also an illegibly written copy of her part, and the request that she would be in Glasgow to commence rehearsals by the following Wednesday.

Evarne smoothed out that most interesting document—the script of her first dramatic *rôle*—and studied it eagerly. She supposed "Caledonia's Bard" was Robert Burns, for references to "Bobbie" were frequent. She could not glean much idea of the plot from her part, nor did the words she was to utter appear likely to call forth any great histrionic talent that might be lying unsuspected within her breast. As far as she could gather, all the scenes of the play took place by the deathbed of "Highland Mary." She read out a speech to Mrs. Burling as a specimen.

"Now lie ye still, bonnie Mary, lie ye still. Sure, Bobbie will greet sair to see ye laid sae low. For his sake, Mary, ye must get the roses back agin into your bonnie cheeks, now sae white, Mary. Oh, doctor, is she no a wee bit better, think ye?"

Thus it went on. "Bonnie Mary" was obviously a most obstreperous patient, and it evidently called forth all "Bess's" powers of persuasion to make her die quietly in bed. "Mary" apparently took to seeing visions as the play waxed more thrilling, and "Bess" was required to employ "gentle strength" to persuade her charge

to obey the injunction, repeated with wearying reiteration, "Rest ye calm, Mary; rest ye calm." Indeed, the
idea did flash across Evarne that she might almost as
well have undertaken to tend lunatics in the privacy of
an infirmary, as she was seemingly to do much the same
sort of thing on the boards and under the public gaze.

"It's not very inspiring, is it?" she said rather despondently, but at the same time she was relieved to find
that no serious demands were to be made upon her—as yet
untried—dramatic abilities.

She went out to buy the brown serge and the blue cotton
material necessary for her two costumes, and on her return
was told that during her absence a gentleman from Scotland
had called and gone.

"It must be my ticket," exclaimed the girl. "Didn't
he leave it?"

Mrs. Burling handed her an envelope. In it Evarne found
the return-half of a third-class ticket from Glasgow to London.

"Dear me, we are going to break the regulations of the
railway company, I see," was her first thought.

However, the arrival of the ticket seemed to make the
engagement real—a settled fact. She was now fully in the
throes of an actress's life. As she sat studying her part
and stitching away at her stage costumes, she recalled the
early days of Mrs. Siddons and various other great theatrical
stars, and tried hard to feel resigned concerning the past
and the present, and hopeful for the future. She determined to force herself to become ambitious. She would
live for and think only of professional success, and dream
no more of Morris.

More of her precious money had to be expended. A
"make-up" outfit was essential, also a small theatrical
touring basket, together with several other more or less
expensive items. Thus by the time she had settled her
final account with Mrs. Burling, there was less than two
pounds in her purse with which to set forth for Glasgow.

CHAPTER XVII

A STRANGE INTRODUCTION TO THE PROFESSION

DEPOSITING her box at the Glasgow station left-luggage office, she set out to discover Sauchie-hall Street. In this, of course, no difficulty arose, but when it came to finding the actual house—well, that appeared a total impossibility. Evarne was almost inclined to believe that she had come to Scotland on a wild-goose chase, for there seemed to exist no such address as that with which Mr. Punter had headed his letters. There was the number above and the number below the very one she required, but between them—where the house she sought would naturally have been expected to stand—was merely a piece of unused building ground.

It was a forlorn, unkempt spot, with straggling grasses and weeds, amid which were piles of bricks and stone, fragments of torn paper, an old boot, and other such débris as will accumulate on waste ground, even though it be in the very centre of the principal street of a big city. As if to make it serve at least one useful purpose, there had been erected on it an enormous hoarding, covered with advertisements.

Here was a regular mystery! Inquiries respecting the address she was seeking were vain. She walked anxiously up and down Sauchiehall Street, half hoping to find the missing number somehow transported from its legitimate numerical position, but all to no avail. Again and again she returned to survey the deserted site where Mr. Punter's residence *ought* to be. Unless he camped in the shadow of the hoarding, as did one or two stray cats—a sudden thought flashed across her! Pushing past the small gate that hung partly open on its hinges, and ploughing her way through the long grass, she penetrated round to the back of the hoarding. There it was, after all—a house sure enough—partly tumbled down, it is true, with broken windows, fallen chimneys, and a general air of having been long abandoned by mankind; still, a house, even though half the roof had collapsed. More than that; close by, on a large wooden frame, hung a roughly painted theatrical drop-scene. The place was found!

But what a habitation for a civilised human being! What sort of a person was Mr. Punter? Was he a gipsy— a tramp? Was he in the last stages of poverty, or merely eccentric? The girl approached the front door. Its upper half was formed of thick panels of stained glass, now cracked and broken in a dozen places, but with brown paper carefully pasted on the inner side to cover the actual holes. Knocking boldly with the end of her umbrella, Evarne waited, though half prepared to receive no answer.

But after a moment's silence there came a sound of a window being thrown open, and a voice called out from somewhere aloft, " Hullo! "

She stepped back and looked upwards. A youth, wrapped in a blanket, was gazing down upon her.

" Oh, I suppose you are Madame Sheep, or Miss Stornway? " he exclaimed. " Stop a minute, and I'll be down."

With these words he vanished.

Decidedly " intrigued," the girl waited patiently. How very unlike was this reception to anything her wildest imagination had anticipated. An inhabited ruin, the occupant thereof clad in the bedclothes, peering down from an upper window to inquire if she was herself or some person who possessed the weird name of " Madame Sheep! " She felt as if it were part of a ridiculous dream.

Finally, the door was opened, not by the blanketed

youth, but by a middle-aged man, small and short, with a head beginning to grow bald and a face clean-shaven, save for curious old-fashioned side-whiskers.

Hailing the girl by name with the heartiness of an old friend, he led the way across the hall and into a large room on the ground floor. It was totally unfurnished, save for a rough wooden table, a bench and a couple of chairs. On one of these Evarne was invited to take a seat.

Yes, this little individual was "the" Mr. Punter in person. He proceeded to hold forth in enthusiastic terms concerning the future prospects of "Caledonia's Bard." The play had never been produced yet, that was why he had advertised for a full company. He anticipated that it would run for years. Not that he expected to be able to retain the original company all that time. Every part was so splendid—practically all were star-parts—that the artistes who had the good fortune to appear in them would soon be tempted away from him by London managers. Oh no, he hadn't written the drama himself. He only wished he was sufficiently gifted. But he was very proud to be able to acknowledge that it was, indeed, the fruit of the genius of one of his family. Such an inspiring subject. He had an intense admiration for Robert Burns. Was Miss Stornway, indeed, not intimately acquainted with the whole of that wonderful poet's works? Oh dear! dear! That was distressing, and must be remedied. She should be lent a book—several books. Mr. Sandy, the great actor who was to play the title *rôle*, knew nearly all Burns's poems by heart, and it was chiefly owing to his appreciation of the acute study of the poet's character in "Caledonia's Bard," that he had resolved to disappoint several other managers in order to join this company. The young lady who played "Highland Mary," the heroine, had not arrived yet. She lived in Northumberland. A really excellent actress, only second to Ellen Terry. Mr. Punter had gone to great expense to procure her services.

Madame Cheape—not Sheep, my dear—was the " Clarinda." This spacious apartment had been retained especially for rehearsals.

Thus he ran on, apparently in emulation of Tennyson's brook, and Evarne had nothing to do but look intelligent, and interpose a brief question occasionally to show that she was attending.

He only ceased when the door opened to admit a little woman who had approached unheard. The newcomer was very pale, and looked fragile and subdued. Her thin hair was drawn neatly behind her ears, her shabby black gown hung in folds over her flat chest, and she slouched in list slippers so many sizes too large that had she ventured to lift her feet in walking, she would inevitably have stepped out of her footgear, and left it behind her on the floor.

" Ah ha ! Allow me to introduce my wife," said Mr. Punter.

Evarne rose and shook hands.

" How do you like your part ? " was the salutation of the lady of the house.

The girl discreetly avoided a direct answer.

" It has made me very anxious to hear the whole play."

Fortunately the little woman considered this response as entirely satisfactory. She smiled complacently, and commenced to nod her head so steadily, it appeared in danger of becoming loosened.

Mr. Punter likewise seemed to swell with pride. At length he could keep the great secret no longer.

" I may as well tell you first as last, Miss Stornway. You are now addressing the authoress of ' Caledonia's Bard.' "

Evarne was indeed taken aback at this piece of information. Barely succeeding in suppressing a start, she murmured something she fondly hoped was duly appropriate to the occasion. Evidently she was successful, for Mrs. Punter ceased nodding, and thanked her heartily.

"And now, where are you going to put up, my dear?"
she inquired. "Do you know Glasgow at all?"

"I've never been here before, but I expect I can find
diggings easily enough. Rehearsals begin to-morrow,
don't they?"

"Well, that was what we expected," responded Mr.
Punter. "But a few of the principals have not arrived
yet. Still, a short delay will enable you to become word-
perfect in your part, won't it? And that is so important."

"Yes-s. But when does the tour open, then?"

"Of course that depends entirely on how the rehearsals
progress. Now, you must have something to eat before
you start house-hunting. You won't mind going into the
kitchen?"

Mrs. Punter slouched on ahead, and Evarne followed to
another room at the rear of the house. This also was
practically devoid of furniture, but doubtless derived its
name from the small oil-stove that stood on the table.

The window looked out on to what had formerly been a
garden, but which now wore that melancholy and desolate
aspect that characterises a once well-tended spot that has
long been utterly neglected. The lawn was a field; the
flower-beds lost in weeds; the gravel walks overgrown;
boisterous winds had snapped the slender stem of a young
tree, which now lay wilted upon the ground. Altogether,
it was a scene in no way conducive to high spirits.

The authoress set about performing culinary operations
with a frying-pan and the oil-stove, and in due course a
repast was evolved of fried ham and stale bread. Evarne
found Mrs. Punter's skill at cookery on a par with the
estimate she had already formed of her literary gifts.
Eating heroically what she could, she rose to leave.

"But first I must introduce you to Charles Stuart,"
declared Mr. Punter, who had joined them.

"Yes. Who is he?"

"He does a little carpentering, and is to appear in the
drama. He is now painting the scenery."

" Useful man," thought the girl, and almost forgave him for adopting such a *nom-de-théatre*.

Wending their way to a tiny outhouse, they there found this valuable personage busily occupied in mixing paint. He turned round at their entry, and for the second time that hour Evarne with difficulty suppressed a gasp. The entire person of Charles Stuart, as far as could be seen, was so covered with black hair that at first glance he resembled a monkey. Quantities of fringe concealed his forehead, falling even over his massive eyebrows. Although quite young still, he not only had a heavy moustache, but a beard and whiskers that lost themselves in the thick mop covering his cranium, while his open shirt displayed a chest like unto a doormat. As he transferred the dripping paint-brush to his left hand and advanced towards Evarne with his hairy right arm outstretched, the girl felt rather like ignobly bolting away. What very extraordinary people she had fallen amidst, to be sure !

But she stood her ground, and spoke to the man as if he had been a natural-looking human being.

" What are you painting now, Mr. Stuart ? I should like to see what you have done, if I may."

" Show Miss Stornway what you are working at, Charlie," suggested Mr. Punter, and as they all went out into the garden he explained—

" Stuart was for years the head scene-painter at one of the leading London theatres. You see, we mean to spare no expense."

Evarne found herself wishing that she had not been apparently the one exception in this determination concerning lavish expenditure.

Hanging against the wall of the house were three scenes— one a cottage interior, another a wild glen, and the third, a rustic landscape, scarcely commenced.

" I should like to watch you work," she said. " I paint a little myself."

"Perhaps you would like to help, then?" Mr. Punter promptly suggested. "All my sons work under Charlie. Come to-morrow, and we will find you an apron and brushes and see what you can manage to produce, eh?"

Laughingly, Evarne promised, and at length was allowed to depart.

CHAPTER XVIII

NEW TRIALS AND TROUBLES

AFTER some search she lighted on a really pleasant room, clean and bright, at a rent of ten shillings weekly. It possessed a true Scotch bed, built into a cupboard in the wall. She had her box conveyed from the station, and that night slept comfortably enough in this curiously situated bed, in which confused dreams of authoresses who inhabited ruins, and hairy men who painted scenery in back gardens, appeared only an appropriate accompaniment.

The next afternoon she wended her way to Sauchiehall Street, and there made the acquaintance of Mr. Punter's six sons, old and young—including Pat, the youth who had first greeted her from the window. Then started scene-painting. She undertook to do a cottage window, draped with snowy muslin curtains. Pots of scarlet geraniums stood on the sill, a big flour-bin was underneath, while a green pasture with a lovely blue sky showed through the open lattice. Her effort evoked ardent admiration from the whole assembled Punter family. Indeed, Mrs. Punter's gratitude was such that she impulsively invited the artist in to tea.

Never had Evarne beheld such an extraordinary chamber as that upstairs one into which—as a guest of the family— she was now admitted. The first impression was of the wildest confusion—house-moving, or spring-cleaning at least. Here, as elsewhere throughout the house, the windows were cracked and broken. In one corner was a

huge bed, covered with a grimy patchwork quilt. Boxes
stood around, some with open lids, others as yet uncorded,
while two large empty crates placed side by side and
covered with a cloth formed the table. There were several
chairs and stools, piles of dishes, cups and saucers of varied
hues and designs; some torn books, devoid of covers;
a number of men's hats and outdoor coats; and a baby's
cradle half-filled with potatoes.

The uncarpeted floor, on which lay a few small rugs,
was decorated likewise by a considerable number of stage
" properties " of many descriptions. The half-dozen large
plaster statues that stood around doubtless came under
this heading, but being all nude, they appeared indecently
incongruous amidst this domestic confusion and makeshift. Evarne was now quite convinced that the Punters
were merely " squatters "—that they paid no rent, that
no public authority knew them to be here, that they had,
in fact, taken up their temporary abode in what was
really a deserted and supposedly uninhabitable house.

" I've been grieving all the night that you've not been
engaged to play ' Highland Mary,' " commenced Mrs. Punter, after supplying her guest with tea. " You're so verra
bonnie, just like what I imagine her."

Evarne was somewhat flattered.

" Will you care to hear ' Mary's ' part ? " asked Mr. Punter,
and he then read aloud those scenes in which this damsel
appeared. Since she breathed her last in the second act,
and " Clarinda " then took her place as heroine, the *rôle* was
but brief.

" Now read her the part of ' Jean Armour,' " said Mrs.
Punter, and the obedient husband started off again.

As he ceased, he looked inquiringly at Evarne over the
top of his spectacles.

The girl's genuine opinion was that never had she
listened to such utter twaddle in all her life. There did
not seem to be any plot at all, no vestige of even a central

thread of continuous story. Yet more and more was proudly read aloud, until at length nearly the whole manuscript had been gone through. It was really immensely funny, but, alas! this was quite unintentional. Its creator laboured under the belief that she had produced a poetical drama in blank verse, slightly bordering on a tragedy!

Evarne felt cold depression steal over her as she listened. Was it possible that such inane dulness would ever attract the public? But, concealing her fears, she inquired in respectful tones—

" Did it not take you a long time to write it ? "

" Oh dear me, no," was Mrs. Punter's lightly spoken disclaimer. " I just dictated it to my husband in odd moments, while I'd be bustling about getting dinner. It was no trouble to me, I assure you."

It was on the tip of the girl's tongue to answer, " I thought not," but instinct whispered that such a supposition might not fall quite prettily upon the authoress's ears. Instead, she was just hypocrite enough to look as impressed as she could have done had Shakespeare himself stated a similar fact.

After this she rose to leave. Amiably enough they insisted on lending her several books concerning the hero of their drama ; a volume of his poems, one called " Burns's Highland Mary," another entitled " Burns's Chloris," and yet another about his " Clarinda." Evarne thought it very unromantic and unpoetical of " Bobbie " to have worshipped at the shrines of so many " ladye-loves," but was well pleased to be supplied with so much reading matter.

Still, while all this was very well in its way, it was not business! Days passed. Mr. Sandy and " Highland Mary " did not arrive, neither did Evarne see any of her other fellow-artistes. As time went on and no rehearsal-call was given, while the demands upon her purse were constant, she commenced to make frequent and anxious inquiries.

Mr. Punter was evidently as much concerned as she was herself.

"But it's no use my gathering the company together here until Mr. Sandy has arrived. You must see that for yourself. The whole play circles round him, as you know. We must all wait a day or two longer. I admit I cannot account for his unexplained neglect, and am much displeased."

Evarne saw nothing for it but to be patient and make the best of a bad job, but it was indeed a very seriously bad job in her case. She had been prepared to find it difficult to make her money last out until she received her first week's salary, and this delay over even commencing the rehearsals was really terrible.

She was lonely as well as anxious. She recommenced sketching, studied Burns and his poems, stared in the shop-windows, visited the Corporation Picture Gallery, read in the Free Library. Despite all this, time hung heavily on her hands.

"What do the remainder of your company do?" she inquired of Mr. Punter one morning, on being informed, as usual, that no news had been heard of Mr. Sandy. She had that hour been forced to produce another half-sovereign for her lodgings, and was seriously alarmed at her situation. "Are the others submitting to be kept fooling around earning nothing and having to spend money every day, as I am?"

"They realise that it's no fault of mine, Miss Stornway," answered Mr. Punter severely, "and they do not add to my worries by reproaching me, even indirectly."

"That's all very well," retorted Evarne tartly. "You say most of them have homes in Glasgow. In that case it's not the same expense for them that it is to me, and they have their friends and families also, while I'm alone."

"As far as that goes, I'll tell you what I can do—yes, and I will do it."

This was stated with such an imposing and benevolent air that Evarne waited expectant to hear in what manner she was to be recompensed for this unjustifiable delay.

" Yes, I can quite do away with any trouble of that nature. I shall give your address in Shamrock Street to the very next of our lady artistes who calls here, and she will doubtless come to see you. It is really too bad that you should have no society."

" It's decidedly worse that I should have no work, and, consequently no salary," retorted the girl as she turned away.

The manager remembered his promise, for a couple of days later Evarne's landlady announced that Miss Kennedy had called from Mr. Punter.

" Oh, show her in, and make tea for two, please," said the girl, and a minute later the visitor entered.

She was a slender little creature, barely eighteen years of age. In appearance she was one of those who seem to have been manufactured in wholesale batches. Her figure was practically identical with that of thousands of other girls, and her countenance likewise had very little that was at all distinctive. The grey eyes were—well, they were what Miss Kennedy looked around the world with, nothing more nor less ! All her other features were equally nondescript. Her light hair, much frizzled in front and tied in a catagon behind, was neither dark nor fair, neither thin nor ample. The little face was not unattractive, but promised very average intelligence and no force of character. She bore not the least likeness to the popular conception of an actress. Her face was entirely free from the least artificial aid to beauty, while her plain serge coat and skirt, scarlet tam-o'-shanter and black cotton gloves were equally unpretentious.

As far as appearance went, she was in every way a contrast to beautiful, stately Evarne, with her aristocratic bearing, yet there was already a bond of sympathy between the two girls, and in less than five minutes they were forming a kind of duet to complain of the perfidious behaviour of the Punters.

"It's really perfectly scandalous," declared Jessie Kennedy. "They promised me the rehearsals were to begin ten days ago. They've got no right to get their company together—or almost together—like this, until they were really going to make a start. And to bring you all the way down from London too! I suppose they paid your fare?"

"Yes, they did that, or I couldn't have come. Still, it's a great shame. They must know people generally can't afford to live in idleness like this. Yet what can we do?"

"Well, I shall accept another engagement in a couple of days if they don't begin, and so I shall tell them."

"What part have you got?"

"I understudy you, I believe, but otherwise I'm not actually in the play itself. I'm the pianist. Of course, we're only a 'fit-up,' and don't have an orchestra, but I'm at the piano all the time between the acts, and I play soft music during the love scenes, the death-beds, and the visions."

"Then I should fancy you're kept very busy?"

"Yes, there is plenty for me to do, but I don't mind that. I only want to start and do it."

"I wonder how the remainder of the company is taking this miserable idleness? Do you know any of them?"

"Oh yes; nearly all, more or less. One, Harry Douglas, lives in my street, and he and I have done double turns at music halls. He's got a voice like a seraph. He's the most glorious tenor you ever heard. He's limes-man in this company."

"Do we have limelight, then?"

"Rather, where 'Highland Mary' appears as a vision, and one or two other places."

"And what does Mr. Douglas think of it all?"

"It doesn't matter so much to him. He's working in a carpenter's shop until we start."

"Fancy! Can't he do a lot of things!"

"But you should just hear him sing. Oh, my! It's angels! It is really!"

CHAPTER XIX

NEW FRIENDS

JESSIE KENNEDY turned out to be a very companionable little person, and after this first interview the two girls spent a good deal of time with each other.

But the question of funds was of infinitely greater consequence than any social intercourse, and with alarming rapidity Evarne had arrived at the point when her resources were no longer represented by even the smallest gold coin of the realm. This thoroughly aroused her, and the very next time she was again put off by excuses, her usual gentleness was swept away beneath one of those torrents of hot wrath that were a heritage from her mother. Her beautiful dark eyes seemed to positively flash fire as she fiercely declared that this sort of thing would have to stop, that Mr. Punter's action in offering her this mock engagement, and so preventing her from seeking genuine work, was absolutely unjustifiable and infamous ; that it was not far short, if at all, from cheating and defrauding ! She concluded by hotly stating that if Mr. Sandy could not or would not come, his part, in mere justice to others, ought to be given at once to an actor who would take it. She finished up by the statement that she was voicing the opinion of others besides her own.

These words did not fall on barren ground. Mr. Punter definitely settled on the evening of the following day for the long-deferred first rehearsal, and further announced that Mr. Sandy had now finally lost his splendid chance, for

Pat should go out immediately and telegraph for Mr. Heathmore, an even better actor, whom he knew to be anxiously longing for the opportunity of appearing in " Caledonia's Bard."

On the strength of all this Evarne allowed herself to be pacified, and was amiably willing to admit that perhaps the real blame rested with the faithless Mr. Sandy alone. Hereupon Mr. Punter had a suggestion to make.

" My wife and I have been talking the matter over, and we have decided to offer you—you, Miss Stornway—the rôle of ' Highland Mary ' in place of that of ' Bess.' It is not a very long part, and you'll soon learn it. Your remuneration then would be twenty-three and six in place of a guinea. There now ! Does not the notion appeal to you ? "

" I don't mind," replied the girl dubiously. " If you could have told me sooner than the very day before the rehearsals are at length to start—but there, if you give me the script at once, I'll commence to study it. But what about costumes ? "

" Quite simple ! Mrs. Punter herself has resolved to undertake the rôle of ' Jean Armour,' so she will buy one of your dresses for the purpose. She says the blue cotton you showed her will serve nicely for you to wear when you go to meet ' Burns ' in the glen, and with the money she gives you for the other you can buy some white stuff and make a robe that will do to die in, and likewise for the vision."

" I agree then, willingly. Who is to play ' Bess ' ? "

" We see no reason why Miss Kennedy should not undertake that inferior part. Madame Cheape—our ' Clarinda,' you remember—will arrive in a day or so, thus all the female rôles will be most satisfactorily filled."

As Evarne walked back to Shamrock Street, she thought somewhat ruefully that she had fallen among a very queer and reckless—not to say shady—set of people. Every-

thing connected with them and their enterprise seemed a
matter of makeshifts. She could not help smiling to recall
the grandiose announcements printed at the head of the
official notepaper. " Company of Star Artistes," indeed !
Fancy herself, then, never having yet set foot upon the
boards or spoken one word in public, being created leading
lady amid these universal stars ! Still, it was such a silly
soft part in such a silly soft play she had to act, that she
was troubled by no apprehensions as to whether she was
sufficiently powerful, or emotional, or capable, or anything
else. She was fully convinced of her ability to rise to equal
heights with the other stars—at all events as far as those
constellations, Mrs. Punter and Jessie, were concerned.

The following evening, sure enough, rehearsals of a sort
did indeed commence. Mr. Heathmore was not forthcoming, and " Caledonia's Bard " without " Bobbie " was
even worse than " Hamlet " without the " Prince of Den-
mark." Still, it was a comfort to make a start of any sort.

Jessie Kennedy at once brought up Harry Douglas, and
presented him to Miss Stornway. He was undertaking two
minor *rôles* in addition to managing the limelight and
helping to shift scenery, and within the first five minutes'
conversation this all-round genius had incidentally remarked
that for several years he had been a professional light-
weight prize-fighter.

Two men—besides the ubiquitous " Bobbie "—had dia-
logue parts with Evarne.

Joe Harold—who played her stage father—she had
heard much of already. Jessie had procured him this
engagement, and had confided to her new friend that ere
the tour ended she hoped to have brought to pass another
engagement of a more romantic and lasting type. He
was absolutely the dearest boy alive, she declared. He
was a Jew, his real name being Joe Moses, but no one
would ever guess it. He hadn't got a hook nose, and he
would share his last penny with a pal. He had only one

failing in the world, sometimes he took a " wee drappie " too much to drink, but she would help him to conquer that weakness. He was a commercial traveller, but, being out of a job, had been pleased to join her in " Caledonia's Bard."

John Montgomery—the stage doctor who had to aid " Bess " to persuade " Mary " to die respectably in bed— had great pretensions to good looks ; moreover, he was both tall and stalwart. But he was no more a professional actor than the remainder of the company—as a rule he earned his bread as a compositor.

There was, indeed, one taller than Montgomery, one whose height numbered two or three inches over six feet, but who paid for longitude by a painful meagreness. Archie —for so Jessie called him—was, in very sooth, a protracted tragedy. The son of a groom, he had been, until the age of fifteen or thereabouts, the tiniest, lightest little chap imaginable. Always amid horses, his one ambition was to become a jockey, and he might have succeeded in attaining this aspiration, had not cruel Nature taken it into her head to make him grow ! He had sprouted almost visibly, beneath the horrified eyes of his horsey friends, and ere he came to eighteen years had reached the proud—yet hated—height of six feet three. Poor Archie's ambition being thus hopelessly blighted, he had made no effort to settle to any less fascinating career, but earned his daily bread by doing more or less badly whatever came next to hand.

Of such consisted the " star company " ! Evarne deemed them all quite suitable individuals to be thus secretly conglomerated in an empty room of a deserted house hidden away behind a hoarding and seemingly forgotten in the very heart of Glasgow. Strange fate that had brought her to form one of the conspiracy !

The rehearsals now proceeded daily, Mr. Punter always giving the cues of " Burns's " and " Clarinda's " parts. The chief difficulty lay in remembering " who was whom " at

any given moment. Without exception, all the men played
a couple of characters, in some cases even three separate
and distinct *rôles*. Mad-looking Charles Stuart appeared
as a prince and as " Clarinda's " footman—a proceeding that
appeared to Evarne as the height of absurdity. Charlie
swore he had no intention of visiting the barber, and no
one, having once seen that weird head above royal robes,
could possibly fail to recognise it again, even though the
appended body might, next time, chance to be clad in
servant's livery. They would at once discern the prince
in disguise in " Clarinda's " establishment, and would accordingly look for intricacies of plot—doomed to be
disappointed.

If it had not all been really a matter of such serious
consequence to her, the girl would have spent her time
during these rehearsals in struggling with inopportune
laughter. As it was, her expression grew habitually more
and more serious as the conviction forced itself like unto a
barbed arrow into her brain : " This play is to fail ! It is
bound to fail ! It can never succeed, never ; and what can
I do then ? "

For the present, at all events, there was neither inaction
nor loneliness. She made the more intimate acquaintance
of Joe Harold and John Montgomery by inviting them,
together with Jess, to her lodging one evening for a little
private rehearsal of the death-bed scene. To her amusement the men had purchased sausage-rolls, cakes and
ginger-beer from the shop round the corner, and the business over, they produced these edibles and invited themselves and their hostess to supper.

The unappetising topic that opened the meal was the
universal poverty that prevailed. All had been out of
work for some time, it appeared, and, like Evarne, were
subsisting painfully on a few paltry and fast-failing savings,
until the first week's salary from Mr. Punter should arrive
to relieve the situation.

It was the second time in her short career that Evarne had been introduced into an absolutely fresh world. Live and learn ! Had the girl given her opinion a month ago, it would probably have been to the effect that all commercial travellers, compositors, and daughters of scene-shifters (for this Jess owned had been her father's avocation in life) were necessarily common and uneducated—even though worthy enough folk. But there was very little either in the speech or ways of her three humble friends that could have appeared either absurd or offensive to the most dainty lady in the land, while Mont, the printer, was remarkably well-informed, handsome, and interesting. Thus for so long, at all events, as Evarne and her commercial traveller and her printer had mutual interests in " Caledonia's Bard," she found them infinitely more congenial than had been the majority of those men in the higher walks of life whom Morris had presented to her.

As a matter of fact, the nature of the society by which she had been surrounded in those bygone days had, from first to last, presented itself as one of the drawbacks of her unfortunate position. Time's progress had, to some considerable extent, blunted the keenness of her susceptibilities in this direction. Still, she now found it passing sweet to receive once again that vague indescribable deference and respect that distinguishes so subtly—perchance so unconsciously—a man's manner towards a " good " woman, from that which he assumes to one whose morals are understood to be " easy."

Yet more strongly did she experience a similar charm in the society of Jessie. The young girl—" who would sooner marry Joe with all his faults and without a penny, because she truly loved him, than marry a lord she didn't care for "—might not have been as witty, as merry, as brightly amusing as some other women whom Evarne could have named, but she was the first self-respecting and respectable member of her own age and sex—save

Margaret—whom the girl had known since she left Heather-ington.

Those years given to Morris—however brightened and redeemed by her pouring forth the most disinterested and sweetest affection—had been really very lonely—very desolate. When she had first been thrown into contact with the female associates that Morris's men friends had been willing to introduce to her, she had instinctively disliked and shrank from them, even although she had been far too childishly innocent at first to realise to the full the depravity of these "kept" women.

Even in the days of her naïve ignorance of the real nature of their purchased love—when the consciousness of her own high impulses, combined with the all-embracing instinct of charity in her disposition, had led her to attribute only her own really beautiful motives and emotions to these other women, who led lives outwardly corresponding to her own—she, and they likewise, had felt that there was really nothing in common between them. They belonged to different worlds.

And even now, between Evarne and her lowly Scotch friends—honest and agreeable though they might be—there was still a barrier, that of caste, culture, habit. It might be totally disregarded amongst them by common consent, but was not thus easily annihilated. They were of an entirely different station—of another stamp—from the daughter of the refined Oxford student, with his lengthy pedigree and old traditions. They and their equals could never have entered thus intimately into her daily life had she not been *déclassée*. In one way or another, Evarne was indeed cut off from all open companionship with those men—and especially those women—who would have been really suited to one possessed of her training, her general refinement, her personal character and nature. Had her few brief years of love's happiness foredoomed her to lead for evermore the lonely life ? Was it partly this that was foreboded in the grim smile of Sekhet ?

But as comrades the four amalgamated splendidly, and at length the date on which the tour was to really start was actually settled. Mr. Heathmore and Madame Cheape were going direct from their homes to Ayr, since " Bobbie's " birthplace was to have the honour of witnessing the first performance of " Caledonia's Bard." The other members of the company were to leave Glasgow on Monday, rehearse with " Bobbie " for the first time that same evening, and open on Wednesday night.

CHAPTER XX

REHEARSALS

BUT before then Evarne was reduced to what was indeed a harrowing necessity—a surreptitious visit to the pawnshop. For some days ere this she had been gradually eating less and less in a despairing endeavour to hinder the steady lightening of her purse. But even porridge and tea, bread and salt butter, rice and brown sugar, however cheap, and alas! correspondingly nasty, cost something.

One terrible morning, on returning from the day's meagre shopping, she sat down to grapple with the fact that all the money she possessed amounted to five pennies and one farthing.

The only article of any value that she still owned was her simple little enamel-cased watch.

The dire necessity of creeping into a pawnshop, to raise money on her father's last gift, distressed the girl beyond measure. She sat playing with the poor little thing, turning it over and over tenderly in her hands, while tears of mingled shame and grief gathered behind her eyelids. At length she was learning the truly humiliating side of abject poverty. She had asked Mr. Punter to advance a portion of her first week's salary, and had been refused. Now, not only was she terrified and appalled as she heard the violent scratching of the gaunt wolf against her slender shaking door, but abashed and mortified at what must be done to ward off these cruel fangs yet a little longer.

However, she talked logic and practical common sense

to herself, and after twilight had shrouded the city in a kindly veil, sought out an establishment decorated by three balls, and as unobtrusively as possible sneaked inside its portals.

An old man behind the counter of the small cubby-hole in which she found herself, looked at her watch and inquired how much she wanted on it? She had half anticipated being called upon to prove that it was legally hers, but questions of any other nature were quite unexpected. On the spur of the moment, fearful of asking too much, she said softly, " Twenty-five shillings, please." But even at this the old man pouted out his lips for a minute, then said :

" We couldna gie ye mair nor fifteen shillin's."

With the colour rising to her cheeks Evarne agreed, whereupon her embarrassment was increased by the unlooked-for fact of her name being demanded. With a half-sovereign and five shillings in her purse, and her watch represented by a horrible pawn-ticket, she slipped from the shop, feeling relieved and degraded at the same time.

She clung to the idea of the ultimate success of " Caledonia's Bard " with a tenacity that was pitiful. It must, it should triumph ! She dared not look onward and contemplate what might be her lot if this unpromising venture should indeed fail. The future had seemed black enough while she still possessed a few pounds and one or two trinkets. Now she had nothing—nothing !

On the company arriving at Ayr on Monday afternoon they proceeded direct to the Drill Hall, where the " fit-up " was to be erected. There—to the frank surprise of some of the more incredulous—they actually discovered both Mr. Heathmore and Madame Cheape awaiting them. The parts of " Burns " and " Clarinda " were not, then, to be undertaken at the last moment by Mr. Punter and Evarne respectively, as had been whispered.

The girls were scarcely prepossessed by Madame Cheape.

Evidently quite a middle-aged woman, she obviously objected to this fact being known, and strove to conceal it by the use of golden hair-dye and face powder, of which quantity endeavoured to compensate for quality. This very forgivable weakness in the lady's nature could have been overlooked, but her affected airs and languid drawl were, somehow, irritating in the last degree.

She inquired if Evarne and Jess were settled in " diggings " yet, and suggested that all three should put up together. The girls glanced questioningly at one another. They had already arranged to divide expenses, and now, on the score of further economy, agreed to the newcomer's proposition.

And certainly, it was largely the business-like capacities of Madame Cheape that enabled them to get rooms for twelve-and-six the week for the three. For this sum they were to have a sitting-room on the ground floor, a double-bedded front and a small back bedroom upstairs. By common consent Madame Cheape was accorded the privilege of solitary grandeur.

The house stood in an eminently respectable street, one end of which opened on to the banks of a canal. The sitting-room was really quite pretty, with clean curtains, pictures, and cheerful coloured cushions. Moreover, in the corner stood a piano, its brightly-polished candle-holders and embroidered key-cover suggesting that it was the pride of its owner's heart.

That evening took place what had promised to be the first real rehearsal, but lo ! it seemed totally impossible to get a full cast together. " Clarinda " and " Burns " were on hand now, sure enough, but that much-needed personage, Charles Stuart—scene painter and shifter—prince and footman—had run away ! He added insult to injury by leaving a message that he was " safely out of it," and " Caledonia's Bard " knew him no more.

His mantle descended upon two of Mr. Punter's sons,

who donned it reluctantly enough. These lads, Pat and Billie, nervous gawks of seventeen and nineteen, were both seemingly of such timorous dispositions as to be unable to speak above a whisper. The lost Charlie had roared his words like the Bull of Bashan. He would have been audible, at all events.

Mr. Heathmore repeatedly assured everyone that he had only received his script that Saturday. Since some of the scenes consisted almost entirely of soliloquies on Burns's part, and since the poet, even in casual conversation, had a little way of giving utterance to speeches of over a page in length, poor Mr. Heathmore was still far from having committed the part to memory. He unblushingly carried the voluminous script in his hand as he acted, but held out hopes of knowing it pretty well by the fateful Wednesday night. But if he really believed this himself, no one else shared his confidence on the point.

Even had the performance been a fortnight instead of a couple of days ahead, the company would have appeared in a hopelessly backward and muddled state. Dismay was universal.

" This is no ordinary theatrical concern, is it ? " inquired Evarne despondently, and thereby aroused a regular storm.

" Heavens, no ! It's a howling swindle ! Ayr will probably see the beginning and the end of the whole idiotic show." All agreed that the play itself was a bit of rubbish, the management a regular humbugging affair, and the prospects of the tour—nil !

" Do let's work hard, though. Do let's make it a success if we can," begged poor Evarne, but indeed no one stood in need of any such prompting. All would willingly have rehearsed from morning to night, but Mr. Heathmore insisted on being left in peace on Tuesday afternoon to try to master at least some of his endless part. Thus the remainder of the company were at liberty to visit Burns's

Cottage, the Kirk o' Alloway, and to wander along " Ye banks and braes o' Bonnie Doon."

In the evening, after another rehearsal, the girls held a reception and supper-party in their sitting-room. It was not a wild extravagance—indeed rather an economy—though maybe there was something of " eat, drink and be merry, for to-morrow we die," in the feeling that prompted it. The supper was a joint-stock affair ; everyone who was invited was in the same breath likewise asked to produce fourpence towards the banquet. Jess expended the fund of three shillings thus raised on bread and cheese, honest unpretentious beer, a monstrous hot rice pudding with jam sauce, mixed biscuits and a couple of bunches of watercress. All the shareholders were fully satisfied, and united in a vote of thanks to the caterer.

After supper an impromptu concert was organised. Everyone was able to contribute to the general entertainment, save Evarne herself, and Pat and Billie Punter, whom nobody heeded. But Evarne fulfilled her share of social duties by presiding over all, and surely never had such a gracious and tactful young hostess held sway over such a strangely mixed gathering.

The piano—the well-tuned, well-polished piano—was an immense assistance. Mont sang, Jessie played, and Douglas was enabled to show off his much-belauded tenor notes. And exquisite they were, in sooth—those tender, heart-stirring and dulcet strains. It was indeed a glorious singing-bird that was confined in this ex-prize fighter's throat.

The hostess's only trouble was Madame Cheape. That languid individual had spent the afternoon with the landlady, Mrs. Sargeant, and the evening likewise, presumably, for she had not turned up at the seven o'clock rehearsal.

And alack ! this protracted confabulation had very evidently not been carried on without the aid of a certain amount of liquid refreshment—and that, too, of a more exhilarating nature than mere tea. Thus, after a bumper of beer at supper, the sentiment of the tenor's love-songs proved too trying. The final strains of "Sweet Géne-viève" were still lingering on the air, when the hush that Douglas's enchanted notes evoked was ruthlessly broken in upon by Madame Cheape. She proclaimed that they were all getting "a confounded sight too solemn," and that she would liven them up with a dance. Thereupon the poor old thing, seizing her skirts, proceeded to "liven them up a bit."

Jess, who was seated at the piano, promptly strummed a merry dance-tune, and all laughed to watch Madame Cheape's absurd caperings. There had been a time when Evarne would immediately have been outraged by the painful spectacle, but now, to behold a half-drunken woman providing merriment for a roomful of men was no longer strange or instantly repulsive. She laughed too, until she suddenly realised that she had been enabled to discover that Madame Cheape wore red garters, and re-membered that she was in the society of presumably respectable men.

She became scandalised, and, springing to her feet, called, to Jess to cease playing at once. Then, since the dancing was continued with renewed vigour to compensate for the absence of music, Evarne laid her hands on the shoulders of the skittish performer, and suggested that "Clarinda" should retire and have a nice long night in readiness for the morrow. But dear "Clarinda," not being taken by this notion, declined to act upon it. She hadn't nearly done her dance yet. Let Miss Stornway be off to bed her-self. But Evarne was determined to get the intoxicated woman out of the room, and rapidly crossing to the door, flung it open as a preliminary to bringing "gentle strength" to reinforce her wise advice.

Outside a surprise awaited Evarne.

She found herself face to face with the flabbergasted Mrs. Sargeant, who was standing on the doormat.

"You were just coming in, I suppose?" inquired Evarne politely.

The landlady stammered, and at length confessed that she had been listening. But her explanation made the action appear forgivable—even touching. Her son was a sailor, she said; he used to sing "Sweet Géneviève," and until this evening she had not heard it since he went away to sea.

Evarne believed her, and was moved to sympathy.

"Would you very much like to hear it again?" she asked. "I'm sure Mr. Douglas won't mind repeating it."

Gratefully the woman entered the room and stood by the piano, her eyes fixed on the singer, as once more his exquisite notes sweetened the air. Then, full of thanks, she went out, taking the unsentimental Madame Cheape with her, and ere long the party broke up.

CHAPTER XXI

THE CAREER OF "CALEDONIA'S BARD"

AT length the feared and fateful Wednesday dawned. The morning was devoted to a final rehearsal that only left everyone more confused—more hopeless —than ever. Not a solitary actor was word-perfect in all the *rôles* that fell to his share. Evarne and Jess, with a single part apiece, were the most promising, but both were absolutely inexperienced, and now rather frightened.

In the afternoon the actors erected the " fit-up," under the supervision of Brown, the baggage-man, while the girls looked on and encouraged their struggles. Evarne, who had only that very morning been able to get the money for her brown costume from Mrs. Punter, had spent it on white butter-muslin for the " vision" gown. She now sat hastily stitching away at the interminable, seams of a flowing, snowy, shroud-like garment, whilst Madame Cheape—sober again—poured into her presumably maiden ear lamentations concerning the woes of married life.

By the evening, the whole company was in a state of irritable nervousness and apprehension. They ate what tea they could—and in some cases that implied what they were able to get—and were all gathered in the hall, with ample time not only to dress, but to stand around in knots, conversing in ominous whispers. Archie, the soured, even went so far as to assert that they were all very likely to be lynched by an infuriated public,

It was difficult to avoid some feelings of sympathy with poor old Mrs. Punter, as she handed each member of the company a leaf from some species of herb, which she confidently declared would bring them luck. She also made it understood that she was going to celebrate the first night by standing drinks all round, and solemnly wrote down on a slip of paper each individual's fancy in this direction.

This did something towards producing a more universally good-natured state of mind, but the reaction was sudden and disgust loud and undisguised, when—after the elaborate ceremony of putting everyone's wishes into writing and duly receiving their thanks—all that did verily make its appearance was one bottle of lemonade—small size !

And the performance ! A fiasco had been anticipated, but it proved to be even worse than the wildest nightmare had pictured. Evarne really did know her part, and had rehearsed her dying scene with Mont and Jess until they presented it—or so they flattered themselves—in a manner that would cause it to come as a refreshing little oasis in the midst of the evening's confusion. But to rehearse in private and to appear in public are two different matters. Jess repeatedly forgot her words, and would then unblushingly demand in loud, flurried whispers, "What's next, for Heaven's sake ? " That was bad enough, but Mont was far worse. He not only forgot his *rôle* as completely as if he had never learned it, but seemingly every other word but one in the whole Scottish language likewise.

At all events, what he did whenever wild glances from both girls told him that he had got to say something or other, was to repeat over and over again a phrase that sounded like " She's champing, she's champing." Evarne felt really angry at his stupidity in describing her as if she had been a fretful mare instead of a dying maiden. Finally, it dawned on her perception that this imbecile doctor was holding out hope to the weeping friends around her couch

—assuring them that the patient was "champion"!—Scotch for "in excellent health." What a monstrous lack of resource on Mont's part, when he knew right well that the curtain descended on the touching demise of this damsel whom he persisted in describing as "champion"!

As to poor "Highland Mary" herself, she was utterly tricked and sold. Where were all the graceful gestures to the perfecting of which so much practice had been devoted? Where those truly dramatic attempts to spring from the bed with outstretched arms, as beauteous visions assailed her dying eyes? Where the pathetic leaning over to one side to gently stroke the bent head of the weep'ng "Bess"? Where all those sweet and realistic little touches which were to have brought tears to the eyes of even a bored and irate audience? All impossible! Out of the question! Had investigation been made, the luckless "Mary" would have been found to be breathing out her last sigh upon a couple of chairs laid over on their sides, with two tin bonnet-boxes between them to render this makeshift couch sufficiently long.

As it was, her toes projected over the end of the lowest chair, while she suffered such anguish from knobs and spikes that it composed a mild form of torture. Yet whenever she dared to so much as wriggle, the tin-boxes creaked loudly, while had she attempted to gain genuine relief by actually shifting from her first position—had she not lain absolutely motionless, propped up on one elbow, which soon ached to distraction—tragedy would have been turned to comedy with a vengeance. Those rickety chairs would assuredly have over-tipped, and the audience would have beheld "Mary" and her improvised couch rolling pell-mell together down to the footlights.

Mr. Heathmore started by explaining to the audience that his part had been sent to him too late to be possibly learnt; then he undisguisedly proceeded to read it. In the "glen scene" Evarne found it truly disconcerting to

have to stand throughout these endless love-speeches, her
waist tenderly encircled by " Burns's " arm sure enough,
but with his head all the time turned right away from her
in order to gaze on the script that he held in his other
hand. As to the rest of the drama, she never had been
able to learn properly who was whom, or what they were all
up to, and even the first public performance threw no
light on the puzzle.

The play was proceeded with to the bitter end, but a
mere sprinkling of spectators remained to the finish.
Quite early in the evening the quieter members of the disgusted audience had, in severe silence, left the hall. The
more rowdy element remained to get what return they
could for their money by hooting, cat-calling, whistling and
shouting.

Jess stuck to her post at the hired piano, and played
away heroically throughout the protracted intervals
between the acts. The young girl was quite admirable,
sitting alone amidst the defrauded audience, strumming
away dauntlessly, regardless of the nutshells thrown at her,
and the jeers and ribald questions by which she was assailed.

All the performers at least were heartily thankful when
the miserable show was over for the night, and midst
many " swear words " from the men and plaintive deep-
breathed " Sh's ! " from the girls, they wended their ways
to their respective lodgings.

And next evening it all had to be gone through once
more, and this time the supply of audience was strictly
limited. It might be owing to the rain, which was descend-
ing in a steady Scotch drizzle. But the despondent
mummers had a shrewd suspicion that the truth concerning
" P. Punter's Magnificent Co." had spread throughout the
length and breadth of Ayr. It was not merely the dejection caused by the snub expressed by the rows of empty
benches that brought such frowns upon usually placid
brows. The abject poverty prevailing in the company

was universal. Several of the young people were almost penniless, and made no secret of their destitute condition. So a deputation had waited upon the manager that afternoon to " protest," or " kick up a righteous row," as they put it—to " try to get the breeks off a Hielander," according to Mr. Punter's version. In plain words, there was a general demand that, in consideration of the long delay for rehearsals, a portion of the company's salary should be now paid in advance—at least sufficient to buy bread and cheese until the end of the week. After much argument, appeals, and threats, Mr. Punter had been brought to promise that the takings on that evening should be divided amidst the company after the show. Thus the tiny audience was a truly serious matter.

The second cause for anxious frownings was the statement of Archie that the eldest Punter boy had been overheard to tell the girl behind the bar in the " Ass and the Thistle," that the company was to be disbanded at the close of the three days at Ayr. No hint of this had been officially given, but it seemed so highly probable that it was generally accepted for fact. Evarne dared not contemplate it. The sorrows of the past seemed already years behind her, overlaid by the painful excitement and interest of the present, and sick anxiety and apprehension concerning the grey-shrouded future.

A little innovation was introduced that evening that certainly made things run smoother. Jess not only played in the intervals, but lifted up her voice and sang old familiar Scottish ballads. This was immediately popular. The audience joined in the chorus of some, and applauded all. Jess sang until her throat must have ached, and was undoubtedly the success of the evening.

After the " rag " had fallen for the last time, the audience dispersed howling, booing and hissing, out into the rain. Then the company gathered expectant around Mr. Punter, who accordingly handed out some coins. It was but

small sums that he distributed, but it was something to
go on with, and Evarne and Jessie came off far best of all
with four shillings apiece.

By Friday morning the girls at least felt too abashed to
willingly show themselves in the streets of Ayr. But
another rehearsal call had been given for eleven o'clock—
which at least sounded encouraging—so exhorting one
another to be defiant and brazen, they wended their way
towards the hall. As they neared it, Jess suddenly stood
still, and clutched Evarne's arm. Three men had appeared
from out the building, staggering beneath the weight of a
piano. This they placed on a cart, carefully covered it
with oil-skins, and drove away.

"Oh my! is that my piano gone?" gasped the little
songstress. Impossible that their resource—their stand-by
—should have been thus filched from them! Yet so it
was. The owner of the piano, it seemed, had been present
on the previous evening, and being perchance a prophet
and able to foresee the future, had taken time by the fore-
lock and demanded in advance the money due for the hire
of his instrument. A quarrel with Mr. Punter had resulted,
which ended by the man ruthlessly removing his piano.

Jessie particularly was in a fine state of distress: with
her it was a case of "Othello's occupation's gone," and
her complaints and lamentations rang loud. "Caledonia's
Bard" unrelieved by music! Terrible! At length,
Heaven bestowed an inspiration upon the troubled Jessie.
What about Mrs. Sargeant's piano? Surely if Harry
Douglas went and asked for its loan, making a personal
favour of the matter, he might succeed. If Mrs. Sargeant
at first declined, and he forthwith broke out into the
strains of "Sweet Génevieve," would he not be irresistible?
Anyway, for goodness' sake let it be tried.

Procuring a trolley, and accompanied by Brown, the
heroic Douglas set out upon this venture. In less than
half an hour they returned. Wonder and delight! then

efforts of the modern Orpheus had been crowned with
success. He had sung " Sweet Géneviève," and had
thereby charmed either Mrs. Sargeant or her piano. Here
it was ! he stood by it smiling—proud and happy singer !

All that day it poured with rain. It was now the
evening of the last performance of " Caledonia's Bard at
Ayr. What were Mr. Punter's arrangements for the
morrow ? So far he had given no clue. The weather
added to the general depression ; none ventured out into
the downpour, but as twilight fell the figures of the actors
and actresses, huddled under umbrellas, might be seen
approaching the hall from various directions.

The conjectures, the suggestions, the hopes, the fears
discussed in the dressing-rooms were of far greater interest
to the members of the company than was the play itself.
The time they spent on the stage—far from appearing
in the light of the most important moments of the evening
—seemed but breaks into the far more serious and enthralling " Drama of Reality " in which all were taking part.

It was now a generally known secret that Mr. Punter
was unable to pay the nine pounds owing for the hire of the
hall. Halfway through the evening it was further spread
around—in mysterious murmurs and with bated breath—
that the instant the curtain fell for the last time everyone
must be prepared to look after themselves—their own
interests—and, as far as possible, those of Mr. Punter.
All were to promptly seize on their respective belongings
for fear they might be claimed by the officials of the hall ;
the " fit-up " was to be rushed down—on the morrow all
were returning to Glasgow, where more prosperous arrangements would be made for the future.

But this programme of events, even if originating in Mr.
Punter's brain, was not destined to enjoy his co-operation.
Suddenly Joe startled the girls by dashing almost without
warning into their dressing-room.

" He's gone—he's off—the blaggard ! " he shouted.

" Who ?   Where ? "

" Why, that vile Punter.   Somebody from the station
has come and told Brown.   Him and Mrs. Punter and the
kids caught the five-to-ten to Glasgow.   He was off with
all the cash while we were finishing acting his rotten play !
He's given us the slip, left us in the lurch without our
salary !   Got clean away with all the rest of the takings,
such as they are ! "

Both the girls gasped, and Evarne, homeless, friendless,
with exactly five-and-twopence in the world, turned pale.
A moment later, a sudden uproar on the stage caused them
to both rush out excitedly.   There, surrounded by irate
actors and stage-hands, stood—or rather huddled together
—Pat and Billie Punter.

" We've got them, anyway ! "   shouted   Brown.
" They'll have to pay something for their pa ! "

Before any further threats could be either uttered or
put into action, two men appeared in the entrance, closing
dripping umbrellas, and with countenances as lowering as
the weather without.   They were the respective owners of
the Drill Hall and of the hired piano.   The latter strode
straight up the gangway to the Punters.

" Here, you young thieving varmints.   Where's my
money for the two evenings you had my piano ?   Five-
and-six a night, and three shillings for transport.   I'll
just thank you to hand over fourteen shillings."

" I'm afeared——" Pat was commencing feebly.

" No jaw !   Hand over my fourteen shillings," repeated
the man.

Pat accordingly remained silent, and fumbled in his
pocket.   The piano-owner's brow cleared somewhat, but
only to cloud afresh as the youth merely produced his
father's visiting-card.

" If you'll take this," faltered Pat, offering the piece of
pasteboard.

" What !   D'you think that's good enough !   You and

your visiting-card be——" the irate creditor was beginning, when the owner of the hall interposed—

"Look here. I shall pay you this fourteen shillings out of my own pocket, and for my security I will retain possession of everything now in the place. Do you all understand ? " —and he glanced sternly round at the assembled company. " You're at liberty to take yourselves off—the sooner the better—but if any of you attempt to remove any properties—yes, I mean either stage-truck, or what you choose to call your own—I will have in the police. Understand that now."

His listeners returned him no response, but unobtrusively wandered off to their respective dressing-rooms. Forewarned, everybody had practically completed their packing, and now the owner of the hall, penetrating behind the scenes, discovered the entire company to be fastening straps and hastily cramming various objects of one sort and another into pockets or blouses. Bags and boxes were vanishing with various figures who were drifting away towards the front entrance—striving to render themselves as small and insignificant as possible—yet departing with all good speed. In an instant he had made up his mind. He whispered to one of his satellites, and in half a minute all the gas was turned off, plunging the whole place into inky blackness.

Evarne was in the act of fastening the padlock to the end of the long metal rod of her basket, when this darkness as of Erebus suddenly descended. Finishing her task, she was groping her way between chairs and boxes to where she imagined the door to be, when she heard the welcome sound of Mont's voice.

" Are you here, Miss Stornway ? "

" Yes, quite lost. What has happened ? "

" He's done it on purpose. Here, Brown, strike that match now. Quickly, which is your box ? We will carry it out for you."

The last match they owned between them flared and died out, and in the darkness the three groped their way from the hall. Evarne went ahead and tried to clear the track as best she could, but all stumbled and lurched against overturned chairs, and tripped over articles dropped in the hasty escape of those who had preceded them.

CHAPTER XXII

POVERTY MAKES ONE ACQUAINTED WITH STRANGE BEDFELLOWS

SETTING down the basket at the corner of a neighbouring street, the men went back to see what else could be thus rescued. Evarne sat on her box and waited. Her umbrella was lost. The rain was still pouring down steadily, persistently; along the gutters the water rushed in torrents, the skies and the earth were alike enveloped in damp obscurity. No living being appeared; indeed, practically the only sign of the existence of mankind was the feeble jet of the street lamp, which reflected its gleam in the wet pavement as in a lake.

So long did the girl wait, that, despite the discomfort of her unique situation, she fell into a sort of vague reverie, and a curious feeling of abstraction from her own personality crept over her. Was it really she indeed—Evarne Stornway—who was out here in the middle of the night in this drenching rain, seated in solitary misery upon the box containing all her worldly possessions, at some unknown street corner of a small town in Scotland? Unreasonably enough, it appealed to her as a most extraordinary thing that *she* should be the individual chosen out of all humanity to be thus strangely circumstanced this night.

She was aroused by hearing her name shouted in the distance. In response to her answering call a couple of figures appeared, and Mont's voice said—

"Couldn't find this blessed corner again in the mist. Jess has sent down a message that she's gone to supper with Joe, and will you come too? You had better. There's always a nice fire there of an evening, and you look soaked through."

"I only look what I am, then. Certainly I'll go, if Jess is there. What about my box?"

"Brown and I will carry it round to Mrs. Sargeant's and tell her you'll both be late. Do you know your way to our diggings?"

"I don't know where I am now, one bit."

Mont explained, and Evarne accordingly hurried off through the downpour.

On reaching her destination she was received with cheers. Most of the company seemed gathered in Mrs. Shiells's kitchen. The house itself was let out in tenements, and theatrical lodgings were obtainable on practically every floor. Thus all the actors were residing in the one building, and the kitchen of good-natured Mrs. Shiells was the general rendezvous.

In due course Mont and Brown returned, and with them came news of fresh complications. Madame Cheape had gone! She had been back to her room, packed up all her belongings and taken them with her, leaving behind only the assurance that the other young ladies had the money for her rent. Mrs. Sargeant had evidently been drinking again, but not to the point of forgetting the piano. It belonged to her daughter, it seemed; it had been lent without its lawful owner's leave, and if it was not in its place when that daughter returned at eleven, Mrs. Sargeant contemplated being half-slaughtered by her offspring, whose temper, when aroused, she described as "enough to make the 'air stand up on your 'ead."

"Oh dear! I forgot the piano," faltered Jess.

"I tried to get it out, I swear I did," avowed Douglas. "The owner of the hall made two men sit on it until the door was locked. He's going to keep it in pawn until he gets his nine pounds fourteen."

" And Madame Cheape never gave us any money, did she ? "

" Not one farthing."

A grim silence prevailed. How were they to face this terrible Miss Sargeant ? One of the lodgers and the piano, both departed—flitted away !

" I advise this," said Archie ultimately. " Let Miss Stornway's basket be brought round here, and you girls go and pack up all your other belongings and bring them along too. Then each pay Mrs. Sargeant your respective shares of the rent you had all agreed upon—twelve-and-six, wasn't it ? That's four and twopence each. Tell her old Cheape has sloped, but that the piano is all right, and will come home sooner or later. Then if she still chooses to kick up a row, she can't stick to any of your props, that's one thing."

" We really oughtn't to be expected to suffer for either the Cheape's or the Punter's tricks, ought we ? " demanded Jess, and so Archie's plan of campaign was adopted.

The interview passed off quite easily. The terrible Miss Sargeant had not yet returned ; the old woman accepted their eight-and-fourpence without demur, and a blouse that Madame Cheape had overlooked as a substitute for the remaining four-and-twopence. Both girls united in assuring her that the precious piano was in safe keeping, and that she was to impress this fact upon her daughter.

They then hastened back to Mrs. Shiells's warm, cosy kitchen, feasted on hot broth and discussed the desperate state of affairs. At last it became needful to return to their own cheerless rooms to sleep. The men in a group escorted them through the dark, deserted roads. But Archie was in a thoroughly furious temper, and Douglas was never a sucking dove. As the group stood for a final chat in the street outside Mrs. Sargeant's house, these two, from angry disputing, set to work to settle their differences of opinion by seeing who could hit hardest.

A general uproar resulted, starting peaceful Ayr from its first slumbers. All along the street, upper windows were flung open, and heads appeared, startled or curious. Suddenly yet another sound was clearly heard above all the confusion—the angry bang of a door, the sharp turning of a key, and the drawing of bolts. The girls were locked out !

A sudden hush descended, and for a moment everyone stood spellbound. Then Evarne quickly sped across the street, and banged with the knocker again and again. The only response took the form of a young woman appearing at an upper window.

" You folk don't seem to know that we keep a respectable house," she cried. " We are not going to have females here who don't know how to behave themselves, and who are thieves into the bargain. If you get over ma, who's a fool, and come stealing my piano—my piano, what I paid for myself—well, if ma lets herself be sucked in by a lot of sneaking scoundrels like you are, all of you, I tell you straight out we're not going to have women here who brawl in the streets in the middle of the night, as well as steal pianos ; so you can take yourselves off, and if either of you two, who call yourselves ladies I dare say, show your noses here again, I'll have you clapped into prison for stealing a respectable woman's piano. You needn't think you're going to sleep beneath this roof to-night, so be off with you, piano thieves."

Here she banged down the window with such violence that the glass rattled in the casement. Dead silence prevailed in the street.

" I'm so sorry," faltered Douglas, quite subdued. " It's all my fault from beginning to end."

" Well, it's no use standing here, I suppose," declared Evarne in rather a shaking voice. " Come along, Jess ;

we'll go back to Mrs. Shiells and see what she can do for us. I'm sure she will let us sit in her kitchen till morning, anyway."

"Archie and I will give up our bed," cried remorseful Douglas, as the glum little procession, under the gauntlet of many eyes, turned to retrace its steps.

"What a bad, wicked creature to shut us out in the streets at this time of night," declared Jess with emphasis, then sniffed, suspiciously close to tears.

"Don't cry till you see the end of it," advised Evarne, stoical from very misery. "How can we know whether it be good or bad angels that have planned all these unforeseen events? Anything that appears to be entirely hateful—like this whole evening has been—may be but a preliminary to happiness!" But her heart was as heavy as lead as she spoke.

"Goodness gracious me! What a queer girl you are to talk like a minister in his pulpit while we are sloshing through the mud and the rain with nowhere to sleep!" laughed Jess, highly amused; whereupon Evarne smilingly inquired what more appropriate moment could be chosen.

Mrs. Shiells was kindness itself. Surely, she would find a haven for the puir lassies, she declared. Let them wait a moment.

After a brief absence she returned, accompanied by another brawny Scotch dame. She had believed Miss Brodie here had a vacant room, she said, but she was mistaken. However, it was nigh two o'clock. There wasn't much more of the night before them. She'd be pleased if one of the lassies would share her bed, and would the other sleep with Miss Brodie?

Gratefully the girls accepted this offer. It was arranged that Jess should stay with Mrs. Shiells, and in less than a quarter of an hour Evarne found herself lying in the darkness by the side of this new good Samaritan who had so recently appeared upon the scene.

CHAPTER XXIII

A FRESH TURNING

MISS BRODIE had apologised for not having a spare bed.

"If it had been the morn's nicht, noo," she explained. "I've got ma sister frae Lunnon stoppin' wi' me, she's in the only vacant room, but she'll be awa' again the morn."

Of course, Evarne emphatically declared that she did not envy the sister the spare room one jot, and soon after this they composed themselves to rest.

But Evarne wooed sleep in vain. In silence and darkness and strangeness; the excitement of the evening, with its sustaining power all past; the company finally disbanded and deserted; everything chaos for the present—and for the morrow——? She had now a shilling and a halfpenny left in the world. Supposing she pawned some of her garments, and thus got back to Glasgow, wherein had she at all bettered her position? What could she do for the next night, let alone the nights to come? How long would it be now before she was both hungry and penniless? Would she then have to go into the workhouse—or what?

She shuddered in bed, and writhed her fingers as if suffering physical agony. The cruel horror of the immediate future seemed to crush her as she lay. For the sake of her bedfellow she forced herself to remain silent and motionless for what seemed an interminable period. But giving way to a sudden invincible panic induced by accumulated reflections on many possibilities, she started up violently, and cried in a voice that scarcely sounded her own—

"Oh Heaven! What am I to do?" Then, burying her face in her hands, she wept unrestrainedly.

An arm crept round her waist, and she was gently drawn to the side of her companion.

"Puir lassie," said the kindly voice. "You're o'errocht. Dinna greet, but lie quiet and see what daylight brings. You've a' had a verra tryin' time here, but you'll sune be hame aince mair wi' your frien's, and mayhap a kind fayther or mither to welcome ye."

"Oh no, no!" sobbed the girl, "I've got no one—nothing—no parents, no home or friends or anything! Oh, what shall I do? what will become of me?"

Miss Brodie leaned out of bed and lit a candle.

"The dark is na cheerie," she declared.

Evarne managed to choke down her grief, and lay back upon the pillow once more.

"I'm so sorry to have awakened you. Please go to sleep again. I'm going to be quite still and quiet now."

"Dinna think o' me," said the kind-hearted Scotswoman. "What o' yoursel', puir bairn? It's a terrible thing for a lassie to be a' her lain i' the world."

Gradually Evarne was prevailed upon to confide the seriousness of her plight. Miss Brodie grew more and more pitying and sympathetic.

"I'll consult wi' ma sister," she said, at length. "Jean has got verra sharp wits frae being in Lunnon. She will advise ye. Anyway, ma lamb, dinna think that I'll turn ye oot a' at aince, though ye had naething in the whole world but a tongue to say 'thank ye' wi'."

Evarne kissed her again and again.

"I do meet kind friends, anyway," she whispered, and encircled by Miss Brodie's motherly arms, she at length fell asleep.

Notwithstanding the disturbances of the night, the

thrifty Scotswoman rose as usual shortly after daybreak, and by the time Evarne had awoke, dressed and wandered out into the kitchen, she found that her difficulties and distresses had already been the subject of careful debate between Martha and Jean Brodie.

The latter, a tall, angular young woman, with a somewhat careworn expression, had justified her sister's confidence by almost instantly producing a suggestion anent the vexed question of earning a livelihood without a week's delay. Waiting only until Martha had ladled out a plateful of porridge and set it before Evarne, she opened the subject without any preliminary remarks.

" Are you at all a good needlewoman, Miss Stornway ? "

" Only pretty fair," was the truthful response. " I've done a lot of embroidery, but scarcely any plain sewing. I made this blouse I've got on, though ; but not without help."

" That will do. Now, if my sister didn't exaggerate, if you're really penniless and don't know which way to turn——"

Evarne cast down her eyes.

" That's right enough," she said ; " go on."

" In that case I can give you a job myself—that is, if you're not too proud to work hard and live humbly."

Here was indeed a surprise.

" Only try me," declared the girl eagerly. " What is it ? "

" Perhaps Martha told you I was a blousemaker by trade. I work for a wholesale house in the City. I haven't got a big business, but I live by it, and I always have a young girl under me as an apprentice to do certain parts of the word. Generally, my assistant lives and boards with me, I pay her half a crown a week and teach her the business. As soon as the girl is past the apprentice stage she leaves me and I get another beginner. My last one left me just before I came away for my holiday. My girls are generally only about fourteen or fifteen; but if you care to take the job for a time, it's open to you at once, and you'll get a better berth presently like the others, if you choose to continue in the needlework line. There's my offer."

"I daursay it seems a bit o' a come-doon i' the world to you," interposed Martha, "but when all's said and done it's a respectable, God-fearin' business that no woman need be ashamed o'."

"Think it over while you eat your breakfast," advised Jean.

Evarne was distinctly startled at an entirely fresh career being thus suddenly dangled before her gaze for inspection. The remuneration offered, two-and-six weekly, likewise proved amazing. Still, board and lodging were included in the bond, and, after the terrible pictures her imagination had painted in the blackness of the past night, the certain assurance of a sheltering roof, and of bread to ward off the pangs of hunger, was alone sufficient to form a bright constellation of stars in her dark sky. Not long did she stop to consider whether these newly-risen orbs were of a colour and design pleasing to her fancy. Between the fifth and sixth spoonfuls of porridge she had signified her willingness to become a blouse apprentice.

"Then pack up your things as soon as you've done eating. We must catch the half-past eleven train, because of my excursion ticket."

"How—I hadn't thought of that—how am I to get my fare?" faltered Evarne painfully.

"I'm going to lend it to ye, lassie, and sure, you can pay me back week by week," declared Martha.

Evarne endeavoured to express her gratitude, but the only answer she got was—

"It's naething at a'. Jist keep your breath to cool your porridge, and make haste too."

Speedily finishing her meal, the girl went upstairs to Mrs. Shiells's. There, in the kitchen, she found a heated quarrel in progress. The " loot " of the disbanded " Caledonia's Bard " was the bone of contention. Archie had carefully packed the limes-box round with stage garments, enclosed the whole in a drop-scene, tied it all up with gas-tubing, and then calmly announced that this was his " little share." Since there was not much left of any description, all the other members of the late company, headed by Douglas, were vigorously protesting.

Already Archie had been discovered trying to palm off upon his landlady, in lieu of money, a couple of long cylinders containing gas—dangerous, explosive, useless objects to which no one would willingly even give house-room. General indignation had been provoked by this attempt at returning evil for good, and amid the general uproar it was some time before Evarne could persuade the excited party to turn their attention to her, and realise that she had come to bid them farewell.

The regrets expressed at this parting were perfectly sincere on both sides. Evarne was being swooped off, leaving many mysteries unsolved. Where was Madame Cheape ? What would befall the piano that day ? Would Mr. Punter try to reclaim any of his stage belongings ? Moreover, it appeared that that gentleman's whereabouts were being eagerly inquired after by a number of the leading tradesmen of the district, who had been persuaded to pay cash down for advertisement spaces on the back of the company's programmes, misled by the assurance of a prolonged local tour for " Caledonia's Bard "—a fact that went a long way toward explaining the whole strange business. Jess and Mont both undertook to write and tell Evarne all the news, but ere she well knew how it had come to pass, she found herself in the train being whirled back to London.

Another act in the " Drama of Reality " had commenced.

CHAPTER XXIV

' STITCH, STITCH, STITCH ! "

THE house in which Miss Jean Brodie rented a single room stood in a by-street in the heart of Camberwell. Despite the knowledge that any feelings of fastidiousness were now entirely unseemly and out of place, Evarne could not avoid a certain dismay at the prospect of actually residing amid such abject poverty, disorder and squalor. Threading their way between the swarming dirty children, who shouted and played and disputed on every side, numerous as rabbits in a warren, they entered a dark, narrow passage and proceeded to mount the uncarpeted stairs.

" My room is on the top floor," explained Miss Brodie, as the first landing was gained. " Rents are very high in London. There are seven separate lots of people living in this house."

At this juncture a voice came from one of the half-open doors they were passing—

" What did I do ? Why, I says quite perlite-like, ' 'Ave a drop o' gin, ol' dear,' but she ups and says to me, she says——"

But what " she " had responded to this invitation was lost in a peal of laughter from several throats. Miss Brodie looked supercilious.

" That's Mrs. Harbert. You won't need to talk to her at all. She's not a very respectable old woman. I'm sure I wonder the landlord has her in the house ; but there, he doesn't heed anything so long as he gets his rent punctually."

Evarne glanced back over her shoulder, and surveyed this wicked personage! She saw a cleanly, neatly-clad, comfortable-looking old dame of about sixty, who still retained traces of unusual good looks. She seemed so good-natured and happy that Evarne inquired with some interest into the character of her misdemeanours. She was more entertained than appalled by the information. The culprit had been an artist's model, and the walls of her room were now absolutely covered with innumerable paintings and drawings depicting herself in the days of her youth, " but with not a decent stitch of clothing among the whole lot, my dear."

Miss Brodie's own apartment, though poor in the extreme, was certainly respectability itself. As was most suitable in a room principally designed for needlework, the floor was uncarpeted, while the bed, with the narrow rug by its side, the washing-stand and the few clothes-pegs, were all huddled as much out of the way as possible. The place of honour in the centre of the room was given to the substantial table necessary for cutting out, while by the light of the window stood the sewing-machine. On the mantelpiece were china ornaments in couples, a pair of pink vases, and some cheap frames holding family photographs. On the walls were coloured texts and several gloomy memorial cards.

And within these precincts Evarne started upon a life the conditions of which she had hitherto never dreamed of, far less realised. Work commencing at eight in the morning, the stretch of hours until eight at night was unbroken save by a brief time for meals. Day in and day out—except for the blessed Sabbath—week following week in slow procession, still found her bent over her needle, stitch, stitch, stitching as fast as her skill allowed.

At first, while yet unbroken to the yoke, she many a

time seriously feared that the day then passing would be
the very last of its kind that she could possibly manage
to endure. The nerve-pangs of irritability and impatience,
of well-nigh uncontrollable rebellion and revolt—all concealed with difficulty, but not thereby conquered—seared
her spirit far more deeply than her left forefinger was
pricked and torn by the needle driven at unaccustomed
speed. Sometimes she would stop working for a minute,
straighten her back, let her hands, together with the
material, drop loosely upon her lap, while she would glance
over at Jean with an expression that said plainly, " Is it
really possible to endure this ? "

But Miss Brodie during work-hours was as a part of her
machine—she never ceased, never looked either to the right
or to the left—so that after a minute or two nothing remained for the as yet unresigned apprentice but to
stifle a sigh—or maybe even a groan—and again take
up the labour at which her whole nature was vigorously
protesting.

She wondered if she was naturally idle, or if all other
needlewomen had had to get the mastery over similar
feelings to those that ramped in her breast, when the
monotonous occupation had to be continued for long weary
hours after it had become thoroughly uncongenial ? Did
Miss Brodie, for instance, not know what it was to feel
every pulse of her body aching and crying for movement—
change—liberty ? Was she never conscious that her brain
was frantically protesting against the maddening monotony
—the unvarying sameness—the crushing tedium of pushing that needle in, then pulling that needle out, again and
again and again, as steadily as her pulses beat or her heart
throbbed ? Did Jean never have to fight against an almost
uncontrollable impulse to scream, shout, wave her arms,
stamp, swear, play ball with her work, tear down " God
Bless our Home," and throw it out of the window ; do something—anything—wild, mad and unseemly, to relieve the

tedium and assuage the awful tumult of overwrought nerves ?

But whatever storms might rage within the recesses of her own mind, Miss Brodie was ever outwardly calm—but then Evarne was to all appearances equally passive, equally resigned. She never once complained. While pitying herself as frankly as she sorrowed over a squirrel upon the wheel ; a wood-bird shut in a tiny cage ; a young dog fastened to its kennel in a walled-in yard, strangling itself frantically against its collar ; she suffered all in total silence.

However, Jean had an outside interest—a hope that beyond a doubt served to lighten and brighten the tedium of these days of toil. She was engaged to be married to a dashing red-coated soldier, and many of the ends of her evenings were spent in his inspiriting society.

Evarne's spare hours were passed in absolute loneliness and solitude. After supper she would wander out, generally along the Embankment, but if she had sufficient energy she would persevere as far as Hyde Park. At all events she would walk about somewhere until she was wearied, not returning home until it was time to go to bed. It was a grey, soul-crushing existence, and she grew depressed and spiritless beneath its burden.

She made no effort to change it for anything better. Miss Brodie was satisfied with her, and was always kind. One thing was as good as another, and incompetence was a drug in the labour market. Everyone, too, by whom she was now surrounded laboured more or less incessantly ; work made up their lives. She was no miserable exception, no victim, no martyr. Her fate seemed but the common fate of all.

" It's a real pity you can't get a young man, Miss Stornway," said Miss Brodie, worried by her apprentice's unconcealable pallor and listlessness. " It certainly does seem to make everything so much easier."

The girl smiled and shook her head. Indeed, Camberwell

was as likely to produce a " young man " for Evarne as was a desert island. Not that she was overlooked by the male sex ; on the contrary, in common with every girl who is at once poor and beautiful, practically every man who had any sort of opportunity commenced, sooner or later, to make love to her. Quite often strange men turned and walked by her side in the parks, seeking to engage her in conversation. But not for one instant was the proud purity of the beautiful face disturbed. Evarne had loved Morris Kenyon as truly and purely as ever any young girl loved. By the shameful arts of the street *roué* she was profoundly repelled. So as far as masculine society went, she lived the life of a young nun.

She seemed to have nothing left save memories, and these were all tainted with cruel bitterness. As the weary weeks lengthened into months the acuteness of all past emotions—joys and anguish alike—became dimmed, and then faded away. What had been once her life seemed now only a story she had read long ago. That brilliant room at " Mon Bijou " ; the lovely garden with its winding mosaic walks ; the blueness of the Naples Bay ; the snow-capped mountains of Switzerland ; her dainty flat and her carriage here in London ; the vivid sun of Egypt—none of this was real, surely ? Reality was scanty fare in a top garret—incessant stitching—loneliness—and nothing else !

And her love for Morris that she would once have sworn could have survived all blows, all passing of time, was as much a thing of the past as were all these other memories. Morris had slain it himself once and for ever. For some time she had cherished the corpse, not knowing it to be lifeless ; but gradually the deceptive outward tokens of vitality faded away. A little longer and the dead thing fell to dust and was no more. The glamour of Morris's presence removed enabled her to see more clearly, not only the unforgivable nature of the insults with which he had cast her off, but the great wrong he had done her in the first place, and which had directly led down to these dregs wherein she was now drowning.

If she had any feeling for him other than indifference, it was hatred. She felt no gratitude—not one jot—for the money or the care and attention he had once lavished upon her. It had been nothing to him. And since she was merely one of many women who in turn occupied those rooms at " Mon Bijou," she had no more call to be grateful for any of the accompanying accessories of the position than had the horses that passed through his stables.

She was utterly discontented and unhappy in her present existence. True, she had safe shelter, sufficient to wear, and enough to eat to keep life within her—but, merciful Heaven, what a price she paid for that doubtful boon ! Morning after morning she regained consciousness with reluctance, shrinking from the joyless, unbroken monotony of the day that stretched its weary length before her— anxious only to get it done and added to those that were already lived through. She never read now, for her eyes ached painfully long ere work was ended.

Tortured at first by her unemployed powers of heart and brain and soul fighting for expression, all too soon she became bitterly conscious that they were yielding to disuse —becoming crushed and deadened. It did seem hard to have to put all her strength, all her active energies of mind and body—all herself—into the making of cheap blouses. She felt she was being wasted, but that it was inevitable. What was being killed in her would not make money.

It was some time before she could realise that she had found her true level in life's struggle, and that needle-work was her doom. At first she was always waiting for something to " turn up," for the unexpected to happen.

> " ' And is this all of life ? ' she said ;
> ' This daily toil for daily bread ? ' "

And as the conviction grew that this cruel question must be answered in the affirmative—that all heretofore had

been but prelude, unstable and fleeting, that this was
life now upon her in grim serious earnest—her heart grew
bitter, and her once sweet, bright expression gave way to
a settled look of sad discontent.

But through all this her resolution to lead evermore a
" good " life never faltered. She would not even contemplate endeavouring to bring sparks of brightness into
her cheerless existence by setting aflame any man's affection, legally or otherwise. Come what might, she had done
with that sort of thing once and for all.

Mrs. Burling she visited once or twice, but her correspondence with both Margaret and Jess slackened and ceased.
Separated and so unhappy, she found it difficult to know
what to say to them, while they both could produce but
heavy and laboured epistles. She liked Jean Brodie fairly
well, but they were very opposed in character, and for the
greater portion of each day the silence of the workroom
was unbroken save for the clipping of the scissors or the
whirring of the machine.

CHAPTER XXV

HARD LUCK

B UT although Evarne would not have deemed it possible, worse still remained for her upon the knees of the gods.

Jean Brodie returned home one Sunday in a state of unconcealed excitement.

" Miss Stornway, I'm going to be married. The banns are to be called for the first time next Sabbath. My young man's regiment is going out to India in six weeks, and he's just got leave to marry ' on the strength,' so he can take me with him."

After suitable congratulations, and so on, the conversation veered round to Evarne.

" If you follow my advice, Miss Stornway, you'll carry on my business. You've done a lot of good work for me, my dear, so in memory of that I'll give you all—well, nearly all—the furniture of the room. I must take a few things with me, and I can't let you have my sewing-machine, but you can procure a nice one on the hire system. Then get a young girl as an apprentice. I'll introduce you to the City firm I work for, and you'll be comfortably settled. What do you say ? "

Evarne naturally thanked her, whereupon Miss Brodie set forth the expenditure of the establishment.

" The work brings in above seventeen shillings weekly. Two shillings is enough to pay the apprentice, a young girl, you know. There's three-and-six for rent, add to which you must allow three-and-six for your machine, that's nine shillings. That leaves you with eight shillings for food for the two of you, candles, a bit of firing, the goose club, the church collection, twopence for a hot bath—everything else, in fact. It seems very little somehow! I know, it's the hiring of the machine takes your money. I've managed to save some every week, and so will you in time."

Thus the matter was settled. Evarne was present at Jean's marriage, and a few days later waved her farewell from the station as the good Scotswoman departed with the other soldiers' wives. Then the girl walked back to her now empty room with a fresh sense of depression. After all, Jean had been a friend in need, and had remained her only intimate acquaintance in London.

As she wended her way upstairs a sudden stumble was heard on the upper flight, and immediately after half a dozen rosy apples came bounding down. At the same time the disreputable Mrs. Harbert's voice was heard calling shrilly—

" 'Ere, Smithkins! Come to the rescue! Buck up! Everything's a-goin'."

Thus abjured, Mrs. Smithkins hurried out from her room and lent her aid. Evarne, having gathered up the apples, joining the group.

" Here's something of yours," she said.

" Good retriever! 'Ave one," was the response.

Somewhat objecting to be thus described, the girl declined the gift, and was continuing her way upstairs.

" Wait a bit. I must give yer somethin' for yer trouble, me dear. I'll learn yer some cookin'. Best and quickest way to make a sausage roll. D'you know it?"

" No."

" Take a sausage to the top of the stairs and chuck it down—like them apples rolled. See? Ha, ha! Shakespeare! No, not 'im this time. That was the clown at the pantomime last year.'

Evarne certainly thought the old dame was slightly
incoherent, and smiling indulgently took another step
upstairs.

" Done it ! " declared Mrs. Harbert triumphantly.

" What 'ave yer done now ? " inquired Mrs. Smithkins.

" Made 'er laugh ! Said I would. I fair 'ate to see a
glum look on a pretty face. You've lost yer friend, Miss
Stornway. Now, won't yer come in an' 'ave a cosy cup o'
tea along o' me ? "

" An' see 'er wunnerful pictures," sniggered Mrs. Smithkins.

" Jist be off with yer. To the pure all things is white as
wool. Shakespeare ! Miss Stornway's a real laidy. She
knows Shakespeare, I bet. You ask 'er."

All this certainly succeeded in distracting Evarne's
mind.

" Thank you," she said. " I shall very much like to
come."

The visit turned out very successful, though it was perforce but brief, as the girl had to be back at her labours
again. Only by uninterrupted industry could the requisite
number of blouses be finished, and Evarne, with only a few
weeks' practice at machining, was far less rapid than had
been Miss Brodie with her ten years' experience. Milly,
the new fourteen-year-old apprentice, was clumsy and somewhat idle, so that there was now less time than ever in
Evarne's life for protracted afternoon calls.

Day after day she worked with a will, and though at
first her uttermost endeavours only brought in about
fourteen-and-sixpence each week, she rapidly grew more
skilful. Milly, too, became quicker and more useful, and
things were thus promising to become decidedly easier
when an unforeseen accident occurred. It was just one of
those foolish little mishaps that nobody can always succeed
in guarding against. This one was very unromantic in its
origin. Evarne was seated on the side of one of the public

baths, polishing and paring and generally attending to her pretty pink feet and nails, when somehow she lost her balance and fell. In saving herself from splashing half-dressed into the water, she contrived to drive the point of the scissors into her finger, right down to the bone.

It only left a little wound, which Mrs. Harbert tied up with a piece of rag, and although it was the right hand, the girl continued her work next day as if nothing had happened. But in the night the pain grew so bad that it awoke her and prevented her sleeping again, while the daylight showed the wounded finger to be ominously blue and swollen. This spread with terrible rapidity and ere long her hand was totally useless. Full of alarm she hurried off to the hospital, and had her suspicions of blood-poisoning confirmed. The poor hand was carefully bandaged up and put into a sling, and, almost overwhelmed by this new anxiety, the girl returned home to see what could be done about her work.

Everything now devolved upon Milly. Evarne contrived to cut out the blouses with her left hand, and to do a little tacking, but all else had to be left to the apprentice. Evarne could but encourage and supervise, and wearying work that proved. Even in these new circumstances Milly was still slow and idle, and if she was pressed to work faster, she ceased sewing altogether and whimpered.

Thus a miserable three shillings was all that could be earned in the first week, and the next six days showed an increase of but ninepence. Evarne had about half a sovereign laid by, and out of this she paid Milly's wages and the hire of the all-precious machine. But in the second week, when the landlord made his usual Monday rent-collecting visit, she was forced to beg his indulgence, showing her blue and bandaged hand as an excuse and explanation. At first he told her roughly enough that he did not run his houses as a philanthropic undertaking, and that if his tenants could not pay they just had to go. But finally he grew more sympathetic, and at last quite kind. He actually promised to take no steps whatsoever for a month, and if she stayed on after that she could make it up at the rate of a shilling a week.

She recovered the partial use of her hand in less than the stipulated time, and resumed her place at the machine. But she had now got thoroughly backward with money matters. Only by pawning everything in the room that was not absolutely essential could she pay both rent and machine hire, and the eight to ten shillings that was all her still crippled hand was able to earn seemed to be swallowed up immediately she received it. Only about eighteen-pence at the outside could she manage to retain to buy food for herself and her apprentice.

Now, Miss Milly was not particular, and had made few complaints at being reduced to a diet of potatoes and bread and scrape ; tea made of leaves used a second time ; rice boiled in water and sweetened by a little condensed milk, and so on. When, however, the quantity came to be also unpleasantly restricted her hearty appetite, unappeased, rendered her decidedly fractious.

Her honorarium had been reduced by Miss Stornway to a shilling weekly, on the promise that it should be more than made up later, but now she was apparently expected to spend even this miserable half-pay on sustaining life. True, Miss Stornway always took far the smaller portion of every meagre meal, but unfortunately even that fact did not fill the cavity in Milly's stomach. So the day came when that damsel, being entrusted with a penny and sent out to purchase an ounce of tea, returned no more. In the evening came a note :

" DERE MISS,
          " i've gorn ome to my mother Because i wants more to eat. it aint your forlt miss nor it aint mine and mother Says its rite if you works ard you ort to ave Enuf

to eat two shillings you Ows me dont trubble about miss
Eat it.

"Yours respeckful,

"MILLY."

Whether a sting or a kindness lay in the closing sentence, Evarne knew not, but all the statements in the letter
were as clearly undeniable as was the fact that Milly had
deserted her. She felt both ashamed and strangely forsaken, and crushing the scrap of paper in her hand, rested
her pale cheek on the bare boards of the table, while tears
of feebleness and helplessness rolled from her weary eyes
and slowly soaked their way into the wood.

Hampered as she was by her still awkwardly swollen
and painful hand, with those terrible debts clinging like
leeches, and with the imperative need there had been for
every penny that she and her assistant had earned by their
united efforts, she could not conceive how she was possibly
to manage without any help whatsoever. Milly might
have stood by her a little longer, she thought sadly.

There was no chance of economising on anything save
food, and to such lengths was she now forced to carry this
disastrous self-denial, that the uninitiated might have supposed she was trying to solve the problem of how to live
without eating. Naturally dainty, she had, in Jean's
day, often left untouched much of the indifferent food
provided. Now she consumed far rougher and more un-
palatable meals to the last crumb with avidity, and once or
twice even ignobly consumed what should have been her
supper at the same time as her dinner.

She bravely persevered with her work, cutting-out and
machining and stitching from early morning until darkness descended. Even then she continued her weary
labours with the work held close up to the light of a gutter-
ing candle, until practical inability to see longer forced her
to cease, to throw herself upon her bed and sleep.

But the night time brought very imperfect rest. Constantly she was awakened by the vividness of dreams of banquets ; well-stored provision shops ; food lying in the very gutter while people held her back from reaching it ; boards lavishly spread, whence every dish faded immediately she thrust forth her hand to grasp its contents.

Scarcely ever did she leave the four bare walls of her room, save for necessary business. Not only had she neither time nor strength, but now the soles of her shoes were worn into great holes and her stockings were no longer mendable, so that her bare feet trod the pavement, and became bruised and blistered.

And every effort, additional to the day's routine, was to be avoided. Scarcely could she drag herself up of a morning, repeatedly would she find that the treadle of the machine was being worked slower and yet more slowly, as a dull stupor and inertness crept like a fog over her mind. Once she wasted a whole afternoon by fainting, and came to herself to find that nightfall had set in while she was lying unconscious upon the floor.

" I wonder if I'm going to die ? Perhaps I ought to warn somebody or—or do something. I wonder ? " She asked herself this question one late afternoon as she finished tying up the parcel of completed blouses, and found that she could not walk across the room with them without staggering and reeling.

She recalled a ghastly account she had read in the paper, of a man who had died in a locked-up flat, and was never discovered until his corpse decomposed and soaked through the floor to the ceiling below.

" Mrs. Harbert is just underneath me. I wonder if she would move if that happened ? " Evarne grimly and wretchedly pondered as she commenced to descend the stairs.

Ere she was half-way down she suddenly stood still. What was happening ? Why was there that vast yawning pit below? It wasn't real—no, she knew it—but all the same it made her dizzy. She grew blind, and her brain seemed to heave madly. Dropping her parcel, she pressed both hands over her eyes. Was she swaying to and fro, or were the stairs rocking beneath her feet? She made a wild clutch at the banisters, but her fingers closed only upon the air. She was falling—falling—yet could not save herself, and a scream of terror rang through the house ere unconsciousness closed in upon her, and she fell with a dull thud down to the landing below.

CHAPTER XXVI

EVARNE'S VOCATION

WHEN Evarne next opened her eyes she was lying cosily enough in bed. What a strange troubled sleep she had had, so full of confused dreams ! Instantly came a fear of oversleeping, and she made an effort to rise. But the attempt was vain ; even her half-opened lids were insupportably heavy. Languidly she let them droop, and then knew nothing more until a spoon was placed to her lips, and she felt some warm liquid meandering down her throat. At this the heavy lids were lifted widely in astonishment.

"Bravo ! My pretty dolly is made to open its eyes ! " cried a cheery voice, and there by her side was old Mrs. Harbert, gazing at her smilingly.

Evarne looked slowly around. This was not her own room—no—all those artist's studies—where was it ? Then she remembered. She must surely be in Mrs. Harbert's own domain.

Her lips shaped the words, " What am I doing here ? "

" Ah, ha ! My dolly talks," was the only answer she received.

The girl tried to arouse herself further, but enthralled by a heavy lethargy, she abandoned the attempt, and gradually fell asleep once more.

When next she awoke the sharp sound of a falling cup had aroused her more thoroughly. She lifted her head slightly from the pillow. There stood Mrs. Smithkins, looking at her with much concern.

" Lor' now, I do 'ope I 'aven't done no 'arm by wakin' yer up ! "

" Am I ill ? " whispered Evarne.

" You've bin at death's door," impressively replied Mrs. Smithkins, with obvious satisfaction.

" I remember. I was going downstairs. Did I fall ? Tell me everything."

" The doctor says yer ain't to speak."

" You talk ; I'll listen."

Nothing loath, Mrs. Smithkins set to and related the story. It appeared that everybody in the house had run from their rooms at the sound of Evarne's terrible tumble, and, lifting up her unconscious form, had laid her upon Mrs. Harbert's bed—the nearest at hand. Her forehead, which was cut and bleeding, had been promptly tied up. But neither lavish sprinkling of water, draughts of un-diluted gin, the burning of feathers nor the tickling of her palms, had sufficed to bring her to her senses, so the parish doctor had been called in. He had said a lot of things none of the hearers had been able to properly understand, but finally had said clearly enough that it would be weeks ere she was well again.

Mrs. Harbert had undertaken to nurse her, and, accord-ing to Mrs. Smithkins, had fulfilled this promise like an angel of light. Sometimes she had been forced to be absent for the best part of the day about her work, but she had always prepared the invalid's diet beforehand, and Mrs. Smithkins had administered it. The doctor had been ever so many times ! Once he even came twice in one day ! As to Evarne's room upstairs, it was let to somebody else. A man from the firm had come and taken away the sewing machine, her bed was here—Mrs. Harbert now slept on it —her chair and table and other belongings were on the landing upstairs.

Left alone, Evarne lay awake for hours pondering. She half regretted that she had not died ; that would so have simplified matters. Now she had the future to worry about once more ; and she felt positively overwhelmed by the knowledge of her poor old neighbour's extraordinary charity. When evening fell, and Mrs. Harbert entered very softly on tiptoe, Evarne greeted her, feeling quite embarrassed by the extent of this debt of gratitude

" Why, my dolly is quite well agin, the Lord be praised," declared the old woman, beaming all over her face.

Placing on a chair the packed market-basket she carried, she proceeded to lay its contents one by one on the table.

" I've got something for yer," she declared, triumphantly holding up a couple of volumes. " I bought 'em from an old bookstall. ' Rose Leaves or Strawberry Leaves ? A Romance of Society.' That sounds real exciting, and will amuse 'er, thinks I, and then ' Gull—Gully somebody's Travels.' That will be instructive, and will educate 'er mind."

" Mrs. Harbert, you are far, far too good to me. I shall never be able to thank you properly."

" Yer can't do nothin' properly till yer gits well, and the doctor—nice old chap 'e is too—says yer ain't to talk."

" Doctors always say that. Why are you so kind to me ? "

" 'Cause I likes it. My gosh, 'ere am I, a lonely old woman, and when 'Eaven drops a nice-spoken pretty gal, bang splosh at my very front door, d'you think I was goin' to just git out my broom and sweep 'er away ? That ain't Philadelphia 'Arbert."

" I'll get well quickly now, not to cause you any more trouble."

" ' 'E goes quickest who takes time by the nose,' as Shakespeare says."

Evarne smiled.

" How did you come to study Shakespeare ? "

" It was this way. Yer know, my dear, I'm a hartist's model. All these pictures on the wall are me. I showed 'em to yer once before, didn't I ? My gosh, when I was a gal—a young woman—I was real lovely. But yer can see that for yourself, though these 'ere pictures is only students' work, and don't do me real credit. Still, jist notice my shapely legs in this one. Nice bust too, eh ! See my back 'ere—there's a fine straight back for yer. Every great hartist painted me in them days. I was a regular queen among 'em—'eaps more work offered me than I could manage. There was one gentleman—oh, a real nice gentleman 'e was too, pore dear, 'e's dead now—and 'e used to 'ave Shakespeare read out to 'im all the time 'e worked. I often posed for 'im, and as I've got a good memory I picked it up, and bits of it is always comin' into my mind. My gosh, Miss Stornway, I tell yer it do make the other old gals in this 'ouse that jealous ! I'm always sittin' on 'em with my quotes, and they can't do nothin' but keep their hignorant old tongues still and look silly."

Thus she rattled on, meantime proceeding to prepare the evening meal for herself and her charge.

Days passed, and having once started upon her convalescence, Evarne gained strength rapidly. At the end of a week she was able to leave her bed. The colour and contour gradually returned to her pale, thin cheeks, the brightness to her eye, all her marvellous beauty blossomed forth afresh. At the end of a fortnight she was strong enough to take her first outing in the form of a short ride on the top of a 'bus.

On returning from this expedition she lay down while Mrs. Harbert made tea, and over the genial beverage the old woman for the first time consented to discuss future plans. Evarne had two or three various suggestions to bring forward, but Mrs. Harbert would not even listen.

" There's only one sensible thing for yer to do, Evarne, my gal, and that's to follow in my footsteps. Needlework

and sich-like may be all right for some, but for you—why,
it's jist a wicked waste of Gawd's gifts.   Now, I'll tell yer,
when yer was ill and me and Smithkins was givin' my dolly
a bath, I says to 'er, I says, ' My gosh, what a lovely
gal ! ' and Smithkins she says—— Now, whatever are
yer blushin' for, my dear ? You are a real lovely gal, and
I speaks as one who knows what's what.   I never seemed
to notice it when yer was bundled up in clothes ; that's the
way with the best of us, we never appears to advantage in
togs.   It's the skinny women with waists the size of their
ankles, what no hartist would so much as look at ; or them
females as is bundles of fat what wouldn't look human if
they wasn't packed up tidy into corsets—they're the sort
what looks best in their clothes.   Beautiful women like
you and me looks better and better as we undresses more
and more.   You'll make a fortune as a model, and you'll
be a bigger fool than I take yer for if yer chucks away
that fortune."

Evarne remained silent, pondering over this suggestion.
Instant objections sprang to her mind, but at the same
time came the conviction that here indeed was a means
of earning a livelihood for which she was undeniably well
qualified.   Her own experience as an artist had taught
her both the value and the rarity of a figure, beautiful from
an artistic point of view.   At the same time .   .   .

Mrs. Harbert broke in upon her reflections.

" Perhaps yer was thinkin' it ain't proper. '

But the girl shook her head immediately.

" No," she declared.   " I studied Art myself, and painted
from the nude, when I was better off, so I should have got
rid of any ideas of that sort, even if I had ever had them ;
but I never had.   I was just thinking that it really was a
brilliant notion of yours, but that I didn't quite like it
somehow.   Still, I believe that if you hadn't spoken just
then, I should have gone on to reflect that beggars can't
be choosers."

"Ah, Shakespeare! But why don't yer like it, if yer ain't shocked? It's the nicest profession in the world. Takes yer among sich 'igh-class people—real ladies and gentlemen—and into sich nice warm rooms. And what's more, yer can go on till yer are as old as old—as a costume model anyway. Of course, while you're young, the sun shines, and yer bucks up and makes yer 'ay accordin'. Yer can earn pounds a week sometimes, quite easy. Look at me—I'm a middle-aged one now, yet I makes a pretty fair livin' by it, and don't overwork myself neither."

"How would I start to get work? Is it difficult to get up a connection?" inquired the girl dubiously.

"Not for the likes of you. You'd only 'ave to show yerself. But yer still looks ill, and you're ever so weak. You've got to be strong to 'stand,' I can tell yer. 'Tain't no use beginnin' yet. I wish we could git yer away to the seaside.

"I'll get well quickly in London now—I will really. I'll go out into the parks every day for fresh air, and be as strong as ever I was in no time. You shall see."

She duly followed this prescription, with the result prophesied. It had been inexpressibly painful to feel that she was being maintained by this hard-working old woman, upon whom she had not the slightest claim, and at the same time to doubt her power of ever making due recompense. Now, with a mind at ease once more as to the future, the open air, the rest, and the ample though simple diet were free to fulfil their good work. In less than a fortnight Mrs. Harbert was able to declare her *protégée* to be blooming as a rose, and a picture unpainted.

Accordingly she set about finding an engagement for the girl, and one morning, a week or two later, she watched Evarne set off for an advanced and important Art school, armed with good courage, a packet of sandwiches and some sage advice.

"Nobody guesses it's yer first sittin', me dear, and

nobody won't take no notice of yer if yer don't tell 'em. Walk out of the dressin'-room as bold as brass, and grumble under yer breath at the pose the master chooses, no matter what it is. If you won't come when 'e calls, or run back agin, or act the fool in any way what ain't usual with models, they'll all remember you're a human bein', and stare at yer, anxious to know what's the matter. Then, likely enough, you would feel rather put out of countenance."

"I'm not going to be silly at all," Evarne had declared with conviction ; and sure enough, when she returned in the evening she was able to state that the entire day had gone off satisfactorily.

She had not expected to be much troubled by inopportune bashfulness, and when she found herself again in a studio, beheld the easels and drawing-boards, canvases and palettes, smelt the characteristic odours and heard the familiar artistic jargon of the students, she had felt herself to be an acolyte in a temple wherein was worshipped the perpetuation of the beautiful. The influence of modern thought and custom had fallen from her with her garments, and she had adored her own fairness.

"I'm sorry if it sounds immodest," she confessed, "but indeed I only felt happy to be in the atmosphere of Art once more. I knew that those young men, who all seemed so much in earnest, would learn much from painting me—for it was a very charming pose—and somehow I felt interested in everyone, and as if I wanted them all to get on, and was glad to be able to help them to progress a little. Oh, Mrs. Harbert! Somehow I feel that if only I came across a real artist—a grand man, you know, but young, who hadn't found himself yet, so to speak—I could inspire him to do such wonderful work, to paint pictures he had never dreamed of before. I don't fancy I should ever have been much of an artist myself, even if I'd been able to keep on—perhaps I should though! Anyhow,

I know I have got something in my heart or mind,
or something vague of that sort, that I could give out
to another if he could receive it, and had some of the
impulse I'm talking about of his own, and then he would be
able to do what otherwise he would never be able to do.
. . . I am getting dreadfully incoherent, but I know
what I mean myself. Did you ever feel anything like what
I've been describing ? "

The old woman would not commit herself to a direct
answer.

" It's a blessing yer looks at it in that light," she commented.

But nothing could possibly have surpassed Mrs. Harbert's
real opinion of the importance of the part played by the
model in the production of any picture of worth, so she was
fully sympathetic, no matter to what heights the girl might
soar on the topic.

And now Evarne found that she had indeed alighted upon
a profession in which she had little to fear for competition,
neither did she require much more aid from Mrs. Harbert.
Before her fortnight at the Art school was completed, she
had already obtained another engagement.

" It's the elder sister of one of the young men," she
explained gleefully. " The youth seems to have waxed
somewhat enthusiastic about me ; so much so that his
sister, who is an artist, came down to the school to see the
wonder with her own eyes. She wants me to start sitting
for her next Monday. Am I not fortunate ? She seemed
such a nice woman, and her brother says she paints beautifully. I am so pleased about it.

And this success was only the beginning. Ere long
Evarne found herself the proud recipient of more offers
than she could possibly accept. Allowing herself to be
guided by the experienced Mrs. Harbert, she discriminated
among them, and also gradually raised her terms. Nevertheless, work continued to flow in unceasingly ; very rarely

was there even half a week day that she could regard as
a holiday.

As time passed she became quite well known in the
artistic world, and sometimes even fulfilled particularly
well-paid engagements out of London. Not only was the
girl absolutely delightful to the eye, both in face and form,
but many an artist found her presence in his studio to be
strangely valuable. It was her sympathy with any aspiring worker—the keen interest she took in the picture
on hand—quite as much as her quick understanding, her
almost intuitive divination of its creator's ideas, unex-
pressed thoughts and half-conceived fancies, that gave her
a unique power that the painters themselves were quick
to feel. Her own artistic instincts and her studio training
had given her the gift of falling easily and instinctively
into poses full of grace and expression. Quite frequently
too, studying the half-completed work, ideas would come
to her which, with a gentle diffidence, she would suggest—
usually to find her thought taken advantage of to the vast
benefit of the picture. Unquestionably Evarne had found
her vocation at last.

Had she been plunged into the career of a model immediately upon leaving her petted, luxurious life with Morris
Kenyon, she would probably have considered it as a truly
miserable lot—and herself as a victim of cruel fate. But
her descent in the social scale had been so gradual, and had
led to such an abyss of abject poverty and humiliation
before she had almost groped her way into the next world
by the gateway of starvation, that this new existence
shone brightly by comparison.

Occasionally she would smile just a little bitterly on
comparing her early dreams of artistic fame with the reality
of settling down contentedly enough to serving as a mere
accessory in the production of pictures. But she had
never been genuinely ambitious, and the pang was not
severe. Besides, the counsels of Socrates could step in at

such moments, and bring contentment and resignation. Poverty she feared and hated, but now that came not near her. True, sweet luxury was also but a memory of the past, but she was well able to live in perfect comfort.

The five years that followed her adoption of this new profession were successful, prosperous, and, in their way, happy. Her beauty was not of the type that wanes with girlhood—each year brought added graces. Her path through life was encompassed with affection, good-will, regard. She made a circle of acquaintances for herself—bohemian, but bright, kindly and amusing. In every studio she entered she was admired instantly and respected ere long. Both men and women artists were considerate and friendly towards the stately young model, and this was all that she desired.

In those five years more than a few men fell captive beneath her subtle charm, but never a one could gain her love, and she ruthlessly made it clear that she regarded unwanted masculine devotion as the most useless and undesirable thing on earth. Neither did the wealth and good position of at least one of her honourable suitors affect her. Evarne was true to her heart, as she had ever been.

She was unfailing in friendship and gratitude towards the old woman to whom she owed so much of her present calm contentment. Very speedily she had discharged her monetary debts to Philia—for so she affectionately abbreviated Mrs. Philadelphia Harbert's somewhat ponderous first name—but that was not all.

Her first upward step had been to move into a couple of rooms in a neighbouring house, furnishing them gradually in a manner pleasing to her taste. After a year or so she grew ambitious, and inviting Philia to join forces with her, migrated to Chelsea. There she took a little house in a poor yet eminently respectable street. Her new domain had a tiny garden in front, a yet tinier grass plot behind, and contained four rooms and a kitchen. True, there was no room for the proverbial swinging of a cat, but Evarne was touchingly proud of her little home, and spent money upon its furnishing with truly extravagant abandon.

Old Philia's engagements as a model had for years past been somewhat difficult to obtain, and as Evarne waxed wealthier, so Philia had fallen into low water. It was accordingly arranged between them, on their first deciding to live together, that when the elder woman was actually earning money she should pay somewhat towards the expenses of their joint establishment. At other times it was to be regarded as fully equivalent if she undertook to prepare breakfast and supper for Evarne, the principal bread-winner and rent-payer ; to superintend the labour of the occasional charwoman, and generally to see to the little home being kept neat and clean and cosy.

As time passed, Philia almost entirely abandoned posing, and devoted herself to domestic labours. Evarne delighted in being looked after, tended and made much of, so she was well content with this state of affairs. As to Philia, she found herself absolutely happy in her old age, and was given to quoting imaginary passages from Shakespeare largely, to show that her first disinterested kindness towards her poor young upstairs neighbour had been as bread cast on the waters, which was now returning itself in the form of cake.

CHAPTER XXVII

IN ARTIST-LAND

ONE winter morning the monotony of the studio in which Evarne was posing was broken by the unannounced entrance of a young man.

Mr. Towning, the owner of the domain, threw down his palette, and greeted the newcomer heartily.

" Why, it's Hardy ! Haven't seen you for ages, old chap."

" Up to my eyes in work. And I see you're hard at it too. Don't let me interrupt business."

Thus adjured, Towning recommenced his interrupted occupation, while his visitor stood by and scrutinised his labours.

" You're making a fine thing of that," was the verdict. " The colour scheme is delightful—absolutely. That touch of blue just there—splendid ! I say, what a splendid model you've got."

Towning lowered his voice a trifle.

" Yes, and that touch of blue was her suggestion, if you please. What do you think of that ? Have you not seen her before—Evarne Stornway ? "

" Oh, is that who it is ? Of course I've heard of her. Only last week some chap was in to see Geoff, and he fairly raved over her. By Jove, he wasn't far wrong either."

" She's quite uncommon, isn't she ? It's not often one finds a glorious shape like that, more's the pity. By the way, what's Geoff Danvers working at now ? "

" He's off to Venice at the end of March.   He's going
to paint abroad till next winter."

" Lucky dog.   It's all right to have plenty of money,
isn't it ? "

" But there are not many who use it as Geoff does.
Heaven knows what I should do without him, and now he
is not going alone to Venice."

" No ? "

" He's taking two young chaps, Melcarp and Thorpe,
with him.   It will be the time of their lives.   They haven't
got a spare penny piece between them, and could as easily
have taken themselves to study in the moon as in Italy.
Geoff is paying all their expenses, and making out that it's
a favour on their part that they're coming.   Vows he would
die of dulness without company.   Melcarp and Thorpe
are half off their heads with excitement."

" Lucky beggars.   What will you do when he's gone ? "

" Oh, plod along in the studio as usual.   I have got a
fine idea for a picture, and I am hunting for a model.   The
subject is a couple of lines of Keates's ' Belle Dame sans
Merci,' and I want a girl with reddish-golden hair and a
palish face ; gleaming eyes, deep set ; and cruel red lips—
all curves.   Not a fine bouncing wench at all, but one of
those weird, fascinating, fragile sort of women—you know
what I mean."

" But you surely don't expect to find exactly what you
want ? "

" Scarcely.   But if I could only get the right coloured
hair with the pale face it would be something.   To tell the
truth, Towning," the young artist avowed, with a moment's
outburst of confidence, " I haven't got as much imagination
as an artist really wants.   I don't get a clear vision of
things in my mind ; I just get a shadowy sort of notion.
But unless I can have some degree of reality before me,
very similar to my vague fancy—well, I am nowhere.   My
idea just dies away."

"Paint portraits. There's more money in that than in anything else, you know."

"Oh, that reminds me of a bit of real luck. When Lord Winborough returns to England in the autumn, he has promised to let me do a bust of him to exhibit. Splendid chance, isn't it? But I am awfully set on doing that 'Belle Dame' picture."

"Perhaps Miss Stornway knows of a girl with red-gold hair and all the rest of it. By the way, it's time."

He ceased working, and slightly nodded to Evarne. She stood up, stretched her arms over her head, gave a couple of tiny kicks to take the stiffness from one of her knees, then slipped behind the screen that formed a temporary dressing-room. She reappeared, clad in a loose crimson wrapper, and sat down by the fire.

The young men joined her.

"You heard what we were talking about, of course, Miss Stornway?" questioned Towning. "Is there a 'Belle Dame' among your friends?"

But Evarne was unable to render assistance. She knew of two models with red-gold hair, but the accompanying round, rosy faces and *retroussé* noses of both were in no way mystic and interesting. All she could do was to promise to remember the requirement, and to send any likely damsel along for inspection.

"Thank you. But you're about the fiftieth person who's on the lookout," returned Jack Hardy ruefully.

When he finally took his departure, he walked slowly back to Kensington, a cloud of discontent upon his brow. His mind was full of his picture, the great work he was longing to commence, yet—morbidly conscious of his own limitations—he was resolutely determined not to start without having found a suitable model for the central figure.

"I *must* get on! I *must* make headway! All my youth is passing!"

He almost snarled these words aloud. Earnest, enthusiastic, patiently hard-working, Jack Hardy was devoid
of one spark of divine inspiration, and knew it but too well
for his peace of mind. He saw his own handiwork without
gloss or glamour ; viewed it as it was in stern reality, good
in composition, in technique, but commonplace—oh !
Phœbus Apollo and all ye Muses—how sadly commonplace ! Not a man or woman, trained and practised as he
was, but could have done equally well. In the ripest fruit
of his hand and brain there was absolutely nothing individual ; scarce a trace of originality ; no magnetism, no
grip. Never had Jack Hardy completed a work, and looking upon it said within himself : " None but I could have
produced just this result. Only the combination of heart
and brain and soul and knowledge that makes Me could
have evolved this picture. I myself am in it."

As a student, a great future had been prophesied for him,
and in those days he had believed in himself. But time
had glided by, his thirtieth year was past, his powers had
matured without enlarging their scope, and with bitter
reluctance he commenced to realise that he now saw the
full extent to which his capacity would ever attain. He
might become more certain, more facile, but nothing else.
No longer could he still look forward and upward, confident
in what would be revealed when the summit of the hill he
so laboriously climbed was reached. He was there, and
lo ! it was but the crowded tableland of mediocrity !

His thoughts were bitter as he walked through the streets
that day. Why had Nature so utterly denied him that
divine " something " that no industry can give, no study
can acquire ? " I can but despise my own men and women,"
he thought. " I am no creator ! I make forms in paint,
but I cannot give them the breath of life. I make them
beautiful—strictly speaking—yet there is no beauty in
them. I am a craftsman, a mechanic—not an artist."

But he had a stout heart and a dogged obstinacy that

refused to yield. Surely this fervid ambition to abandon himself to imaginative work must be the outcome of some fire of inspiration, however small and smouldering. Let him only find that woman with the gleaming pale face and the sunlike hair, and he surely could and would produce his masterpiece.

He looked around as he walked. Even if he discovered his personified dream out of the ranks of professional models, he meant to leave no stone unturned to persuade her to sit for his great picture.

He shivered somewhat as the chill winter blasts rushed by. Money was far from plentiful in Jack's pockets. In true artistic style he inhabited a garret in Bohemia, and it was only by the strictest economy that he was enabled to exist on the work he sold, aided by the small sum of money he had inherited from his mother.

Yet the studio belonging to the top suite in the handsome block of flats that he entered, and in which he was obviously quite at home, bore every sign of ample wealth. A spacious and lofty apartment, it was obviously no makeshift, but had been destined by its architect to behold artistic labours. This was clearly shown by its top-lights, and its one very huge window, unusually wide and deep.

From the front entrance of the flat of which it formed part, this studio was reached by crossing a wide hall, on the left side of which opened the living-rooms of the suite. But the entire right-hand half of the flat, looking north, was devoted to the requirements of Art. At the farther end of the studio itself a door opened on to a short passage on each side of which was a quite small room. That on the right was the model's dressing-room ; it communicated also directly with the studio, but the other little room had its only opening into the short corridor. It was destined for the storing of plaster and other materials used in model-ling, and possessed the useful addition of a tiny sink with hot and cold water. A door at the farther end of the dividing passage gave access to a flight of stairs which ultimately led out to Langthorne Place, where was the back entrance of the block of flats.

The studio itself was verily a fascinating spot, with its exquisite replicas of classical statues ; its curious swords and armour ; its plaques ; its Damascus shawls and Eastern draperies ; divans and lavishly carved chairs and tables. Vases of curious build, harmonious outline, or rich colour stood around, several—despite the wintry season—filled with pink and crimson roses.

But for all this luxury, it was obviously a workshop. The scent of the flowers struggled feebly through the stronger odour of oils and turpentine, while a couple of the vases were utilised to hold spiky clusters of innumerable paint-brushes. The statue of Venus was next to the life-sized lay figure ; the Salviati mirror reflected, besides a bronze Mercury, a grim skeleton and a plaster cast of a head with the outer skin removed to show the facial muscles. Numerous studies and unfinished sketches decorated or defaced the walls, while heavy-looking books on anatomy and perspective were to be found by the side of daintily-bound poets and some of the newest novels. There was quite enough of dust and disorder to show this *atelier* to be the haunt of earnest workers, and the young man, clad in a much-besmeared painting overall, who stood before a large canvas, scarcely glanced aside as Jack entered.

In this industrious artist Jack beheld his best and truest friend. It was to the good-nature of Geoffrey Danvers that he owed the privilege of working in this splendid studio from morning to evening, and making it practically his home ; it was Geoff's generosity that freed him from any difficulties concerning the cost of canvas, colours and models.

Meeting at an Art school in Paris, a close comradeship had sprung up between the two young Englishmen, and when Geoff returned to London and took up his abode in this flat with its fine studio, he was not slow in suggesting that Jack Hardy should continue to be his brother-in-art.

He knew his friend's poverty, knew that without some such help he would be condemned to waste many of his days turning out " pot-boilers," and was heartily glad to be able to save him from this embittering employment. For the present, at all events, Jack was quite freed from every expense connected with his work. He procured all his materials from Geoff's colour dealer, and never even saw the bills, while each week the fee for his model got itself paid in the same convenient manner.

But money was indeed scarcely an object to Geoff. He was possessed of far more than enough for the simple life that was his choice. He really could not see that any unusual kindliness or generosity lay in his favourite diversion of playing " fairy godfather " to other young artists, clever yet needy. All his aspirations for the future, all his interest in the present, lay in Art—his life's occupation—and he pursued it with a devotion, an ardour, that could not have been surpassed had he known his whole ultimate welfare to depend upon his success.

And surely the gods loved Geoffrey Danvers ! Not only did he bring to his labours a brain in which the capacity for unwearying endeavour co-existed with ever-active enthusiasm and alert intelligence ; more than that—to him had been given an imaginative soul that swam easily and always in a boundless sea of fantasy and dreams. His good right hand followed instincts, obeyed emotions and up-welling thoughts, all unguessed-at and undreamed-of by plodding, heavy-minded Jack Hardy. Thus came forth work pulsating with that power, that appeal, that life, for which Jack yearned, that he struggled for, prayed for— in vain—all in vain.

An hour later the two young men sat down to lunch. Jack's opening statement was startling.

" I've seen the most beautiful woman alive."

"That's a big order. Your 'Belle Dame'? No, you couldn't have kept that great fact to yourself for so long."

"I should think not. No, it's that Miss Stornway whom Flinders spoke of. You remember—the 'Diana' of Montford's last year's Academy picture. She's sitting for Towning now. She is lovely—really. She looks as strong and lithe and graceful as the goddess herself. Never worn corsets in her life, I understand. Her face is perfectly exquisite too—pure Greek. Her hair waves back from halfway down her forehead, like that of Venus there."

"Dark, is she?"

"Almost black hair, big brown eyes, quite a brunette really; but one might think she was fair, she has such a clear complexion, such a smooth, satin-like skin. Go out to Towning's and see her. It's really worth while."

"We'll have her to sit here. I can see you are anxious to paint from her."

"I must confess I am."

"You had better write at once then. Since she is such a paragon of beauty I expect she has a waiting list of engagements."

A couple of days later proved Geoffrey to be a true prophet.

"We have indeed got to wait our turn, it seems. Miss Stornway can't come until the middle of March," announced Jack, studying the response to his letter. "Ten weeks ahead. Why, that is about when you'll be going away."

"That doesn't matter at all. If I have got my 'Death of Orpheus' finished I might make a few studies of her, to use up my last few days here; but she is coming for you, you know."

CHAPTER XXVIII

GEOFFREY DANVERS

THE spring morning on which Evarne was to make her first appearance in this new studio dawned fresh and crisp. On the outward journey she purchased a bunch of daffodils, and slipped them between the revers of her warm squirrel coat. A little cap of the same grey fur perched itself jauntily upon her thick hair, beneath which her clear, calm eyes looked forth upon the world with a certain sweet and serene complacency.

She had allowed herself more than sufficient time for finding her goal, and was ushered by an elderly charwoman into an empty studio. She sat down patiently to wait, picking up the day's newspaper to pass the time until Mr. Hardy should arrive.

Gradually the feeling assailed her that she was being watched. At length the conviction became sufficiently strong to cause her to lower her paper and look round. There, sure enough, in an open doorway, stood a young man.

She rose rather suddenly to her feet. This was presumably Mr. Danvers.

"Excuse my staring so hard," said Geoff rather awkwardly, as he came forward. "I didn't mean to startle you."

"I'm here to be looked at, you know," was the smiling retort, and then a confused silence prevailed.

Any embarrassment before strangers was an unusual experience, and Evarne found herself consciously casting around in her mind for something to say.

"May I put my daffodils into water—I should be sorry to see them fade?" she asked at length.

For answer Geoff impulsively seized a bunch of roses by their unhappy heads, whipped them out of their vase and flung them aside.

" Put your flowers here," he said.

" You need not have done that," suggested Evarne somewhat reproachfully. " There was plenty of room for my daffodils beside your roses."

There was another pause.

" Do you believe in omens ? " asked Geoff suddenly.

" I hardly know," was the uninspiring response.

Once more came a pause of considerable duration. Conversation between these two, neither usually gauche or dull-witted, seemed to consist of brief, somewhat inane remarks, interlarded with long periods of silence. But these protracted intervals were strangely devoid of any unpleasant feeling of restraint.

Meeting Geoffrey's grey eyes fixed full upon her, Evarne instinctively smiled at him, slowly and serenely as was her wont. The young man rose from his chair with an abrupt start, and, crossing over to his easel, commenced to sort out brushes.

" I, too, am going to paint from you, Miss Stornway," he explained with his back to her, " but my friend must arrange your pose. He has got an order for the picture. I can't think what is keeping him."

Even as he spoke Jack swept in like a whirlwind, full of explanations.

" Have you been here long, Miss Stornway ? Well, never mind, only be as quick as you can in dressing, there's a good girl. I want you to wear this. Where on earth is it ? Have you looked at the costume this morning, Geoff ? "

" Which costume ? "

" The one you helped me twist up yesterday, of course."

From the recesses of the plaster-room Jack produced

what was apparently a white rope, but as he proceeded to shake it out, it expanded into a loose sleeveless gown. It was made of almost transparent muslin, and had been damped, twisted round as tightly as possible while still wet, and thus left to dry. As a result it was now covered with innumerable little folds and creases, delightfully reminiscent of the draperies of antique statues.

Before to-day had Evarne worn just such a robe, and knowing that nothing was better calculated to emphasise her commanding beauty than was this graceful simplicity, it was with considerable satisfaction that she took it from Jack's hand and retired to the model's room. A white ribbon was provided to confine the falling folds beneath her breast ; the only touch of colour was the rich blue of the cornflowers and golden yellow of ripe wheat-ears that composed a wreath for her head. She did not hurry in the least over her toilette, but took as much time as ever she required in arranging her hair graciously beneath the light garland, and in carefully coaxing and smoothing into artistic folds the masses of snowy drapery, and moulding it to her form. She felt strangely, unreasonably excited—peculiarly anxious to look her very best for Mr. Hardy's benefit. She gazed at her reflection critically ere leaving her retreat, and having an artist's eye, her lips inevitably curved into a soft smile of satisfaction.

" Well, you do look ripping ! " exclaimed Jack impulsively, as she appeared and stood motionless for a moment to be surveyed.

Geoff was silent, but Evarne's glance had somehow wandered towards him, and his eyes had spoken. Half-unconsciously she gave a tiny happy laugh, as, scorning the step, she sprang lightly upon the throne.

Never had a day sped with such magical rapidity. For the first time in her whole experience as an artist's model she was genuinely sorry when twilight fell and work had to be abandoned. Strangely, strangely attractive was the

mental atmosphere of this studio, wherein luxury and ambition blossomed side by side.

She had received in her life not a few personal lessons
concerning the uncertainty of Fate and mutability of
Fortune, while from Philia's teachings she had learned it
all over again second-hand. As the old woman put it—

"Yer goes out innercent and unsuspectin' for a quiet
walk, and perhaps you're brought 'ome on a shutter dead as
a doornail, from a chimney-pot 'avin fallen and cracked yer
skull; or you've been squashed by a motor; or shot by a
lunatic; or bit by a mad dog. All them things 'appens
to some folks. Maybe your turn next, maybe mine. Or,
more ordinary like, a bit o' grit blows into yer eye all in the
twinklin' of a second—no warnin' at all—and yer goes
gropin' 'arf-blind for the rest of the day."

Evarne returned home that evening with a metaphorical
"bit o' grit" having blown in her eye, "in a twinkling of
a second—no warning at all." Many a studio had she
entered, many an artist had she known, clever, young and
attractive, who had been kind and considerate to her, even
as Geoffrey Danvers. What quality did he possess in any
superlative degree to mark him out from all others? What
was there about him that awoke such—well—such a keen
and ardent interest in her mind, not only for himself and
his work, but for everything with which he was even remotely connected? He had not said or done anything
at all original or particularly interesting, yet she found herself dwelling upon his every word, every action, recalling
and musing upon his most casual unprofessional glance.

Perhaps, after all, the deep and engrossing impression
he had made was but the natural outcome of the ardent
admiration she had felt for those of his paintings that were
still in the studio. Instantly had she realised that here was
work of no common order—that there was a combination
of charm and of force, an instinct for the dramatic, together
with a certain dreamy mysticism, a poetic treatment of

daring realism, that could not possibly have been evolved by a banal, uninteresting mind. Surely a man's self can often be better read in his works than by years of ordinary acquaintanceship?

When Philia made her usual inquiries regarding the personal appearance of these new employers, Evarne had described Jack Hardy well enough, but her recollection of Geoff was apparently vague.

" Well—let me think—he has fair hair, but he is clean-shaven, and he was dressed in light grey."

" Yes ? "

" There is nothing much to tell, really. He is a bit taller than I am—I noticed that when he stood up on the throne to make some alteration in my wreath. When he is work-ing he wears a painting overall of blue linen, which betrays vanity."

" Pore young man. Why should yer say that ? "

" I'm sure he knows the colour suits him. Now, Mr. Hardy only has brown holland."

" Is Mr. Danvers good-looking ? "

Evarne reflected a moment, then temporised.

" I thought so," she answered.

Days came and passed. A whole week went by, but her mental vision in no way recovered its normal equipoise.

" Whatever 'as took yer, Evarne ? " inquired Philia at supper one evening, when some blatant act of absent-mindedness proclaimed that her companion's thoughts were far away. " There's no tellin' now what you'll be up to next. You're anticking about jist as if you'd fallen in love."

" Fallen in love ! " Evarne had never liked that term ; it had seemed to her somewhat cheap and light. But, after all, was it not strangely descriptive—full of realism ? Only last week she and " that other " had been total strangers. Now—ah ! now—what a difference ! Only a few mutual glances ; a tender pressure of the hand ; a stolen smile, so full of meaning—at once the whole world bore a different face, was lit by a new glory ; all life's hopes and possibilities sprung forth anew, richly scented, brightly hued. " Fallen in love " indeed ! What other imaginable phrase could so forcefully express both the suddenness and the personal irresponsibility of that which had brought to pass this all-wondrous change ?

Evarne pictured love as a seething, rushing torrent. It had nigh drowned her in a maelstrom once, but she had scrambled out, and the last drop of its cruel waters had long since dried from her garments. Now she had walked quietly along as if on its flat, dull, safe banks for many a year, merely smiling serenely, somewhat scornfully, at those who—dabbling their feet where its eddies were calm and shallow—had stretched forth their hands, inviting her to join them in their child's play. But in the fated hour a pair of grey eyes had gazed up at her from out the depths of the stream ; she had looked a moment too long, too intently, and had fallen sheer into the flood and was swept helplessly along in its wild current. Surely it was far safer to retain one's balance always and ever, to keep a steady head and avoid even this divine fall ? Mayhap ! Yet so far—drifting lightly and unresistingly—she could not regret. The touch of these waters was indeed pleasant ; they tasted sweet within her mouth. Rocks there were indeed—cruel, menacing boulders—yet she came not nigh them. Surely it was better here, far better, despite dangers cruel and manifold, than on those level arid banks.

A fortnight glided by, and not a day but saw fresh verses added to the poem of which these two had, all unconsciously, composed the opening stanzas at the very moment of their first meeting. So far this song of love ran in simple cadence—easy of construction and rhythm. Not a line had yet been sent forth into the air. Strophe and antistrophe were sung in silence, yet with perfect mutual comprehension and harmony.

Never since those first few minutes—given over to apparent tongue-tied embarrassment—had Geoffrey and Evarne been together without Jack making a third. While this was certainly in the ordinary course of events, it was also, in some degree, the outcome of deliberate design on Jack's part. That young man had the greatest fear of love. He viewed it with apprehension and misgiving, a disease, a madness, to be warded off and avoided desperately—at all events by an artist. He might not know very much about the matter, or the symptoms by which it made its terrible presence manifest, but very soon indeed he was assailed by an alarming suspicion that Geoff regarded Miss Stornway differently from other models, dangerously differently.

Jack was uneasy. He felt a sort of responsibility for having introduced the young woman into the studio, much as he would have held himself guilty had he brought home fever from one of his searches for " La Belle Dame," and thus prostrated his friend upon a bed of sickness. He had a vague idea that his presence might somehow suffice to nip any growing feeling of affection in the bud. Thus he conscientiously hovered around.

And Geoffrey—a prey to many conflicting emotions—raised no objection. There were reasons that made it very desirable that he should not grow to seriously care for this fascinating model. Not being of a nature that could treat emotional matters lightly, for some time his delight in Evarne's presence was largely diluted by an ardent wish that he had never seen her fair face. But this marvellous wisdom did not have things all its own way.

The date was rapidly approaching when he had arranged to leave England. Geoff's two young travelling companions were continually dropping in, full of eager talk of the journey and the work that was going to be accomplished at Venice. Day by day his gradually growing dislike of this proposed absence from London increased.

At length a mental crisis came. His many conflicting thoughts settled themselves into a resolution.

"I say, Jack," he announced one evening, " you had better go to Venice with those boys. I have just made up my mind that I'm not going. You can be ready in three days, can't you ? "

Jack absolutely gasped.

"Why not ? Why are you not going ? "

"I prefer to stop in England. I—I—well, I suppose I may as well tell you. There's no reason for secrecy. I've seen the woman I want to marry."

Jack tried to look mystified and at a loss, as if thereby he could ward off the evil hour.

"Who is it ? " he inquired.

"Why, you blind old bat, who should it be but—Miss Stornway ? "

The blow had fallen.

"Geoffrey Danvers ! " and Jack's voice was full of horror. "You must not be so idiotic ! "

The young man laughed lightly as he answered—

"Object, argue and discuss as much as you like. I'll talk to you for hours about her. Why should I not marry that sweet girl ? Tell me ? "

"Well, after all she's only a—only a—— "

"Only a model! What on earth has that got to do with it ? "

"It's a very serious objection on earth, whatever it may be in heaven," retorted Jack, flattering himself he had been rather smart.

"And don't you know where marriages are made ? I tell you she is the one woman Heaven intended for me. Don't think I love her only for her beauty—though she is lovely beyond all words. But if her eyes were small and squinting, yet had that same beautiful soul shining out of them—— "

Jack interrupted. Even his limited imagination was capable of supplying the conclusion of this sentiment.

" Look here, Geoff! Do see reason."

" I prefer to see Evarne."

" But you cannot—you must not—marry an artist's model whom you haven't known for three weeks—— "

" That's a mere detail. It's my misfortune, isn't it, not my fault, that I didn't meet her years ago ? As to her being a model—what of it ? It's an honest enough profession when a girl is obliged to earn her own living, and you know when her father died and left her penniless she had to do something. Everybody knows that needlework is a starving occupation, and I think that old woman who suggested her taking up this business was a paragon of wisdom. There's nothing at all in Miss Stornway's life that anyone could take exception to, unless they were utterly bigoted. You can't find any story to her discredit in any studio, or on the lips of any artist. Everyone speaks well of her, she is entirely admirable — brave, beautiful—— ! "

" Oh, she's a nice girl enough, and I don't doubt she's straight as a die. But don't—don't rush into this affair madly and hastily. You were going to Venice. Well, for goodness' sake go."

" I will, later on, and take Evarne with me. I say, I take it all very much for granted, don't I ? But she does care for me—you think she does, eh ? "

Jack discreetly suppressed the retort that rose to his lips.

" How can I tell ? But, of course, I meant go alone to Italy, to test the reality of your feelings. Six months out of a lifetime—why, it's nothing, if it be really an affair for a lifetime. And if absence shows it to be but a passing fancy—well, you will have done no harm to her or to yourself."

" If I didn't see her for twenty years, I should never change, never forget her."

" And it's only six months that's in question. If she

really is the woman above all others for you, then, I'd say, make her your wife even if she were a beggar in the streets. But be sure first, Geoff! You're twenty-six now—not a hot-brained boy. Do submit your fancy to this small test before you fly in the face of society. You know what a general row there will be, and how all your own set will disapprove. You are the heir to a title, though you never seem to remember it, so that your marriage is a matter of real importance."

" I've thought of all that. Don't think I've overlooked any of the arguments my family would be sure to bring up. But I am not going to let my vague prospects make any serious difference in my life. Why, I dare say the title will never come to me. Winborough quite easily might live longer than I."

" It's hardly likely since he's about a quarter of a century older. Anyway, there's the possibility, not to say the likelihood, that your wife will one day find herself a countess, and that your son will be the future Earl of Winborough. It really is no light matter, old fellow. Don't disappoint these boys ; go to Venice with them, and see how you feel toward Miss Stornway when you come back."

" And have some other lucky beggar with more gumption carrying her off in the meanwhile ? "

" If she married anyone else in six months it would most certainly prove that she had not got the same true depth of feeling for you that you have for her. You ought to be sure, both of yourself and of her, before you make her your wife."

Thus Jack continued, arguing and discussing, talking the profoundest of common sense, yet with enough of sympathy to add weight to his words. And again Geoffrey saw the dark side of the shield, noticed the shadows athwart the roseate path. Finally he resolved not to alter his plans for the summer. Six months would soon be gone, and the passing of this time of test would sweep the last lingering scruples from his mind.

"It is a serious matter, and ought to be treated seriously. I'm glad I've resolved to go," was his ultimate conclusion.

"I shall often write to you, Evarne," he declared, holding the girl's hands as they bade each other farewell. "You will answer my letters, won't you?"

She did not look up, not able to trust herself to meet his eyes.

"Yes," she replied very meekly, yet gloriously gladdened at heart. "I will write if you wish me to."

Impulsively Geoffrey bent down and kissed first one of the hands he held and then the other. Thus they parted.

CHAPTER XXIX

SEKHET SMILES

UNTIL the end of the week Evarne posed for Jack Hardy alone. She had now acquired an entirely fresh interest and new importance in that young man's eyes, and he exerted himself to amuse and cheer her during these early days of separation. Geoffrey was not much mentioned between them. Prudence on the one side, and an instinctive restraint on the other, prevented this. Nevertheless, Evarne was conscious of an added loss when she left this studio to sit for a woman artist, and her surroundings were no longer imbued with the magnetism of the absent one.

But letters from Geoff promptly proceeded to rain down upon her. Within twenty-four hours of his quitting London came a brief note, and apparently his first act on reaching Venice was to write to her for the second time.

" I shall let four full days go by before I answer," she decided. But ere that time had passed, a third very lengthy epistle had arrived, which concluded with the gentlest of reproaches for her unkind negligence in not replying sooner. Thus, when she did sit down after supper one evening to write her first letter to Geoffrey, many pages covered with his handwriting were spread out before her gaze.

The correspondence thus commenced rapidly developed into the most engrossing, enthralling, and delightful feature in the existence of these two. They exchanged ideas, sympathies, experiences, hopes and fears; and their uttermost frankness on any and every subject but served to show with increased emphasis how harmonious were their innermost natures, how naturally their minds trod the same paths.

Both wrote well and easily, although for some time Evarne, with true feminine discretion, retained a firm grip upon the too frank display of the strength of her affection for Geoffrey. But the days in which she forbade her written words to adequately express what she felt were very speedily left behind. As to the young man himself, all his cautious scruples had exhausted themselves in leading him out of England. From the first he was troubled by few restrictions, and within a month he was avowedly writing love letters.

He had never made any abrupt and startling declaration of his feelings, let alone of his intentions. It was just a case of swift yet easy drifting. He appeared to deem it a matter of course that Evarne knew and recognised the fact that he loved her, and that all else was to be taken for granted. She was both amused and attracted by this simple and unobtrusive change in their correspondence from comparative formality to tender truth. She expressed no surprise, but took it all quietly and without comment. Indeed, it seemed really but a natural and ordinary thing that she and Geoffrey should acknowledge their love. It was a continuance of a pretence of mere friendship between them that would have seemed extraordinary. To abandon any disguise was not only easy and comforting—it was instinctive.

Thus all those fresh vague thoughts, those dominating and ardent emotions that love brings into being, and which suppression causes to torture the brain wherein they are conceived, were granted free scope and outlet in the heart-to-heart letters that they wrote so gladly one to another. And their love grew and strengthened steadily from this use and outgiving.

It had been some time before Evarne had got to the point of responding with equal frankness to Geoff's ardent epistles, but she did arrive at last.

"You tell me to think of you, Geoff," she sat happily writing one evening. "I do, indeed I do, remember you as steadily as even you yourself could possibly desire. To say I think of you every hour is not enough—you are never out of my mind or my heart, night and day. I don't mean that I think actively and consciously of you *quite* all the time, but the sense of your personality, the deep thought of you, is *incessantly* with me. It has become a part of my mind, I fancy; for I think of you without realising it, simultaneously with thinking deliberately of other matters.

"Have no fear. I love you—love you utterly! I never seem to get tired now, however long the day; for the hours fade into nothingness in dreams of you. You know how ready all we lazy models are to jump down from the throne directly 'time' is called? Now I often surprise people by not moving when the magic word is spoken. I have not heard it, for I have been—where?—out in Venice—or in Paradise—I know not; but wherever the place may be, I have been with you! How, then, can I be expected to hear, unless people shout to startle me back to earth? In the 'rests' I read as usual, or, to be exact, not as usual; for often on reaching the end of a page I become aware that I know nothing at all of what it is about—the thought of you, my dear tormentor, has come 'twixt me and the words, and for very shame's sake I have had to start again and try to banish you for just a few minutes."

"Whatever you find to say to Mr. Danvers is more than I can make out," declared Philia, as Evarne, having completed writing her letter, proceeded to put its pages into order. "You scribbles sheets and sheets, and every day almost—why, you writes books, and 'e's as bad. If I was the postman I wouldn't 'ave it! Now, jist look at the size of that billy-do."

The young woman made a little grimace.

" It is rather long, isn't it ? But the difficulty does not lie in finding what to say. It is in obliging one's self to stop."

" Are you goin' to marry 'im, Evarne ? "

" I—I suppose that is an allowable question ? I don't . . . No ! I believe—how can I tell ? I never think of anything ahead."

" Give me somethin' I can swoller better'n that. 'Ow startled you look. What's to prevent ? "

" Marrying ! That's—oh, he will marry someone of his own rank."

" Go on with yer. Ain't you a laidy—a perfect laidy, says I ? "

" I'm an artist's model. Nothing more nor less," was the somewhat haughtily spoken rejoinder.

" Then I 'opes to goodness you'll be careful what yer writes. It's a jolly dangerous game, I tell yer, puttin' silly talk into writin' and then chuckin' it into the pillar-box. Lord only knows what may come to it before it's safely burned or tored up."

Evarne smiled.

" You unromantic old dear ! What harm do you think can come of it ? "

" 'E could spoil your chance, if 'e was so minded, with any other gentleman as might want to marry yer."

" That doesn't frighten me. Is there nothing else ? "

" 'Ow can I tell ? I ain't no Mother Shipton. But I knows well enough it ain't a wise thing for a girl to do. There ain't a day as passes without reckless letters making trouble for someone or other."

" Is it an equally unwise proceeding for men too ? "

" Yes, my gosh, it jist is. Never 'eard of breach o' promise cases ? Nobody didn't ought to trust nobody in this 'ere wicked world. If yer contents yerself with jist speaking like an idjit, you can always deny it after-wards——"

"Oh!"

"But when you've bin and gorn and acted like a born natural, by puttin' the stuff into writin', well, 'tain't no use denying it then. You're done for. 'Out damned lines'—Shakespeare! But they don't come out—not for all the cussin' and swearin' in the world."

Evarne laughed outright.

"That's true enough. I know it, and of course Geoff must know it too."

"Oh, 'e's a hartist. They don't know nothin', none of 'em."

"Geoff knows he can trust me, Philia, and I value and appreciate the blessed belief he shows in me by writing as he does. Perfect love casteth out fear of every description. He believes that I shall know the right thing to do with regard to his letters, and that I shall ever and always do it."

"It don't need much wit for anyone to know they're safe in your 'ands, my dear. But do you write to 'im jist all that comes into yer 'ead, trustin' 'im to know the right thing to do, and do it?"

"Indeed yes—oh yes!"

"That's the very frame o' mind as ruins 'undreds o' girls. You git rid of it, my dear."

"I won't. I shan't even try. No"—and a wilful head was shaken vigorously—"I shan't pay any attention to your sage advice, not the—least—little bit. Not trust Geoff absolutely and entirely! Why, I'd as soon mistrust myself. Though I ought to know better by now—oh, indeed, I ought!"

Bitter thoughts of past blind trust made ridiculous, brought a note of anguish to the low, sweet voice. But she went on almost defiantly—

"I like to write to him recklessly, and without a single

thought of possible future regret. It pleases me to think that he possesses letters of mine that people might say a woman should only have written to the man who was to be her husband. I like to feel that he and I are, to a certain extent, in one another's power—dependent each on the other's honour. Through those letters he has seen into the innermost recesses of my soul, in a way that no other human being has done. Think, when you truly love, of the delight that lies in such abandonment. But don't you trouble, Philia. I've not told him everything—not shown him quite the full extent of all I feel for him. There is still plenty in reserve. There remain sealed chambers that will not open readily."

"Well, everyone must go their own ways in sich matters. 'Tain't no use advisin'. Common sense and love never seems to flourish longside o' one another, more's the pity."

"You see, love is not a question of ' reason.' It is just ' unreason.' Surely it is better to grasp that truth at once, and so reconcile one's self to thinking and acting quite unreasonably ? "

"Oh, you silly young fool ! " snorted Philia as she lit her candle preparatory to retiring to bed.

On the threshold of the door she stopped and looked back ; Evarne was gazing across at her with a sweet smile playing around her eyes and lips. The old woman shook her fist in the air.

"You silly young—— " She stopped abruptly, sighed, and shook her head portentously. Then in a changed voice : " My gosh, but 'ow I envies yer ! "

She banged the door violently, and went slowly upstairs. Evarne remained for a few minutes rapt in deep thought. Then, rousing herself, she pressed each individual page of her letter to her lips, folded it up with scrupulous care and exactness, and went out to the post.

Many a year had passed since she had known such perfect peace and satisfaction as that which now coloured and perfumed the routine of her days. Living in the present only, she held in her clasp practically all that is needed for happiness. Since her first success as a model she had suffered no physical deprivation such as had characterised that hateful year spent at needlework, but only now were her emotional and intellectual requirements equally and at one time satisfied.

This voluminous correspondence with Geoff was in every way delightful. They thought and wrote much upon topics not altogether personal, Evarne bringing her whole intellect as well as her heart to bear upon the composition of her letters, and, for the first time for many years, revelling in communion with a mind at least equally as reflective and well-informed as was her own.

"What should I have done," she wondered, as she dropped her letter into the pillar-box, "supposing that, loving Geoff as I do, he had not cared for me, and had never wanted to write? I should have died! I don't mean really and truly, I suppose, but my heart would have drooped, my hope and energy and happiness would have faded. I can never be too grateful to him—no, never— for saving me from so much suffering." Then she smiled softly. "Sekhet is gracious and good to me again!"

She walked home with that free, light step that betokens unlimited vitality and buoyancy of spirit. First-love may be indeed unique, unapproachable, but that which is born later in life—the emotion springing from the rich, ripe heart and brain, the ardent affection of the human being in the fullest physical and mental perfection—is every whit as dominating, and it is more inspiring, ample and satisfying than that which came when the heart was young and life a fairy-tale. Evarne had blossomed forth afresh beneath this renewal of love, which had led her again from the monotony of shade out into the vivifying heat of the sun and the glory of white light.

The power of intense loving was perhaps her greatest

and most perfect force. It was not of the type that can be portioned out into a series of petty passions. Since Morris died to her, she had met with none other who held the secret by which to possess himself of that unlimited fund of devotion lying dormant and neglected. Some of her best and most desirable years had melted away devoid of all emotional interests, and simply to feel herself loved—to have her long-unneeded capacity for loving called again into active use—was all-sufficient to create the most perfect happiness.

Her whole nature reawoke, rejoiced and sang, not merely because her love was returned—though from that certainty sprang triumph and the sweet exaltation ever attendant upon this greatest of all possible successes—but because she herself once more gave her love lavishly. For the present this was all-sufficient. She rarely thought of what must be its result—what ultimate end could be attained. Blinded by the light of the never-setting brilliance that now lit her path, she could see clearly only what was close at hand, and that was indeed fair. She would not look backwards over that long stretch of desert-land to where lay that dark and fearful forest, with its hidden morasses, evil haunts and poisoned plants through which, led by the hand of Sekhet in cruel mood, her track had passed long since. Against her better judgment, against her will even, Hope unfurled his wings again within her breast. Why endeavour to look forward into the ever-shrouded and unknowable future? She lived only for the present, and in that she rejoiced.

CHAPTER XXX

A GREAT RESOLVE

AT the end of three months she sat again to Jack
Hardy. He wrote an imploring appeal that she
would somehow contrive to spare time for him
just to put her arms and hands into a wondrous
allegorical picture he was painting. She did arrange it,
for not only were all Geoff's friends her special care, but
she wanted to behold that dear studio again. She was also
rather curious to see young Frank Pallister, of whom Geoffrey had spoken as sharing it with Jack during its rightful
owner's absence.

She found him to be a rosy, fair-haired, somewhat
smartly-clad youth, looking even younger than his twenty
careless years. His work was distinctly promising, but
at present quite elementary—very much that of an Art-
student. Still, he was but a boy, and, being fairly well-to-
do, would probably not have fretted over his still sadly
low standard of execution had he not been goaded onwards
by a gadfly of another type from that by which Jack was so
constantly harried.

In one of the smartest squares in the West-end of London
resided a certain dainty damsel with a stern, unreasonable
dragon of a father. Maudie Meridith, in her seventeen-
year-old wisdom, fully agreed with Pallister that they were
both of ample age to be at least engaged—even if not actually married. Stern, prosaic dragon of a father begged
to differ. After many prayers, many pleadings, he had
given vent to this appalling ultimatum—

" When you can show me your name in the catalogue
of any of the big exhibitions, my boy, I'll consent to your
engagement with this baby. Otherwise, you will have to
wait until she is actually twenty years of age. Cruelty
to children, isn't it ? Be off with you both, and don't
bother me again."

The youthful suitor had confided this unheard-of tyranny
to Geoff, for whom he cherished an affectionate admiration.
The response had been to the effect that if Pallister was wise
he would not shoot himself or even sink into a decline, but
would see about endeavouring to fulfil the conditions that
would shorten these three years of probation.

" If, as you say, you are unalterably convinced that Art
schools keep you back, you had better go and work every
day in my studio," Geoff had written. " It is a big one,
as you know, and only Jack Hardy is there at present.
You would find him an enormous help to you—but don't
bother him, there's a good lad. If you want to try your
hand at a picture right away, there is ample room on the
throne for two models ; if you think a few months hard
preliminary work would be of most value, you can make
studies from Jack's model. Good luck to you in any case."

This kind offer had been accepted, and every morning
Pallister punctually appeared and painted away steadily
for a few hours. He did not know the meaning of real hard
work, but under the influence of Jack's friendly aid and
advice he certainly improved week by week.

Evarne found a certain satisfaction in being again in
Geoff's own home, despite his absence, and although his
name was scarcely mentioned. On the wall was a painting
of him done by Jack a year or so previously. It was a
marvellously good likeness, although the background and
accessories were unfinished. Portrait-painting was Jack's
forte, would he but have believed it.

" I'm going to smuggle away that picture of Mr. Danvers
when you are not looking," declared Evarne ; whereupon

Jack, when he paid her at the conclusion of her sittings, smilingly handed her also the canvas in question already tied up to be taken away.

She hung it in her room, with a little bracket on either side, whereon stood vases which she kept filled with fresh flowers. Night and morning she pressed a gentle kiss upon the painted lips.

"Come back soon, Geoff—come back soon," she once whispered impulsively. And perhaps her wish was wafted away over land and sea to the City in the Waters, for within four months of leaving England Geoff had endured quite sufficient of this test of absence. Thus he wrote :

"DEAREST, DEAREST BEYOND ALL EXPRESSION,

"I am returning home the day after to-morrow ! Sweetest lady that heart ever adored, I am coming back to see you, to breathe the same air with you, to tread the same pavements, to kiss your hands, your lips, your feet.

"Will you welcome me ? I left England loving you. . . . I thought, to the uttermost of my capacity. Perhaps it was so then ; but now I love you . . . oh, infinitely more . . . because I think of you always. . . . your exquisite letters have taught me to know you far more perfectly ; and all knowledge, all thinking, leads only to fresh love.

"In a way, I shrink from meeting you again. I am fearful now. In you is all the good and true, the pure and beauteous. How can I or any man be worthy of you ? Suppose, after a while, I read disappointment in your face?

"But be kind to me, gentle and compassionate. I kneel at your feet, and beg you to give yourself to me and to take me for your own, heart and mind and body, for ever and ever. No other woman could ever be my wife, Evarne, for no other woman could I love.

"May God bless you !

"GEOFF."

Evarne let this letter drop on the table, then bowed her head upon it in silence.

"What—what am I to do? " she murmured after a long pause, filled with a turmoil of mingled bliss and suffering. Had she been perfectly free to follow the promptings of her own heart, not one moment for reflection would have been needed. As it was, a secret indestructible, albeit so well-guarded—seemed to rise up as a hideous, pitiless spectre, bidding her set aside any idea of a future spent with Geoffrey.

"I see now—didn't I know it before?—I ought never, never, to have let him grow to care so much for me," she thought, weighed down by genuine though somewhat tardy remorse.

She saw that utter selfishness had ruled her so far, with the result that now it was not only—not chiefly—her own happiness that was at stake, but that of one for whom no sacrifice could be too great to be sweet.

In the abstract, the memory of the three years she had spent with Morris Kenyon formed no burden upon her conscience. Versed in the secrets of her own heart—strong in the certain knowledge of the generous, even if misguided, motives that had prevailed with her—she had been absolved at the bar of her most earnest and sincere judgment from all stain of deliberate doing of evil. How was it possible that she should find cause to reproach or condemn herself, remembering that supreme hour of test, when she had held so loyally fast to her innate convictions of what was right and what was not; when she had refused to barter a mockery of love for the reality of continued wealth and protection? She thought, too, of her life since then, chaste amid greater temptations than a man would ever realise. Deep in her heart was the feeling that she had been tried and not found wanting. Surely, then, she was every whit as fitted as any ordinarily spotless woman to marry a good man?

Still, so long as the likelihood of such a desire on her part
had seemed far remote, she had been firmly convinced that
she would never allow herself to become a wife with her
secret unconfessed. But now she was faced by a problem—
a torturing doubt—that was quite unforeseen. Would it
not be morally a greater wickedness, an additional wrong,
should she remorselessly shatter such perfect trust ; smear
and deface the happiness of this man who loved her so
ardently, revered and honoured her with such glad confidence ?

Was it indeed Honour's command that she should dig
up this loathsome, long-buried corpse, to thrust it under
those very nostrils wherein it would most stink ? Was
such a cruel and unscrupulous bowing down to the conventional idea of right and wrong unquestionably Love's
duty ? She had never been much guided by mere con-
vention. Was she to begin now when so much was at
stake ? Surely not.

She started suddenly from her chair in bewilderment
and distress, and commenced to pace the room. What
ought she to do ? Earnestly she tried to put all care for
herself and for her own desires out of her mind—to think
only of Geoff. Setting great importance upon the emotional side of life, she scarcely heeded any difference of
position that might exist between herself and him. Unconscious of his future prospects, believing his marriage
to be a matter concerning himself alone, her one doubt and
difficulty lay in how best to cope with her hidden past.

Reason and common sense bade her guard her secret in
silence, now and forever. But her feelings told her plainly enough that never could she hope to know perfect peace
until she had confessed this thing—confessed, implored and
obtained forgiveness. But would that not be an end of all
peace of mind for Geoffrey—ah, poor Geoff ! She had
learnt his nature so well. His was a love that gloried in
placing the beloved upon a lofty height, there to be crowned

with stars and worshipped. Could she thrust him out of his paradise ?

If she shattered his natural and spontaneous love, would a fresh type, all unknown to him now—that which is founded on pity and kindly indulgence—rise from out the ruins ? Suppose not ? What if that other kind of love— tender and divine though it may be—was impossible for him ? She did not fear that he would repulse her cruelly and scornfully—that he could never do, surely. But suppose his love was killed, while hers remained alive ? Ah ! Merciful heavens !

With eyes filled by a sudden horror she stopped short before the painting of Geoff that hung upon the wall. Long she gazed, and her wild glance grew gentle with unutterable affection—with an almost maternal yearning. Would life be endurable were it not henceforth consecrated to this man ? Ten thousand times no ! Both heart and intellect anguished to be allowed full scope to expend their uttermost capacities in the service of love.

And was she not verily endowed with gifts both mental and physical that would enable her to make existence infinitely more delightful, more full, interesting and com- plete for him, than could possibly be his lot with Art for his sole mistress ? Surely herein lay her foreordained life's work ? Who could be so cruel, so pitiless, as to wish her to be made an outcast from this her heritage ? She stretched forth her hands imploringly to the dear pictured face. Would he wish it ? Oh, surely not ! She felt now that her very cause for existence was explained—she had dis- covered the end whereunto she had been created—the duty for which she had been placed on earth, and for the more perfect fulfilment of which every previous experience of her life, glad or sorry, had been but essential preliminary training.

Geoff was sweet-natured indeed, and ever kindly, yet all artistic temperaments need understanding. It would

require true insight and discretion, perchance a deal of
patience and forbearance, to render any lifelong union
naught but an added inspiration, an unfailing stimulus,
an additional happiness to this now ardent lover. Could
there be any other woman more fitted to this task than she
was herself—more capable of taking Geoff's whole existence into her tender keeping, and thereby blessing and
enriching it day by day ?

Surely if he never learnt this—her one and only secret—
it would be impotent as if it had no existence ? And never
would it be revealed to him by outside agency ; at least,
so far as human foresight could discern. Who among
those who had known the truth in those bygone years
was in the least likely to again cross her path ? Not a
single individual. Surely it would be well for Geoffrey to
be so far deceived—to be tricked, and, if necessary, lied to
on this one point ? Would not his ultimate greatest
happiness be thereby ensured ? Since he wished her for
his wife, should he not have his will ? Looking to her
unhesitatingly for all the good and true, the pure and
beauteous in womanhood—was he to be disillusioned ?

Long and earnestly she reflected, endeavouring to weigh
impartially and fairly every argument favouring confession. If Geoffrey could know, would he deem this
secrecy to be her crowning blemish—the greatest, most
personal and unforgivable wrong of all ? Not if he could
read her heart, and judge by her motives. Her own welfare
was indeed not first in her mind. The shielding of his
happiness was verily her chief thought. Alas, that deception should be necessary for its preservation—yet surely
this was so ? Alas ! alas !

At length the final doubt ceased to clamour. The decision had been protracted and difficult. It left her lovely
face somewhat drawn and pale ; but in her soft, eloquent
eyes gleamed a light almost superhuman in its intensity
of love and desperate resolution.

" What would I not do, dare, defy for your sake, my best and dearest ? " she murmured aloud. " Never, while I have strength and power to ward it off, will I bring grief and suffering and agony of mind into your life. Never ! "

CHAPTER XXXI

JOURNEYS END IN LOVERS' MEETINGS

NEXT morning came another little note from Geoffrey. He would arrive in London at noon that day. When and where could they meet? Would she come to the studio as soon as her day's work was over? Might he come to see her, or should they meet out-of-doors somewhere? Anything she decided—though she was implored not to put him off until to-morrow. Would she please telegraph?

Evarne looked across the breakfast table.

"Philia, in what costume do I look nicest of all?"

The answer was prompt.

"You looks nicest of all in yer own skin, and nothin' else."

The girl smiled.

"But that hardly does for this occasion, all the same. I'm going to supper with—with Geoff."

"Beg yer parding. 'E's really 'ome, then? Wear anythin' yer choose. 'E won't never notice!"

Evarne feared she was a most restless and impatient model that day. The hours seemed interminable. But they were got through somehow, and at seven o'clock in the evening she stepped from a hansom and proceeded to mount the three flights of broad stairs that led up to the studio. Her heart was throbbing so wildly that even before the first landing was reached her breath came with difficulty, and a feeling almost of faintness obliged her to stand still for a few moments, to reconquer some degree of calmness.

The door of Geoff's flat was already wide open, and just within the hall stood the young man himself, awaiting her coming. The instant he caught the first glimpse of her approaching, he bounded downstairs and seized both the hands she held out to him.

For a minute they stood motionless and speechless, more than content to once again feast their eyes upon one another's faces. Then, still without a word, they mounted the last flight of stairs, holding hands like children, and the door of the flat closed behind them.

They were alone together for the first time.

Evarne went into the sitting-room. The curtains were drawn, and two rose-pink shaded lamps cast a warm, softening glow upon the heavy oak furniture. Calmly enough she took off her hat, carefully stuck in the pins, and placed it on a chair. Then she turned round suddenly, and all her wealth of hidden feeling quivered in her voice.

" Oh, Geoff, Geoff ! How sweet beyond words it is to see you again ! "

In a second his arms were around her, and she was strained to his breast with a force that was almost painful. In silence he looked, eagerly and intently, deep into the limpid brown eyes so near his own. Such ineffable tenderness and devotion frankly answered his ardent, searching gaze, that the force of his worship for this beautiful woman grew not only unspeakable, but nigh too overwhelmingly great to be borne. His brows contracted, and all unconsciously he uttered a deep-breathed " Oh ! " that bordered on a groan of pain ; then suddenly sinking on his knees before her with the abandon of his artistic temperament, he seized both her hands, covering them with kisses. At last, pressing her soft palms hard against his cheeks, he rested motionless, and scarcely could she hear his murmured broken words—

" How I adore you ! I can scarcely endure it. You are more perfect even than I remembered. Evarne ! Evarne ! "

She was already bending slightly forward, for unconsciously he was dragging her hands downwards. She
leant lower, and lightly brushed his fair hair with her lips.
A divan was close by. She sank down, and, still kneeling,
Geoffrey rested his folded arms upon her knees and looked
up into her face.

The turmoil of strong emotion was still so far beyond
all possible expression, that to both speech could have
been merely a mockery. For a protracted period nothing
was said in spoken words. When Evarne finally broke the
long silence it was with tones so soft, so appealing, that
they were in themselves a gentle caress, although the actual
words were commonplace enough.

" You won't leave me again ? You won't go away
any more ? "

" Not without you, my dearest, my dearest! Never
shall I go without you—no, not even to the end of the
street—if I can persuade you to come with me."

" And I would follow you willingly, whatever might
await us at the end of the street."

" You really love me ? "

" You want to hear my voice tell you what you know
so well already ? "

Geoff answered only with his eyes. Evarne put out both
hands and drew his head to her bosom, pressing it so tightly
that he felt the throbbing of her heart against his cheek.
After a minute the gentle whisper floated to his ears—

" I loved you yesterday. I love you to-day, and I shall
love you to-morrow." After a little pause she added,
" I'll tell you something more too."

" Nothing else seems to matter. Still, do tell me ! "

" It's just a little nothing. Only this—that I cared for
you before you ever cared for me."

" No, 'twas just contrariwise ! It's no use to shake your
perverse darling head. I can prove it."

" You mean you can try."

" Now, listen. Remember that I saw you before you ever saw me. You were reading the paper, but I was reading your face. I had loved you for at least three full minutes before you ever beheld me. How now ? "

Evarne laughed happily.

" Yes, you have won after all. Do you know, I like so much to be told that your gaze was never coldly critical, or even indifferent to me."

" I can't imagine love that does not come at first sight," declared Geoff with enthusiasm. " Not in all its full force and power, naturally, but at least as an immediate conviction that here at length is the one who is to become dearest in the whole world. Yet one hears of people knowing each other for years before they learn to love. Isn't that so ? What sort of feelings do you suppose fill the space of time between the first seeing and the first loving, when the two are not almost simultaneous ? Just interest and liking ? "

" It is no use looking questioningly at me," Evarne replied, shaking her head gently. " Besides, I thought men had always had so much past experience in that direction that they knew just everything."

Geoff smiled at her.

" Oh, you did, did you ? I'm afraid that branch of my education has been shamefully neglected. And you— you cannot teach me ? "

" Can't I, then ? I know every whit as much concerning love as did Diotima, who instructed Socrates in the art."

" And who taught you, pray ? "

" Don't be jealous. I never had to learn ; it's a natural talent. Perhaps it was a gift from my fairy godmother."

" Then it is all theory ? "

" Oh yes."

For half a minute Geoff did not speak. Painfully conscious that she had now told him her first deliberate falsehood, Evarne glanced into his thoughtful eyes with sudden apprehension. Then she hastened to break in upon this silence, in which another such terrible question, incapable of truthful answer, was perhaps being formulated.

"You must have thought you cared for somebody before you saw me, Geoff. Do tell me?"

"Very well. Now this is the solemn truth. Not only have I never loved any other woman before you, but I've never even made the mistake of thinking a passing fancy was the real thing. I've never burned incense at the shrine of any false goddess. In my heart I've loved you all my life—that is, the idea of you, Evarne. I've worshipped you and waited for you, sweetheart, and now, thank God, I've found you."

She answered very gently and slowly, her heart glowing with triumph and delight at his avowal.

"If it were possible, I should care for you even more after hearing you say that. But how can I love you more than to the very uttermost of my nature, and I believe I have done that from the first."

Geoffrey found this frank and unaffected confession more adorable than any coquettish hesitation could have proved.

"But even if I had not been able to win your heart, I should still have loved you always and ever, and held myself your knight, ready to obey your slightest or your most difficult command, my queen," he avowed with boyish enthusiasm. "I feel that it was preordained that I should love you, and I should have readily fulfilled my fate, even if you had never been able to care for me in return."

She sighed and shook her head.

"Ah, Geoffrey, do you love me indeed? Almost I doubt it."

"You doubt it? Evarne!"

"You can't imagine what I mean? Sit by my side and I'll explain."

Reclining delightfully in Geoff's arms, her slender arched feet curled up on the couch, she expounded her startling statement.

"When you say that it would not make any—well, not much—difference in your feelings towards me if I did not care for you in return, I wonder if you are not indulging in a state of mind peculiar to poetic temperaments such as yours, my dearest, and I feel jealous."

"Dear child—jealous of whom ? "

"Cannot you guess ?   Why, of Love itself.   I believe you are so happy in having me to care for, simply because you delight in loving.   You are a worshipper of love in the abstract ; you fairly glory in that frame of mind people call ' being in love.'   The possession of the emotion means more to you than the possession of any particular woman. There are some terrible people like that.   They would rather their mistress died than that she should destroy the love she had awakened in their hearts."

"Now, fair Diotima, just please name one single individual who ever felt that way."

"Easily !   What about Dante, the patron saint of such sinners ?   Do you suppose he could have had any ordinary personal affection for his precious Beatrice ?   Why, he only saw her twice, or something of that sort, and she was respectably married to somebody else, yet she coloured his whole life, and he seems to have been quite contented. And he is never without disciples—a few.   Oh, I know you—people who are in love with Love itself."

"Yes ?   Go on telling me about them."

Interested though he was in her slightest word, Geoffrey, man-like, was not giving all his mind to Evarne's ideas. He was enthralled by the contemplation of her sinuous, supple form, her tenderly waving hair and satin-smooth skin, and the live beams of her glancing eye ; he was glorying in the dulcet music of her voice.

"Well," she went on, feigning discontent, while her very heart seemed pulsating in notes of perfect happiness— "well, you find some woman whom you can idealise and adore, and if she be but passably gracious to you, you proceed to make a world of happiness for yourselves merely from loving her, dreaming of her, writing poems to her or painting pictures that you think she has inspired—though really it is nothing but your own capacity for loving that she has made active that is the true source of your inspiration. Even if you rarely see her it seems to make very little difference—you still dream, still find inspirations, still do great work under the divine influence of Aphrodite. You live in the enchanted Palace of Love, and once safely there, are horribly independent of the woman who opened its magic portals to you. Oh, sorry fate that led me to love an artist! So long as I condescend to exist and remain tolerably young and beautiful, all is well. I cannot possibly feel that your entire happiness depends upon my presence or my absence, my smile or my frown. Now do you see my grievance?"

"I can't believe you know it, but you actually seem to imply that you care for me more sincerely, more humanly, than I do for you, which is obviously impossible."

"I don't see the 'obviousness.' I should rather like to."

"I'll soon tell you. You won't laugh at me?"

"Laugh! Oh, my darling!"

"Well, then, the fact that it is you, your own dear self, that I so glory in, and not any mere abstract mental condition, is proved by this. I confess I always hoped the time would come when I should be genuinely in love. That's what you are not to laugh at, by the way! I knew somehow that I had all the capacity for intense devotion, and naturally enough, I suppose, longed to exercise it. So if practically any young and attractive woman would have served as the sort of figure-head you describe, should I have been forced to wait—unwillingly enough, I can tell you—until you, my only possible beloved, appeared upon the scene? Of course not."

"You had to wait for me—for me—for me!" sang

Evarne, keeping the time in her little song of triumph by clapping her hands.

"It is very wicked of you to be so pleased about it. Why did you not come along earlier, my blessing? It is a perfect misery, nothing else, to be empty-hearted. It is terrible to feel a thousand emotions seeking desperately for an outlet. Why did your star linger so long in crossing mine?"

But no sympathy was to be extracted from Evarne.

"It has all been just as is best. You have been most fortunate," she declared. "Love is not the be-all and end-all of any life, you know, and when you think of your chosen work—which is the real thing—I'm sure you can't regret any emotional experiences, however distressing they may have been in the learning. They are all needful training for the production of soul-stirring pictures; as necessary, in their way, as is the enchantment of loving and being loved that is now going to help you still further. Mental turmoil of every type bears its own special fruit that may be garnered by an artist to his own advantage. Stagnation, ignorance and lack of variety in emotions brings ultimate failure in imaginative work. Thus speaks Diotima the Second."

Far-away, curious echoes seemed ringing in Evarne's brain. When and where and in what familiar voice had she heard such sentiments spoken long, long ago?

"Well, it certainly is consoling to put all one's mental worries into the same category as freehand drawing and perspective," declared Geoff; and being both ardently happy and therefore easily amused, they laughed merrily.

After a moment's pause he went on—

"But don't you think the secret tragedy of many a seemingly commonplace and prosaic person is the lack of someone to be earnestly and devotedly adored? Don't you think many and many a heart suffers from a craving to exercise strong powers of loving forever ungratified?

I'm speaking of a spiritual demand—not of the universal
desire to find a mate that is just part of Nature's artful
little scheme for ensuring the due arrival of the next genera-
tion.   Do you think that demand of the spirit proves a
man merely a willing follower of Dante ? "

" Oh, no no !—I suppose not.   But, despite your specious arguments, I still maintain that you, individually, are
one to rate love higher than any object.   Obstinate, am I
not ? "

" Absolutely wicked, you dearest.   I love you, my
Evarne—you yourself—in every possible way under the
sun, including the ordinary human love of any man, artist
or not, for the woman he seeks for his wife.   There is perhaps a tiny atom of truth in one of the charges you have
hurled at me, but—— "

" I knew it, my dear commonplace lover.   Confess, and
I'll see if I can forgive you."

" I think, perhaps—dearest, I don't iike even to speak of
it — but perhaps even your — I mean, if the world lost
you, my own beloved—— "

" If I died ? "

He flinched even at the words that expressed the possibility, but went on—

" That it would cause a more—how can I express my
meaning ?   Well, in one way, possibly, even that would
cause a less ever-present gap in my mental life than would
the destruction of my love for you . . .   It's no use
hitting me," he laughed; " I can't help it, sweetest ! "
Then he clasped her closely with sudden eager passion.
" But do not think that your dreamer is at all content to
worship only in spirit, Evarne."

Then, impulsively, he poured forth a flood of words, ardent,
impassioned, throbbing with that fiery sex-love that dominates the entire world—selfish, unheeding, remorseless—
words of that terrible overwhelming passion that will not
be long denied.

" That s now I want to be loved," she whispered, but flung herself away from his grasp just in order to be drawn close once more.

He seized her convulsively, held her in a cruelly fast grip, covering her cheeks, her brow, her mouth with kisses, violent and tender in turns. At last, pressing his face against hers, he rested motionless. She felt the influence of the contact spread itself slowly throughout her entire frame, subtle and concentrated as electricity, and under its power her breast heaved, and she breathed only in short troubled gasps. The whole room, the whole world, seemed to be throbbing, to be trembling—perhaps it was only the arms that enfolded her that quivered—she neither knew nor cared to know.

A deep silence held sway. The only moment's speech was when Geoffrey murmured a sudden question about their marriage, begging, imploring for an early date. It should be quite soon, Evarne promised. It should be within six weeks, five weeks, a month, less still, if he so desired.

She had hesitated perceptibly before she answered. This definite and verbal plighting of her troth was opposed— actively, violently—for a few moments, by the resurrection of those scruples she fancied had faded away once and for all—false and misleading will-o'-the-wisps of chivalrous truth and honour, leading the unwise into bogs of wild despair and utter misery. When at last she did speak it was in a voice fraught with tremulous emotion, low, yet inexpressibly thrilling—notes softer than the cooing of wood-doves, and which reverberated upon the young artist's highly-strung nerves with subtle emphasis.

More than once Evarne had thought that his nature now was not unlike what her own had been originally, before three years of constant effort to please a jaded, middle-aged man, added to unbroken association with coarse, depraved minds, had sullied her soul, blunted her finer susceptibilities, ruined her taste for the more delicate viands of love's feast. Once upon a time she had sought with all her strength to keep the affection that was offered her free from all savour of passion ; now, when devotion, as poetical, refined and idealistic as imagination could devise had been laid at her feet, she had felt starved, chilled, unsatisfied.

But as she looked into her dreamer's altered face and saw its new expression, saw the grey eyes so strangely gleaming, the slight occasional twitching of his lips, the distinct though almost imperceptible veil of moisture that covered his brow, she felt for a moment strangely degraded—curiously identical with the early Christian Fathers' estimate of women. A moment's bitter regret of her own personality cast its shadow. Geoff was too good for her. Ought he not to love a young, innocent girl—one of those sweet maidens who are to be found here and there even in this grimy world, with thoughts white as snow-drifts, and surely invisible halos around their meek downcast heads—pure spirits that were scarcely conscious of possessing bodies, and would assuredly never miss them ? Ought not one of these to have been Geoff's bright particular star ?

" Are you certain you love me ; that you're not deceiving yourself ? " she asked again and again, and each time the only response was a long kiss that penetrated to her heart's core ; a speaking, all-answering gaze ; a closer, almost frantic tightening of the arms in which she reclined.

And her moods changed as a kaleidoscope. Suddenly she laughed aloud in triumphant satisfaction at herself, all that she was, all that she could be. Of course Geoff loved her, and he should love her yet more. Placid snow-maidens—you must be content to shine in heaven ; not yours is it to make men thank God for life !

Now to the man who loved her Evarne appeared the very acme of all perfection. And indeed, in that hour she verily was all that is most appealing—most adorable—most exquisite. Her beauty was transcendent, and her expression remained more noble, more respect-compelling than she knew. And yet, all the while, her soft brown eyes, whether swimming in happy, purposeless tears or shining with inward fire, told, with more convincing eloquence than lies within the power of speech, of the utter abandonment of the soul they mirrored to the domination of the most ardent and enthralling affection. She was all tenderness, passion, charm, fascination. Her powerful magnetism encircled her as an invisible cloud. Who, amid mortals, coming within the radius of its influence, could have saved himself from worshipping this fair woman to the very uttermost limits of his capacity ?

The stress of her own emotion was exhausting ; a delicious languor, a placid dreaminess, tinged with melancholy ; crept upon her. She felt incapable of further movement or speech, and allowed her long-fringed lids to veil her eyes. When she lifted them again it was to behold her lover's gaze fixed upon her in a fresh access of passionate adoration that could not be left unanswered. She smiled up at him, a gentle little smile ; it seemed serene and calm, but behind it, like unto a powerful naked figure veiled in gauze, gleamed love that was resolute, indomitable, heroic.

Her inarticulate little murmurs, her half-sighs, all her tiny actions had been enchanting, enthralling ; but her smile—always sweet and moving—was now provocative of ecstasy. Dazed, unconscious of his own personality, again Geoff knelt before her, his arms clasped around her waist, his face pressed against her soft body. Oblivious to all of life save love alone, he bathed his spirit in this inexhaustible fund of the gods' best gift.

What said Evarne's most-admired philosopher ?

" I say then of all in general, both men and women, that the whole of our race would be happy if we worked out love perfectly, and if each were to meet with his beloved."

Was not Diotima, who taught Socrates, a wise woman

indeed, capable of imparting the truest, the most divine of all wisdom ?

Thus the winged hours sped past.

A dainty little supper was ready, and finally they sat down side by side and played at eating. Over the little meal the conversation became really quite practical and business-like.

Geoffrey had said nothing of the prospect he had of succeeding sooner or later to his childless cousin's earldom. That startling piece of information seemed to him to be best reserved for discussion on some other less idyllic occasion. But it was partly this that gave emphasis to his inquiry.

" You will not continue posing now, will you, dearie ? "

" I have not any choice," laughed Evarne. " There are some people who make me. Let me see, there's the landlord and the tradesmen and—— "

" Then come here, won't you ? Really, I not only want you—I need you. I'm going to start a big picture—any number of figures in it."

" What is the subject, and who am I to be ? "

" I want you for Andromache. I'm going to paint the captured Trojan women."

" I shall make a realistic captive, Geoff, being one in very sooth."

" And I verily believe I was inspired to paint such a subject by the consciousness that I was free no longer, my captor. I shall make a great thing of this picture, Evarne ; at least, I ought to. Everything will be in my favour. Poor old Jack ! He is still lamenting his unprocurable model—his ' Belle Dame.' "

" How different his work is from yours ; poor old Jack ! "

" I am going to try hard to persuade him to take up portrait-painting definitely. He really is very clever, you know. He ought to do well. Or sculpture ; he's quite strong at that. But he will insist on trying to be imaginative, and he doesn't shine there.   Now, when is the earliest day you can come ? "

" It so happens that I finish to-morrow with the man I'm sitting for at present.   That's Thursday, the twentieth, isn't it ?   Then I have nothing to do until Monday the twenty-fourth, when I ought—it's all arranged—you see I didn't expect you home until September ! "

" A lot of engagements, have you ? "

" I've only a few spare days here and there for the next seven weeks."

" But we're going to be married long before that time. Look here, Evarne love, give them all up !   Don't sit for anyone else but me.   Come, spoil me a bit.   Let me be selfish.   My picture is all ready and waiting for the model."

" It's terribly unfair to the others, but—— "

" Never mind them.   Seriously, I mean it."

" It's a shame, when they've been waiting, but there— it's delightful to be unkind to other people, and treat them badly for your sake.   It shall be as you wish.   It is wrong, though !   Aren't you ashamed ? "

A little later eleven o'clock struck.   Evarne pinned on her hat.

" Oh, don't go yet !   It's far too early," cried Geoffrey. But Evarne only smiled.

" On the contrary, it is rather late.   Say good-bye quickly," she responded.

The timepiece ticked on placidly, neither faster nor slower than its usual steady wont.

" Goodness gracious, Geoff, you must send that silly old clock to be mended.   It actually has jumped a whole quarter of an hour !   It is no use its pretending we have been twenty minutes saying good-bye.   Do call a taxi quickly."

" And to-morrow I'm coming to supper with you.   Oh dear me !   twenty-four hours to wait ! "

" Only about twenty now ; and remember, if our stars

in their courses had not chanced to touch, we might have both lived twenty-four years more—and more still—and been lonely to the end. See what we have escaped."

By midnight Evarne was safely alone in her own little bedroom. She studied her reflection in the mirror before removing her hat, and smiled with pleasure to behold cheeks blooming as a blush rose ; lips made up of happy curves ; and eyes shining for very joy as brightly as the most brilliant stars in the summer heaven.

CHAPTER XXXII

FRANK'S BRILLIANT IDEA

ON Friday Evarne was free to give her time to Geoff, and the big Greek picture was duly commenced. Again she wore flowing white draperies, but of a more ornate and ample description than the very simple robe in which she had previously posed in this studio. Her head was encircled by a barbaric fillet, studded with roughly-cut, albeit gleaming stones, and high up on her arms were wide bracelets of chased gold ; for although a captive, fair Andromache was a princess. Yet those same arms bore delicate fetters around the wrists, for Hector's widow was now a slave.

On her shoulder was to be borne a terra-cotta vase of classical design. It was very beautiful, both in contour and workmanship, but it was far from small, and Geoff was troubled lest his dear model should grow weary.

" You must stop as soon as you even begin to feel tired ; don't wait for the ordinary rests. Will you promise ? " he demanded, and smiling her assent, she took up the required position.

The robe she wore was so fine in substance that where the material actually touched her body it appeared to become vaguely hued with the most delicate, the most tender pink. On her arched feet were elaborate many-strapped sandals ; her classically beautiful head, inclined meekly downwards, showed to perfection the gracious line at the back of her neck. She was indeed sufficient to arouse and inspire the most negligent of artists.

But it so chanced that Frank Pallister had just received an added impetus to his industry from another quarter.

A day or two before Geoff's unexpected return to England, Frank had paid a solemn afternoon call on Mrs. Vandeleur. This stately matron was Mr. Meridith's widowed sister, who kept house for him and chaperoned pretty little Maudie. She viewed Frank and his suit with a favourable eye, yet approved her brother's decision with regard to the postponed engagement. Thus, while a sense of duty prompted her to hover around with considerable persistence, it was often quite easy for the young people to make opportunities for whispered flirtations.

Thus, after duly listening to her complaints at being still in sultry London when August was practically at hand, from the necessity of Mr. Meridith's remaining in town until Parliament rose, Maudie and Frank found opportunity to exchange secret groans over the unendingness of three years.

" I wish to goodness I could shorten it ! " sighed the youth.

" Then why don't you ? " demanded the girl. " You know what dad says about it. Now, Frankie, why don't you do something grand, superb, incomparable—something that would cause the whole world to admire and wonder, and make your name famous for ever and ever ? I would, if I were you, but you're a lazy boy, I know you are."

" It's easy to talk," was the rueful response. " But you just listen to what I've got on hand. Some day soon, Jack Hardy is to be allowed to do a marble bust of Lord Winborough. I told you, didn't I ? If the great man will consent to be so far victimised, Jack is going to start proceedings by taking a life-mask of him. Very well, then, I'm going to watch, and perhaps assist, and when I've learnt how to do it, I shall start and do a bust of somebody or other who is well known. Then I have already got three new pictures and two statuettes on hand. Some of the galleries are bound to take some of them when they're finished, I should suppose."

" Dear Frankie," was the answer given in all seriousness, " I am so terribly afraid you're a genius ! "

" Afraid ! "

" Yes, for then you'll never get on in the world. It is only the second-rate people who reach the top of the ladder ; the real born geniuses stick on the bottom rung, just because their work is too superior to be understood and appreciated by the common mob. There ! What do you think of that ? Dreadful, isn't it, poor boy ? "

" I'm afraid you needn't upset yourself over my misfortunes in that direction. Who told you all this piffle ? "

" Nobody exactly. I overheard two men talking at an ' at home.' "

" Were they neglected geniuses ? "

" I don't know. I asked dad what they did, and he said he believed that one composed poetry and that the other wrote tragedies."

" Wouldn't you like Frank to see Sir James's painting of you ? " interposed the voice of Mrs. Vandeleur.

The girl sprang to her feet.

" Fancy my forgetting ! It's finished at last. It's in the dining-room at present. Come along. But don't expect much. It's not a bit nice ; it's really ugly."

And indeed, on beholding the celebrated portrait-painter's production, Frank's loud exclamations of surprise and disdain were as profuse as the most disappointed of sitters could desire.

" Isn't your dad annoyed ? " he demanded at length.

" Indeed, he's really vexed. He is paying so highly for it too. You remember the one of my mother that hangs in his study ? That was done when she was seventeen, and he thought it would be so nice to have a companion one of his only kiddie at the same age. He wouldn't have minded the big price in the least if the picture had been satisfactory.

This has been altered ever so many times, and now Sir James has got tired, and swears it is exactly like me ; but it isn't, is it ? "

" The old boy must be getting in his dotage. Now, I could paint you just beautifully, I'm sure. You would be such a jolly subject. I say ! "

" What ? "

Pallister glanced round to make sure that Mrs. Vandeleur was safely out of earshot.

" Don't you think your dad would consent to our engagement without any delay if I made a perfectly lovely picture of you ? He would have to believe there was something in me then, wouldn't he ? "

" Oh, Frankie, what a perfectly fine idea. I dare say he would. Let's ask him."

But the originator of the idea, with a frown of thought upon his brow, shook his head.

" To really have the proper effect it ought to be sprung upon him as a complete surprise—quite finished. ' Splendid ! magnificent ! superb ! ' he will exclaim, when he sees it—at least, I hope that's what he will say ! Then he will go on : ' Only tell me what artist has produced this masterpiece.' "

" And then you'll answer—— ? "

" Nothing. I shan't speak a word—not a word ! I shall just quietly and modestly point to my name in the corner. Oh, isn't it just a ripping plan ? "

" Lovely ! Perfectly delightful ! "

" But you'll have to come sometimes to Geoff Danvers's studio and give me sittings, won't you ? "

" Then auntie is to be in the secret ? "

" It wouldn't be a secret for long if she knew. No, you must come alone. Do ! It will be quite all right— really it will. Jack is always there, and we almost always have a woman model, so there would be a sort of a chaperone. You'll come ? Remember what depends on it."

" It is awfully venturesome, but I'll do it," promised
the girl after a moment's hesitation.

At this point Mrs. Vandeleur approached, and the remaining details of the conspiracy had to be hastily whispered at parting.

" You'll come as often as you can, duckie ? "

" Yes, but I shan't be able to let you know long beforehand."

" I'll get the canvas ready at once. Come to-morrow."

" Can't. I'll let you know when. What shall I wear ? "

" Any white frock."

" I'll remember. Good-bye."

This arrangement had been entered into over a week ago,
and as yet no word had come from Maudie. Nevertheless
Pallister was working away with renewed ardour, living in a
state of eager expectation. Of course, the little idea had
to be confided to Geoff, since he had so unexpectedly reappeared upon the scene. Strangely enough, it did not
appeal to him in the light of an unquestionably brilliant
notion preordained to success. He was inclined to advise
decidedly against it, but finding that his opinion, although
formally asked, was in reality not wanted in the least, he
raised no actual objection to the carrying out of the plan.

" But, Geoff," persisted the somewhat crushed Pallister,
" surely it is an awfully fine idea, so enterprising and original. Don't you think so really ? "

" I've told you I fancy it's quite as likely to vex Mr.
Meridith as to please him ; but of course I may be mistaken. Who can tell what will melt a stern father's stony
heart ? You know him much better than I do, anyway."

" Well, it's awfully good of you, old chap, not to mind.
I hope it won't interfere with your work too much. You
know, I rather feel I ought to clear out at once, now you've
come back."

" Not a bit of it. Stop at least until Miss Meridith's
portrait is done. You couldn't ask her to go to any strange

studio, you know. It's quite different here, where her father knows the whole lot of us."

So much for Frank's enterprise.

Jack Hardy also was working with increased ardour, with renewed interest and hope.

On the afternoon of the very day of his return from Venice, Geoff had called at the Albany to make inquiries regarding Lord Winborough's whereabouts. However far afield his cousin might happen to be, he almost invariably returned to England in the late summer and paid frequent visits to London.

Geoff was anxious to persuade Lord Winborough now definitely to arrange to fulfil his promise of sitting to Jack Hardy. It had not taken Geoff long to discover that his friend was unhappy and dispirited. The allegorical picture had been so far a miserable failure, and had left Jack in exactly the frame of mind to follow the dictates of worldly wisdom. He knew in his heart that portraiture, whether in oils or marble, was his *forte*, and the news that Lord Winborough was expected at his chambers in the course of a few days had served to brace him up anew. He would follow up the advantages in obtaining paying " sitters " that would probably result from his exhibiting a successful bust of the earl, and the long-dreamed-of " Belle Dame " picture should really be the last of its type, as far as he was concerned. Having definitely made up his mind to this, he was rewarded by a renewal of enthusiasm and belief in the future.

Saturday was devoted to work, but Geoff and Evarne spent the whole of Sunday up the river. To both it was a time of unmitigated delight. Sunshine, fair placid scenery, youth, health and love—what could have been added to render the hours more idyllic, golden, divine ? If Evarne knew much sorrow, she had, as if in recompense, an intimate acquaintance with a far deeper, a more intense happiness than ever falls within the lot of many. She and Geoff agreed that next Sunday should be passed in the same manner. Quite definitely this was decided—" unless it rained ! " That was the only possible obstacle that presented itself. Ah well ! the mere decision was pleasant, and served to soften the hour of parting.

CHAPTER XXXIII

THE SHADOW OF COMING EVENTS

MONDAY morning dawned. Evarne looked more radiantly lovely than ever after her day in the open air, and work was re-attacked with general ardour. The only interruption to the proceedings was a ring at the door, which came as lunch-time was approaching. It proved to be a man with a letter for Geoff.

" This is rather interesting to us all ! " he exclaimed as he read it. " Winborough arrived in London on Saturday. I left a note for him, you know, Jack, and he says he will come at three o'clock on Wednesday to be ' life-masked,' but he is coming in here this afternoon just to see us."

Jack flushed with sudden excitement and apprehension. Geoff laid down the letter and looked at Evarne. These few days of their engagement left her still ignorant of his position and relationship towards Winborough. Geoff could hardly have given any reason for his reticence— there could, indeed, be no rational explanation forthcoming—it was just a purposeless fancy that had not mattered hitherto. But now she must know. She always lunched with him in his sitting-room, while Jack and Pallister sought their mid-day repast out of doors. He would tell her then; and Lord Winborough himself must no longer be kept in ignorance of his heir's forthcoming marriage. There seemed to be an ample dose of " tellings " before Geoffrey that day.

But Pallister all unconsciously relieved him of one.

' I'm really awfully excited," he declared.   " I've never seen his lordship, but Mr. Meridith knows him quite well. Maudie calls him a ' dear.'   And I'm awfully thrilled, too, at the prospect of taking a life-mask.   I shall be longing to try when once I've seen it done.   Will you let me practise on you, Miss Stornway ? "

" Well, I don't know.   It's rather terrible, isn't it ? "

" I don't think so.   Only a bit unpleasant.   Nothing to hurt."

" Have you done many, Mr. Hardy ? "

" Several.   It's a wonderful help towards getting a likeness, especially if the sitter's time is precious.   Still, it is uncommonly hateful to go through."

" Don't tell Lord Winborough that !   How do you start ? "

" Well, you rub cold-cream or some such decoction well into the skin."

" For the sake of the victim's complexion, I suppose ? "

" Partly.   Next you put a couple of quills into his nostrils."

" To breathe through ? " chipped in Pallister.

" Precisely ; and very careful you have to be, I can tell you, considering that it's the one and only way in which a supply of fresh air can be obtained, for the next step is to pour moist plaster all over the face."

" How clammy !   Much of it ? "

" Not at first—only a thin layer ; but after you've laid a piece of string downways on either cheek, you add more plaster until it's about an inch thick.   There it has to remain until it hardens.   Then you draw up the two strings, thereby cutting the mask into three parts, and take it off, a firm and absolute replica of the features."

" But it does sound rather dangerous," declared Evarne after a moment's thought.

" Not with ordinary care and attention.   It's quite safe," Jack assured her ; " but it feels much worse than it is really. One's whole life undoubtedly depends on those two breathing-quills. I went through it once myself, and I couldn't help thinking of what would happen if by any accident they got choked up. The operator always keeps a pair of scissors handy to snip off the end in case by any chance a splash of plaster happens to settle on it. Still, it needs a deal of nerve, I must confess. You can't .hear a sound except an indistinct sort of rumbling and the thud of your own heart like a sledge-hammer. I should think it's a bit like being buried alive. I tried to lift an eyelid, but the plaster held it in an immovable grip, and of course your lips are so sealed that it is impossible to speak a single word. I assure you, it did make me feel queer!"

"I wonder," inquired Pallister meditatively, "what would happen if you just *had* to sneeze?"

But Jack declined to venture an opinion.

"I'm afraid I can't promise to be done," Evarne declared with some degree of emphasis.

"Now, would you expect anybody to consent after that lurid description, Jack?" inquired Geoff, laughing. "It's a good thing Winborough can't hear your vivid reminiscences, or he would suddenly recall some other imperative engagement for Wednesday afternoon."

"Perhaps he won't come anyhow," suggested Pallister, bent on teasing. "You should just have heard a Socialist gentleman—one of your pet pals, I dare say, Jack—who was addressing an attentive and admiring audience in Hyde Park yesterday. 'These bloated haristiscrats, pampered from their cots upwards,' he declared, were, without exception, fickle and false and altogether unreliable, and 'ought to be wiped off the face of the globe altogether!'"

"But Lord Winborough hasn't been 'pampered from his cot upwards,'" returned Jack unperturbed. "He only came into the title about five years ago, so you see he is scarcely one of those whom 'my pet pal, the Socialist,' was referring to."

Pallister ceased grinning at his own wit.

" Oh, of course, I know. He will keep his promise right enough," he said seriously. Then, suddenly recollecting himself : " I say, Geoff, I didn't mean to be personal. If your cousin goes and dies without children, we don't expect you to alter, and be fickle and false and all the rest of it, just because you become Earl of Winborough, eh ? "

Evarne's lips parted, and, turning her head, she gazed at Geoff with eyes filled with utter amazement and incredulity. That young man threw down his brushes.

" Look here," he said lightly, " it's a quarter to one. I think we had better stop work and have lunch."

" Right you are," cried Pallister the lazy.   " Come along, Jackie, my boy ; we had better take plenty of t me to strengthen ourselves for this afternoon. We have both got to make a good impression, you know."

Jack partly understood Geoff's evident anxiety to get them gone. He promptly pulled off his painting overall and put on his coat. Pallister, with no such change of costume to effect, was already awaiting him, and in a very few minutes they were both out of the place.

Already Geoff had freed Evarne from her golden fetters. They fastened by means of snaps, and it needed the use of both hands to open them. The long connecting chain was quite unbreakable, though charmingly light and delicate in workmanship. He occupied the time while his friends were dressing in subjecting it to a series of vigorous little tugs, as if to test its strength ; but directly the studio door had closed, he cast it aside and turned to Evarne.

" Surely I didn't understand rightly ? " she queried, in tones of ill-suppressed anxiety. " I thought Mr. Pallister seemed to say that Lord Winborough was not only your cousin, but that you were his heir ? "

Geoff acknowledged this to be verily the truth.

" I'm sure I don't know why I didn't mention it long ago," he continued apologetically. " It's very silly of me to appear to have made any sort of a mystery about it, for naturally it's no secret. It can't be exactly termed a misfortune in itself, can it, while of course it does not make the slightest little bit of difference in our feelings for one another ? "

" I am not so sure," rejoined Evarne sadly.

With slow steps she walked across the room and sat down by the open window, gazing out into vacancy with troubled eyes. She felt no pleasurable excitement, no eager interest, in this marvellous piece of news. On the contrary, the fact that her lover held a position of so much greater importance in the estimation of the world than she had for one moment suspected, appeared to her simply and solely as an unqualified misfortune. Viewed in the light of this new discovery, his marriage with a woman who was, after all, only an artist's model, and, moreover, one weighed down by a secret that a very few inquiries on the part of the curious might reveal, became a matter of entirely different import. Such ominous forebodings, such fresh doubts and apprehensions crowded upon her, that tears burned under her eyelids, while an expression of utter misery settled upon her features.

Geoffrey sped over to her side.

" My own dearest darling, please, please don't look so worried about it. I'm so sorry I didn't tell you at once, but left you to find out so suddenly. I was an idiot. If you look like that, I shall never forgive myself. Why does it make you unhappy ? I should have thought you'd be rather pleased, if anything. What a sigh ! After all, it's not so wonderfully important. It will not make the least bit of difference to us for years and years to come—perhaps never—who can tell ? "

Evarne did not answer. The longer she reflected the more overwhelming appeared this unforeseen complication. Of course, as soon as her engagement became common knowledge, all sorts of people would want to learn all about her ; the events of her whole past life would probably be delved into—and then—what ? She wished Geoffrey would leave her alone for a time. She wanted to think.

But the more anxious and depressed she appeared, the more concerned and self-reproachful he grew.

" I'm not vexed with you personally, dear," she was at length compelled to explain. " You mustn't think that for a moment. Only—only—— "

" Only what ? "

" I was thinking of a part of Mrs. Browning's translation of ' Prometheus Bound.' Do you remember it ?

> " Oh, wise was he, oh, wise was he,
> Who first within his spirit knew,
> And with his tongue proclaimed it true,
> That love comes best that comes unto
> The equal of degree !
> And that the poor and that the low
> Should seek no love from those above . . .' "

She broke off suddenly.

" Oh, Geoffrey, that is true ! I know it is, and it does seem so suited to us now."

" I noticed you discreetly ceased before reaching the last lines, which would make the application I suppose you intend far from complimentary to me, Mistress Evarne. My soul is neither ' proud ' nor ' fluttered by rows of ancestral lights,' or anything of that sort. Nothing ' flutters ' it except your sweet self, so that verse does not suit at all. How dare you shake your head ? Don't you believe me ? "

" Yes, yes ! I do, of course. But there is your cousin to consider. I shall never gain his goodwill. He will never give his consent."

" Our marriage will be legal without that, my own dearest. But really," and Geoff came out boldly with a thundering big lie, " really I don't anticipate his raising any serious objection. You see, it would be too absurd, considering that it's the merest chance that he has got any title at all. When the old earl and his brother, and both

his sons and his little grandson all died within three years,
it was necessary to go back over a century—if you ever
heard of such a thing—before they came to the point at
which the line from which we are descended branched off.
Why, for my part, I scarcely realised we were related to the
family at all. We didn't even know the old earl personally. It would be too absurd of us to put on airs and
graces as if we were superior sort of creatures born to wear
strawberry-leaves. It's just simply the merest chance.
Now, after that long explanation don't let's talk about it
any more, since it worries you."

" I must say one thing. We have never spoken at all yet
about money or position, or anything of that sort, have we ?
Still, I have known all along, and you also must have known
full well, that in choosing me you were marrying in every
respect far below yourself and what your people would
deem—— "

" Oh ! " broke in Geoff, " please, please don't talk in that
manner. It isn't generous of you, Evarne. It isn't like
you."

" I must finish, though. You are proposing to marry
far below what your relations would consider seemly in any
case, and most undeniably you have not made a fitting
choice when one remembers what the future probably
holds for you. You don't see things quite as other people
do, you know; but I am more worldly-minded and practical.
I think—I do really—that this engagement between us is
scarcely suitable, and that it ought not to exist."

Geoff placed his hands heavily on her shoulders with a
somewhat frantic grip, and looked at her in serious alarm
for a moment. Then he spoke with forced carelessness.

" So you really think to persuade me of your claim to
be considered ' worldly-minded ' by trying now to get me to
give you up, do you—you darling ? Listen to me. I shall
marry you or nobody ! If you won't have me, I shall go
down to my grave a morose, disagreeable old bachelor.

I shall always be doing my level best to make all around me utterly miserable, and although everyone will fear and hate me, a few discerning folk will explain, ' Oh, don't you know ?   That poor old man was crossed in love in the days of his youth, and has never got over it ! '   Would you like to have that on your conscience, Evarne mine ?   Now, come in to lunch, and we won't speak another word of cousins or earls or prospects or anything of the sort.   We will just talk about ourselves.   We are by far the most interesting topic in the world, aren't we, darling ? "

He caught her hand and commenced to draw her across the room.   He looked so young, so happy, so full of life, that Evarne forcibly thrust all her own miseries back into the depth of her heart.   She could not endure to see the glad look fade from his eyes even for a minute.

" Very well, Geoff," she said in all meekness.   " As long as you are sure that you really want me, I will never leave you of my own accord."

" That's a promise ? "

" Very well, it shall be.   But remember this, if you do come to believe that perhaps you would do wisely to listen to what I feel convinced your cousin's advice will be, you must not hesitate or think of me at all.   I only exist now to please you, and I'm not afraid of spoiling you by telling you so, dear.   My first and only wish is that everything shall be well with your life.   Remember."

He bent his head and kissed the hand he held, but declined to even discuss this subject with any seriousness.

" Come," he said lightly.   " I'm starving hungry !   More than anything else in the world at the present moment I want you to give me my lunch."

CHAPTER XXXIV

SEKHET WHETS HER TEETH

NO one felt able thoroughly to settle themselves steadily to work that afternoon, for Lord Winborough had not timed his visit, and might be expected at any moment.

They laughed and chatted for some time, but gradually painting was beginning to engross somewhat of its usual meed of attention, when the electric bell rang out.

"That will be Winborough," declared Geoff as he left the room immediately to admit his visitor.

The studio door swung to, so that only a confused murmur of voices came from the hall. In a minute it was opened again, and Geoff was heard saying—

"Oh yes, we're all much the same as usual. You remember Jack Hardy, and this is Frank Pallister."

Evarne was standing with her back towards the door, and as the two young men had at once crossed over in that direction, they had passed out of the range of her vision; for, despite these interruptions, with the instincts of a thoroughly good model she had not stirred unbidden from her pose.

She heard Jack make a brief speech in his most polite style, though obviously with considerable nervousness.

"I want to thank you, Lord Winborough, for so kindly consenting to spare some of your time to sit for me. I know how busy you are, and am more than grateful."

The answer came in smooth, even tones.

" Indeed, Mr. Hardy, it is a pleasure to be able to assist in any degree so talented and——"

At the sound of this voice an icy hand seemed to lay itself upon Evarne's heart, chilling her blood. With parted lips and eyes staring with terror she turned round. There, in the centre of the little group, stood—Morris Kenyon !

Well may the rapidity of thought be employed as a synonym for the uttermost conception of speed. Simultaneously with the tremendous mental shock of beholding this man again under such horrible, such undreamed-of circumstances—above the resultant seeming cessation of all the wheels of life within her body, the sudden uncontrollable shivering that shook her from head to foot—she became conscious that her brain was frantically urging her to instantly do something by which to account for this physical agitation—something to explain this uncontrollable display of emotion. It prompted the method. She followed it without a second's hesitation. Before any of the men had turned their gaze upon her, she had deliberately let go of the vase she carried. It fell heavily, and was smashed into a dozen pieces.

Down on her knees she sank, bending her head low, as, with trembling hands, she gathered together the nearest fragments. Her actions were quite instinctive ; her whole mind was bent on the recovery of her self-control. And she succeeded. When, after a minute's respite, she did dare lift her face, it was marked by no traces of greater concern than could easily be accounted for as the result of this embarrassing accident.

If Morris Kenyon, seeing her again with equal unexpectedness, had been guilty of any dramatic start or exclamation, it had passed quite unnoticed. All attention was turned upon Evarne, and Geoff was already by her side.

" My dear, what is the matter ? "

She would not meet his eyes; her own might be too full of emotion. She sought to speak, but no words came.

Geoff grew alarmed.

"Are you feeling ill? Can I do anything? Never mind those silly broken pieces. Tell me!"

She made a tremendous effort. She could—she should —answer him rationally and calmly.

"I'm frightened, Geoff," she whispered quickly and very softly—"after what I learnt this morning. You understand? His voice sounded so hard, and he looks so stern. I was frightened."

He put his hand over hers and pressed it sympathetically, but no more could be said in confidence. The three other men had approached.

"What's happened, Miss Stornway?" inquired Jack.

Geoff explained.

"She's tired, that's all. She ought to have rested long ago."

Evarne spoke for herself.

"I'm so dreadfully grieved to have broken this beautiful vase. I can't think how I came to drop it. Oh, I am so sorry."

"It doesn't matter the least bit," Geoff declared emphatically.

Evarne was now seated on the edge of the throne, and for a minute the four men stood in a semicircle, silently surveying her. She could have wrung her hands in agony under this scrutiny.

"Please don't bother about me any longer," she cried, and there were traces of rising excitement in her voice. "I am so sorry to have made such a stupid disturbance. Please, please leave me alone now. There's nothing the matter with me."

Geoff took her at her word.

"Come over here and look at the beginning of my new picture, Winborough," he suggested, after a final keen and anxious glance at Evarne.

While the scarcely-started canvas was being explained, and attention was thus entirely distracted from herself, Evarne brought all the force of her will to bear on gaining complete self-mastery. And for this she had need to call upon that emergency fund of strength, endurance and resolution that a woman's fine nervous system almost invariably produces when great necessity demands. Every moment the horror that assailed her appeared to grow more crushing, more unendurable, yet she sat there silent and motionless, with an unruffled brow and an expression of perfect calm upon her beautiful features.

She could not keep her fascinated gaze from the spectacle of the two cousins going the round of the room together, Geoff chatting gaily as he displayed the various little oddments and curiosities that he had brought from Italy Finally he produced a portfolio of water-colour sketches and handed them to his cousin one by one, describing, explaining, pointing out various parts that were to be especially noticed. Morris nodded, questioned, admired, held them at arm's-length to be better judged, all apparently without another thought in his mind beyond Art and Venice.

As the two men stood thus side by side, Evarne could most distinctly see traces of the relationship between them —more in the demeanour, the general build and outline, than in feature—but kinship, clear and unmistakable. There was exactly the same carriage of the head, much the same walk, while their hands—slender, long-fingered and especially well-tended—were practically identical.

Morris had changed very little in the seven years that had been lived through since the stormy scene that had marked that final parting on that spring morning in Paris. His dark hair was thinner, perchance, and turning grey upon the temples ; there were a few more of Time's scratches upon his brow. But although he must be now somewhere about fifty-five, his figure—thanks probably to his devotion to fencing—was still as slender, as trim and upright as that of any of the younger men in the room.

Evarne had opportunity of studying his appearance at leisure, for not once did he glance in her direction. She knew this must be intentional, and was so far grateful, though such a mild emotion could find scant place in her mind just then. It was almost unendurable to see those two men standing side by side thus. Not only was the instinct of self-preservation on the alert, but every refined impulse in her nature was outraged by the spectacle. Unconsciously she caught hold of the slightly overlapping edge of the floor of the throne, and dragged at it with such unsparing force that the muscles of her arms stood up terse and hard.

The sketches all surveyed, the conversation turned on Jack, his work and the bust that was to be undertaken.

" I've just finished a life-size statue of a child," Jack said. " It's only in clay at present, but I am going to work it out in marble—perhaps as a memorial-stone. You think it is good, don't you, Geoff ? " and he turned anxiously towards his friend for confirmation.

" Indeed it is splendid," was the ready answer " You should see it, Winborough. It is in the plaster-room yonder. It is a dreadful weight to lift. Will you go in there and look at it ? "

Winborough cordially assented, and escorted by Jack and Pallister he left the studio.

Geoff did not accompany the trio. He was anxious about Evarne, and, sitting down beside her, he slipped his arm around her waist as he declared in a tone of raillery—

" Well, sweetheart, you have surprised me ! I had no idea you were such a little coward. I thought you were as brave as anything."

She hastened to account for this sudden weakness by numerous excuses. It seemed to her that it must necessarily have aroused some suspicion, although Geoff's manner showed not the slightest trace of any such feeling.

"I don't like you to think me cowardly," she said, " so please remember all I have had lately to upset me. First of all, I have not really been feeling fit to pose lately. I'm weary! The engagement I finished on Thursday was a terribly trying one. I stood for that wretched artist for the figure for nearly six weeks without missing a single day except Sundays. He wanted to get his picture done before he went away for his holidays, and he succeeded, but it made me quite ill."

Geoff was properly indignant.

"It was enough to kill you; you should not consent to do such things. You must not play with your health like that. You ought never to have sat at all for such a selfish brute."

Evarne shrugged her shoulders.

"You see, you don't know what it is to have to earn your own living," she declared with a little smile. "I certainly did intend resting for the remainder of the week, but you were so anxious to start your picture, dear, that I went right on without even a day's interval."

Now Geoff was indeed repentant.

"Oh, my darling, I didn't understand! I didn't know! It's all my fault. How horribly thoughtless I am! Why didn't you tell me?"

"I didn't think it would matter. I am very strong, you know, as a rule. But what I learnt this morning so suddenly worried me seriously; and then—I told you—I got so frightened when your cousin was really here, that my silly hands trembled, and I broke that vase that I know you value. So altogether, if I was a bit pale and not quite myself, it wasn't without sufficient cause, was it?"

Even as she spoke she found herself wondering why she took this trouble to blind Geoffrey's eyes. If he did not immediately learn the true reason of her alarm at the sight of his cousin, he would know to-morrow—or the day after

—or the day after that ! It could be only a question of a more or less brief time. Why not give up the struggle at once ? Her heart ached as she listened to his expressions of self-reproach, knowing as she did that he had been unfailingly kind and considerate towards her from the hour of their first meeting.

"Evarne, dearest, do forgive me. You have made me feel terribly remorseful. One thing after another for you to endure, and all my fault ! If that is the best care I can take of you, I don't deserve to have you, that's certain. Dear, say you forgive me this time. I will try and be more thoughtful."

He drew her closer to his side, and right gladly would she have rested there and endeavoured to forget the world, its deceptions and its difficulties. But this was most decidedly not the time for such indulgence, and she was in the very act of withdrawing herself from his encircling arm, when exactly that which she was seeking to avoid came to pass. Jack must needs choose this psychological moment to throw open the door and conduct Winborough back into the studio.

It was an awkward moment for everyone. Geoff rose to his feet, but did not loosen his arm from around Evarne. It merely slipped upwards from her waist to her shoulders.

Jack looked absolutely aghast. Pallister gave vent to a silly inopportune little snigger, while Winborough demanded somewhat sarcastically—

"Do you spend much of your time studying art by such methods, Geoffrey, my boy ?"

"Let me explain," said the young man without a moment's hesitation. "It may come as a complete surprise to you, Winborough ; but Jack, and even Pallister, who have been here with us in the studio, must be fully prepared to hear of my good fortune. I mean that I have asked Miss Stornway to become my wife, and she has consented."

That even under these difficult circumstances Geoffrey would make this startling announcement publicly, on the spot, without either warning or preparation, was as un-looked-for by Evarne as it could have been by any of the others. But the emergency did not find her wanting. With this new demand came fresh strength. Instantly rising to her feet, she drew herself up to her full height, lifted her head proudly, and without the slightest trace of fear or faltering, advanced a couple of steps forward. Then, by sheer force of will she compelled Morris Kenyon to meet her eye, and resolutely concentrated the whole of her mental strength to its uttermost limits in sending forth a wordless message—a command—that this man should not speak to betray her.

And silence prevailed in the room!

Evarne remained motionless, her soft robes falling around her in gracious dignified folds, her beautiful head haughtily upraised. She made herself, by mere force of character and dauntless determination, absolute mistress of the situation for the time being.

But the fetters were still around her wrists!

The silence was finally broken by Geoffrey. Turning from the cousin with whom he had but little in common, he looked across at his chosen friend, and asked somewhat coldly—

" Well, Jack, have you nothing to say ? "

Thus adjured, that young man pulled himself together.

" My dear Geoff, I—I really—I do congratulate you—both of you. I'm sure you'll be happy."

" You've completely floored me," cried Pallister gaily, recovering his breath. " I'm so surprised, you can come and knock me down with a feather if you want to. I'm sure I congratulate you heartily. Three cheers for Mr. and Mrs. Danvers ! Hurrah ! Can I be best man ? "

But Evarne scarcely heard anything of this. She and Morris still stood separated by the length of half the room, gazing sternly into one another's eyes, each reading and sending forth defiance, antagonism, mutual hatred.

Yet when Winborough at length spoke it was in tones that were quite light and casual.

" If marriage wasn't such a confounded knot to untie, there would not be the same need for careful consideration beforehand that undoubtedly there is now—more's the pity ! When you do marry, Geoff, I wish you every happiness—that you know."

Evarne returned to the throne and sat down again. Having averted the danger of Morris speaking out on impulse at first hearing Geoff's announcement, she felt herself safe for the minute. He would indeed be strangely altered if he now suddenly burst forth into accusations, making a scene in the presence of Jack and Pallister, and running the risk of ensuring public talk and scandal. Besides, she still retained sufficient faith in his honour to believe that he would not deliberately give away her secret to men whom it did not concern.

But before long her apprehensions were again up in arms.

" You are inhospitable here," announced his lordship. " Do artistic aspirations do away with parched throats, even on sultry July afternoons ? If so, that's rather an important point for temperance advocates. For my part, fancying I remember where you keep your whisky and syphons, Geoff, I'm going to see if I can look after myself, eh ? "

With the utmost nonchalance he strolled out of the studio. As Winborough had anticipated, Geoffrey promptly followed him.

As soon as they were alone in the sitting-room, Winborough rounded on the young man sharply.

" Look here, what folly is this ? Is it possible you are really thinking of marrying that girl ? "

" I told you so plainly enough, didn't I ? "

" Preposterous ! Do you suppose you can be allowed to take up seriously with any stray creature who happens to please your fancy ? The idea is absurd—utterly absurd ! "

Geoff's eyes flashed, but he kept his temper. He had fully anticipated that Winborough would at first oppose this marriage. But of course all objections were founded on mere prejudice and ignorance, so he answered quietly in the hope of explaining and thus conciliating his cousin. He tried to express the admiration, the respect and the affection he felt for Evarne, in a manner totally devoid of any exaggeration or seeming blindness, but with unmistakable clearness and certainty.

" You are prejudiced against Evarne because of her profession, Winborough ; but when you have known her for a little while you will be forced to acknowledge that, despite it, she is in every respect as near perfection as any human being can possibly be. In culture and refinement, in mind and manner, she is the equal of my own mother. She is absolutely honourable and straightforward and high-principled, and I love her. Now, I ask you, what more can one want ? If she is a bit below me socially, that is the one and only drawback—such as it is—that anyone can possibly adduce ; and after all, it is her personality and my feelings that are the matters of real consequence. Isn't that so ? "

" Not entirely. Her character and her past record are of the utmost importance. Now, what do you know of her ? Not much, I'll be bound. No, my boy, when you do finally decide to marry, you must choose some nice girl in your own station of life. One who has been properly brought up, and about whom there can be no question, which is more than can be said for Miss Stornway."

" You presume most abominably upon our relationship," Geoff was commencing angrily, but both his sentence and the remainder of the conversation were doomed to remain

T

unfinished. Hurried footsteps were heard in the hall, and
Jack charged into the room, crying—

"I say, get some brandy or something quickly! Miss
Stornway has fainted."

With a feeling akin to despair had Evarne watched the
two men leave the studio. It had been so obviously a
mere contrivance on Morris's part to speak to his cousin
alone. Now the blow was to fall, and what possible means
had she of preventing it? A sudden consciousness of her
own weakness, her utter impotence, swept across her,
bringing something not unlike resignation in its train.
She would change her costume and go away—everything
was over! She stood up, but with the more commanding
attitude the fighting spirit rallied again. She would not
yield yet. She would strive till the very last.

The imperative need of the immediate moment was to
end that *tête-à-tête* now proceeding. Morris and Geoff
had been alone scarcely a couple of minutes. No harm
was perhaps done yet, but every second might be of consequence. How was it to be stopped—how—how? She
cast about in her mind for an inspiration. Ah! was there
any wisdom in belonging to that sex that men designate
" the weaker," and yet never taking advantage of it in
emergencies such as this? Without a second thought she
gave a low cry, raised her hand to her head, let herself
drop heavily upon the floor, and there lay just as she had
fallen—motionless, helpless, with closed eyes and scarce
fluttering breath.

The anticipated result ensued. Half a minute later
Geoff was on his knees hanging over her in an agony of
dismay, while Winborough might have been absolutely
non-existent for all the attention he was able to command.

Every device known to man for the conquering of a fainting attack did Evarne allow to be vainly essayed before
finally lifting her languid eyelids. A look of relief passed
over three anxious countenances. Winborough stood lean-

ing against the door, surveying the scene. His features bore
an expression that might have puzzled the uninitiated, but
Evarne understood. Meeting her eye, he smiled at her.
Their mutual glance was scarcely more than instantaneous,
but it was all-sufficient. She knew right well that not for
a moment had he been deceived by her pretended swoon.
Geoff's gaze, fixed intently on the face so dear to him, saw
a shadow of distress pass over it as a fleeting cloud. He
looked rapidly at Winborough over his shoulder, but no
explanation was forthcoming from that quarter, and he
turned all his attention again to his "Sweet Lady."

She was supported to the open window, ensconced in an
arm-chair ; cushions were arranged behind her head ; a
footstool was brought for her feet. More than once, as
Winborough watched all this care and attention, the same
mocking smile hovered around his lips.

"Don't leave me," murmured the invalid, laying her
hand upon Geoff's arm.

But even as she spoke she stole a glance at the man
standing by the door. He it was with whom an undisturbed interview was essential. Each must learn the
other's mind—it was imperative.

"I have an idea that if I could say a few words to your
cousin while I'm so ill, it might soften his heart towards
me," she whispered, after a brief period of perplexed
thought. "Do arrange for me to have a minute or two
alone with him, to see if I cannot persuade him to think
more kindly of me."

"I will call him over if you like."

"But I can't talk about you while you're listening.
That would be embarrassing for me, wouldn't it ? "

But Geoff was reluctant.

"Oh, he is in a nasty temper. He would very likely
say something to wound your feelings, and you have
borne more than enough lately. Don't bother about
him."

"I can't endure to make trouble between you. Do let me try. He doesn't look very stern now," she declared.

Winborough was engaged in conversation with Jack and Pallister, and was obviously making himself as pleasant as he so well knew how to do when he chose. Nevertheless, Geoff frowned slightly and shook his head.

But with a very little more perseverance, Evarne, as usual, got her own way. A few minutes later she found her enemy standing by the side of her chair in an otherwise empty room, and heard herself directly addressed by that voice which, above all others, she had hoped and believed would never fall upon her ears again.

"Will you accept my compliments upon your really admirable presence of mind."

She sat erect with amazing alertness.

"Morris! So you are his cousin?" she cried, for the first time allowing the full horror she felt to appear in both tone and expression.

"Most unfortunate, isn't it?" he agreed. "If it had been any other man whatsoever I wouldn't have spoiled your little game. As it is, of course—well, I'm sure you will understand."

"Do you really suppose I'm going to give him up quietly, simply to please you?" she demanded—then added hastily, "But we can't talk about it here."

Morris raised his eyebrows.

"Is there anything to discuss? Oh, I understand. Pardon my dullness. We'll make that all right. I'm not ungenerous. Where are you living? Where can I come and see you?"

So he was actually taking her words to imply that she wanted money. She opened her lips, ready with an indignant denial, but stopped short. Let him labour under this delusion for the time being. It was a decided advantage.

She gave him her address.

" I am posing here all day," she explained. " You can come in the evening at half-past seven."

" I am engaged to-night. Expect me to-morrow. I'll drop in after I've dined. Somewhere between eight and nine. I say, Evarne."

" What is it ? "

" You won't throw the furniture at me, will you ? "

She found no answer for this taunt. Leaning back in the chair, she turned her head wearily away, while a couple of big tears gathered in her eyes. He was very brutal— very heartless. What was she to do, or say to him ?

In another minute the door had swung to behind him, and Geoff was bending over her.

She looked up mournfully, while the big tears overflowed and trickled unrestrainedly down her cheeks.

" It was quite useless," she murmured brokenly. " He is absolutely determined to prevent our marriage. Oh, Geoff, my dearest, I am so unhappy. What am I to do ? I love you so much."

CHAPTER XXXV

THE STROKE OF SEKHET

THE resonant strokes of great clocks boomed forth the third hour after midnight; the sounds faded away languidly upon the heavy air, and silence reigned once more over the sleeping city. Evarne wandering downstairs, leaned out of the landing-window counting the tones, listened until they had died into nothingness, then, with a shuddering sigh, continued her way to the sitting-room.

Hour after hour throughout this seemingly endless night had she wandered over her little house, pacing to and fro distractedly in every room in turn. Morris Kenyon had come again into her life, and to stop her marriage would, if necessary, ruthlessly betray her secret to Geoff. It was beyond any possibility of doubt. That brief interview with him had clearly shown his intention. What power had she to prevent it ? He would tell all—and then—what then ? Even in imagination the results were well-nigh insupportable. And this approaching blow would not—could not—fall on herself alone ; and in this reflection there lay a sting potent as that of the torturing gadfly that drove Io of old wandering over land and water seeking peace in vain.

Why, why had she ever risked this calamity ? She ought to have told Geoff the whole truth about herself directly she saw he was growing really to care for her. But now, as an additional offence, she had been guilty of such brazen lies ; had deceived him both by words and by

silences so continually and deliberately. Her whole conduct towards him must now appear shameful, utterly dishonourable. It was almost impossible to hope that his
affection would endure in the face of such dire discoveries,
it was quite out of the question to expect him afterwards
implicitly to believe even her strongest assertions. Strive
as she might to explain her motives, to excuse trickery that
she could not deny, however earnestly she should plead,
mourn, regret, she could never do away with these damning,
irrefutable facts. What would Geoff think and say and
do ? Surely his revulsion of feeling would be terrible and
complete ?

And if, despite all, he could not cease to care for her—
why, so much the worse for him ! He who so desired to
reverence where he loved could feel but contempt, or at
least mere forgiving, generous pity. In place of trust and
glad confidence—doubt, surmise, unrest. Better far for
her " dreamer " if all memory of her could fade entirely
from his thoughts. To love with the heart and despise
with the intellect—it could be done. But it was cruel
suffering ; it bordered on the unendurable ! She herself
knew only too well the mental torture that such complex
emotions imply. Was she to be the means of forcing Geoff
to acquire this bitter knowledge ?

During the passing of the weary hours her thoughts had
travelled widely. Not only had she shuddered at the reve-
lations of that day, and sickened with horror for the future,
but memories of the hateful past had pressed upon her with
resolute persistency.

And in that retrospect it seemed that bygone days had
failed to show her the uttermost possibilities of mental
anguish. Not throughout the long-protracted pain of
striving against Lucinda Belmont's successful rivalry ; not
in that moment of humiliation and agony of spirit when
Morris had bade her leave him for Tony ; not the year of
grinding poverty and overwork that followed—none of all

this had brought the cruellest last drops of the cup of misery so near her shrinking lips as did the present hour. She knew now that she could taste of these final dregs by one means only—by seeing her own deeds used as the weapon wherewith to shatter the happiness of the man she loved far more dearly then life.

" Geoff, Geoff, forgive me ! " she cried aloud, and buried her face in her hands.

How cruel it all seemed ! Could it be mere chance that so often made a sport, a mockery, of just the highest hopes and prospects—of the sunshine of the present—of the sweetest amidst past memories ? Hot rebellion awoke within her heart, so surely did it seem that some subtle malignity, some deliberate spitefulness, had been at work shaping her life from the very day of her birth, when she lost her mother, guiding and controlling events until they culminated in this coil of torment. Or perchance it had all been preordained by some Supreme Being as a test, a needful trial. Yet again, may be, she, and Geoffrey too, were but working out their own salvation, fated to endure in order to expiate evil wrought in some forgotten exist-ence ; that she ought to be resigned, and, rebelling no longer, to submit patiently to sorrow both for herself and for him.

Ah, mystery of suffering ! Can blind mortal eyes pierce the veil ? Can a heart torn with ardent earthly love find comfort in the shadowy dreams of philosophers or mystics ?

Evarne flung herself upon the couch, pressing her face despairingly into the cushions. And in the blackness arose, clear and distinct, a mental vision of that little Temple of Sekhet far away in the land of Egypt. How minutely could she recall the terrifying aspect of the goddess who held dominion over Love, over its joy and its cruelty. Almost with the vividness of reality could she see those ominous features—that flat head with its receding brow, beneath which no wise benevolence, no tender charity could ever find place. And in the mental picture, the narrow gleaming eyes seemed reading the agony of her spirit with malicious deliberation, the long lips were parted over sharp teeth with a devilish smile of amusement and gratification.

She started erect and gazed around the familiar room, seeking to clear her mind of such spectres. But the train of thought was not to be got rid of so easily.

Surely those long-dead priests of Egypt had been verily inspired when they represented this divinity under the guise of a cat-headed creature ? Ah, " Crusher of Hearts " supreme, with your sheer delight in torturing all that falls helplessly within your power—with your eyes that have the gift of seeing clearly how and where to strike when the vision of all others is dulled ! But they should have given you cat's paws, Sekhet—cruel, tearing talons concealed in sheaths softer than velvet !

There was surely the " Mark of the Beast " upon this fate that had befallen her. After so many years of dull monotony, to be allowed once again to behold prospects of the truest happiness—to enjoy so brief a spell of love and joy—just a taste of life's sweetest possibilities. Then this crushing blow, this darkening of the heavens, this blight upon the earth, this upheaval of the depths !

She moved restlessly around the room for a few minutes, then wandered upstairs again. She longed for the temporary forgetfulness of sleep, but how vain to seek it with a mind in so wild a turmoil. The very atmosphere seemed stifling. Half lifting aside the dressing-table that stood before the window, she flung wide the lower sash, and bringing a chair, rested her folded arms upon the sill and gazed into the night.

Out of doors all was quiet and peaceful indeed. The moon still rode high, flinging clear-cut fantastic shadows upon road and pavement. No sound was to be heard, no human being to be seen.

Yet the mere sight of the street brought a fresh pang to her already overburdened heart. While Philia was away posing at the Polytechnic Art class that evening there had come a knock at the door which Evarne had disregarded entirely. A second rap was treated with like contempt ; the outside world with its demands was non-existent to her that night. But the current of her thoughts had been disturbed, and at the third attempt she became sufficiently interested in this perseverance to stand concealed by the window-curtains to watch who went away.

After a time a figure had appeared and walked slowly down the street. It was Geoff himself. He had driven home with her at five o'clock, and here, but a few hours later, was apparently already anxious for fresh news. To see the road, brought this little incident vividly to her memory. Was she to lose such care and devotion ? And to think that Geoff—with all his kindness and unfailing tenderness towards the weakest living thing, his trust and his true love for herself—was to be nothing more than one of Sekhet's innumerable victims !

She dragged down the blind sharply, to shut out the sight of the road, then made up her mind at least to lie dcwn and strive to sleep. But early risers were already abroad before her eyelids even closed, and she seemed scarcely to have lost consciousness before Philia aroused her.

The old woman had not been as blind to the girl's troubled state as Evarne supposed. Far from sleeping complacently all night, she had lain awake long, listening to the gentle footsteps in the house, grieving over the sorrow that had so evidently descended upon the one who was dearest to her of all the world. Thus her voice was quite apologetic as she called out—

" I'm sorry to wake yer, my pet, but I've let yer sleep as long as ever is possible if you're goin' to be at that studio by nine. It's jist on eight o'clock already."

" I'll get up at once," Evarne answered, and she went
so far towards carrying out her good intention as to immediately sit up in bed. But as the memory of the events
of the previous day came upon her, she promptly sank
down again with a renewal of despair.

But although lamentation and fear were permissible in
the night hours, with the morning must come a renewal of
courage and energy—so she told herself, at least ; and with
the determination of acting up to this resolution, sprang
lightly out of bed, and, crossing the room, drew up the
blind.

But either the energy of her uprising after such a night,
or the sudden blaze of morning light, rendered her suddenly dizzy. She shut her eyes and leant for a moment
on the dressing table. When she opened them again the
first thing she saw was her own reflection in the mirror.
She surveyed it with stern disapproval. What a sight she
was, with pale cheeks and those blue circles under the eyes !
She looked every whit as ugly as she felt—dazed and sleepy
and silly. Suddenly she made up her mind to stay at
home. There was no real need to call upon her resources
until the evening brought the interview with Morris. She
would avoid the unnecessary effort of concealing her distress and anxiety from Geoff.

She went out on to the landing, and, leaning over the
banisters, called for Philia. The old woman opened the
door of the kitchen, from whence issued the hissing sound
of frying.

" Bring me up a cup of tea—nice and strong. I don't
want anything to eat. I'm not going to the studio this
morning."

Then returning to her room, she sat down and wrote to
Geoff.

" DEAREST OF ALL,
        " Will you mind very much if I don't come

to-day ? I have had such a restless night, it has made me look so ugly I don't want you to see me. There's vanity ! Really, I do feel quite unwell—not actually ill, you know, but not up to posing. I feel sure I should only break more precious vases, so I had better not come, though it is hard not to see you for a whole day, my Geoff.

"Your lazy

"EVARNE."

As she took the tea from Philia's hands she gave her the note.

"Send this by district messenger. Go at once, there's a dear."

"Won't yer tell me what's the matter, my pet ? It's all troublin' me, it is, straight."

"There's nothing to worry about in a bad night, is there, now ? When you come back don't wake me. I'm going to sleep again if I can."

But Evarne did not leave it to chance. When she had nearly finished her tea she produced a tiny blue bottle from the drawer of the washing-stand, carefully counted out five-and-twenty drops, shook her cup round several times, then swallowed tea and chlorodyne together to the last dreg. Lowering the blind she got back into bed and was soon fast asleep.

It was three o'clock before she descended to the sitting-room. On the table was a cluster of sweet-peas and roses, together with a note.

"Did Mr. Danvers send these ? " she inquired, as she tore open the envelope.

" 'E brought 'em 'imself. My gosh, dearie, 'e is properly careful of you. 'E knocked so soft I 'ardly 'eard 'im, and 'e looked that worried."

"So I've already started to grieve him," reflected Evarne grimly, as she proceeded to read his letter.

" MY POOR PRECIOUS DARLING,

"I can't tell you how terrible it is to me to think of you as weak and suffering . . . my bright-eyed, rosy-lipped Evarne. And I feel that really it is all my fault in one way and another. . . . I'm sure it is not surprising that yesterday should have upset you. . . . It's a delicate, sensitive soul, I know, for all the glorious vitality of the flesh. Only get well quickly, my best and dearest, and I'll guard you better in future. Get strong quickly, for my sake, who love you so, and you shall have permission to smash every vase in the studio to your heart's content . . . you darling !

" GEOFF."

She put this little note in the bosom of her gown, as she went out to the kitchen in response to Philia's call to dinner.

After the little meal she got out her drawing materials, and made some pretence at working. But her pencil moved almost mechanically over the paper as her mind rehearsed all she could possibly find to say to Morris—the pleas, the arguments she could place before him to turn him from his present purpose. Slowly though time crept, she watched its steady progress with dismay, and as the afternoon waned there arose within her an ever-increasing fear, not so much of the interview that loomed ahead, as of its result. She tried to force herself to think only hope-fully regarding its issue, but all the time in her innermost consciousness she seemed to know that failure was a fore-gone conclusion. How futile to strive to alter Morris's set determination—above all when, for once in his life, he would be able to flatter himself that he was standing firm in the cause of right and justice.

CHAPTER XXXVI

A FRESH VOW

B Y six o'clock the sedentary occupation had become too trying. Evarne changed her dressing-
gown for a coat and skirt, and went out.

All this erratic behaviour caused Philia not a
little concern and alarm. As a general rule Evarne was
so very placid and level-headed, that this disregard of all
precedent, this wandering about in the dark and sleeping
in the daylight, this neglect of work, meals at extraordinary
hours, and all the rest of the disorganising of respectable
routine, was not an occurrence to be treated lightly.
Still, in Philia's experience of human nature, directly a
girl must needs go and fall in love, troubles and upsets and
excitements followed as an inevitable corollary, while calm
quiet contentment took unto itself wings. Thus she did
not consider the root-cause of the present state of affairs
to be enshrouded in unsolvable mystery. Although she
was rather hurt at not being made a confidante, she evinced
no curiosity, being fairly satisfied that clouds of such a
nature almost always pass away in due course.

But when half an hour later she answered a knock at the
door and discovered Geoff, she greeted him with anything
but an amiable countenance.

" How is she now ? " he inquired.

" Guess she's better agin, for she's gorn out to git a
breath o' fresh air. Will yer please to step in and wait.
I dare say she would like to see yer when she comes back."

Needing no second invitation, Geoff followed Mrs. Harbert into the house.

The pretty little sitting-room was full of Evarne's personality. Here were the flowers he had brought her; here too were her books, her drawing-board, her writing-case; there was the embroidered footstool on which she had sat during his previous visit. Everything sang to him of Evarne. There were the really charming pictures on the walls, signed with her initials, that she had amazed him by showing as her own handiwork. There was her little work-box, and across it lay the long strip of embroidery on which he had seen her diligently creating silken blossoms. Moved by a sudden longing to hold in his hand something that she had touched, Geoff picked up this and surveyed it with the minute scrutiny of an apparent connoisseur in art needlework.

Philia was speaking to him somewhat reproachfully. She imagined that now, having the culprit under her thumb, she could, with all due regard for politeness, give him a " piece of her mind."

" I must tell yer first that I ain't bin told who it is worryin' my pore gal, but I warrant if they'd bin 'ere to see 'er last night they'd 'ave bin fair ashamed of themselves. She was roamin' the 'ouse like a wanderin' spirit, and in the mornin' she was jist as white as 'er nightgown. It seems to me that to make anyone really un'appy without rhyme or reason—and I won't believe Evarne is in the wrong—as I was sayin', to make anyone real miserable is a big thing to 'ave on one's mind in this 'ere world o' sin and woe, full o' the slings and arrers of houtrageous fortune as it is—Shakespeare! In plain talk, sir, a world where we're all certain to 'ave quite enough trouble to digest without them as we cares for most forcin' a hextry dose down our gullets. And no stray flowers, nor' even rings nor sich-like, makes up for unkindness—not to the noble mind—Shakespeare! I've lived with Evarne for five

years and more, and she's never 'ad one hour's sorrow
through my fault.   Hexcuse me if I'm takin' liberties I
didn't ought, but you've bin 'ome from foreign parts less
than a week, and for some reason or other now she's made
fair miserable—by someone or other !   I'm not sayin' by
who, but it's very 'ard for me to see it and not say nothin'
at all."

Philia paused, somewhat apprehensive at having thus
let her feelings carry her away.   But Geoff was not displeased by this ardent championship.

" My dear Mrs. Harbert," he said seriously, " if it is my
fault—and to a certain extent I'm afraid it is—believe me
that it was both unintentional and indirect.   Evarne shall
never have a moment's trouble that I can save her from,
be very sure of that."

He walked to the window and looked out.

" I wonder where she is now ? " he went on.   " Do you
think she will be long ? "

" Can't say where she is.   She jist says, ' It's suffocatin'
indoors,' she says, and out she goes.   Most likely she'll be
back by seven.   Anyway, I'm due at the ' Poly ' at 'alf-
past."

" You've always posed, haven't you, Mrs. Harbert ? "

Philia was decidedly a trifle aggrieved by this query, and
answered in wounded tones—

" Now, sir, if yer was a few years older, yer wouldn't
need to ask that.   There was a time when every hartist in
London knew all about Philadelphia 'Arbert, and it wasn't
sich a great time ago either."

" Evidently I don't know much ? " queried Geoff with
a good-natured smile.

The reply was certainly cutting.

" You never 'eard tell of Philadelphia 'Arbert as a model,
and you don't know 'ow to keep yer sweet'eart's eyes dry.
Well, sir, askin' yer pardin', but you 'ave got somethin' to
learn ! "

The young man bit his lip and did not answer. This silence melted his outspoken critic immediately, and she set to work to be amiable.

"Hexcuse me if I'm rather sharp, but it is 'ard to 'ave bin famous once and to find yer 'ard-earned fame all gorn. Why, I can remember the time when any hartist gentlemen as wanted to bring Venus or any other of them 'eathen young women into a picture, didn't feel 'e'd done all he could to 'elp 'imself until 'e'd got me to pose for 'im. That's a fact, sir! I'd a lovely figger when I was a gal. None o' the young women now, only exceptin' Evarne, comes up to what models was in my young days, and I— well, my gosh! I've 'ad a long string o' great painters waitin' their turn till I was disengaged and could oblige."

"It must have been both pleasant and profitable to be in such demand."

Mrs. Harbert looked down with becoming modesty, and smoothed her apron as she replied—

"Well, sir, it was, but I never let myself get huppish about it. I was only as the Lord chose to make me. I used to say sometimes, 'Beauty is as beauty does,' and 'Beauty is but a vain and doubtful good, a gloss, a glass, a flower; lost, faded '—I forget the rest—' within the hour '—Shakespeare. I've sat for Lord Leighton and Millais and Watts and 'eaps of others."

"Then you have posed for some quite well-known pictures, I suppose?"

"My gosh! a picture painted in those days, when Hart was properly understood, 'adn't much chance of bein' thought 'ighly of if the hartist 'adn't taken care to git me to collaborate with 'im."

"Now, that's a really original idea of yours, Mrs. Harbert—that a painter and his model collaborate. Did you tell it to the men you sat for, and what did they say?"

"Well, sir, truth is, I doubt if any of the hartists that I've 'elped to gain positions they'd never 'ave got to without

me, would be willin' to acknowledge it.   But there, that's
only the way o' the world.   Shakespeare 'e wrote a
song about hingratitude, as I dare say you've 'eard
sung.''

" Isn't it very interesting to be able to look back on the
famous pictures you've posed for ? " inquired Geoff, with
another fleeting glance out of the window.

" It is that !   Why, I was that proud the first time I was
in a picture that was the 'it of the season.   I was ' Harry—
Harry—hadney.' "

" Whom ? "

" Ain't yer never 'eard of 'er, pore gal ?   She's bin deserted on a island by some skulkin' brute, so she knelt down
with next to nothin' on, and 'eld out both 'er 'ands to the
sea.   It was like this."

Rendered enthusiastic by her reminiscences, Philia sank
down on the carpet, leant forward, flung back her head
and imploringly extended both her hands.   The effect had
probably been charming when the model was youthful and
fair, but now it put a severe demand on Geoff's good
manners not to smile at the old dame.

"It was real touchin'," she declared, as she rose to her
feet with some difficulty, " but it nearly gave me 'ouse-
maid's knee !   Then there was another picture that made
a lot o' talk.   It was called the ' Race of Hatalanta.'   She
was runnin' fit to catch the last train 'ome.   I shan't
forget that pose in a 'urry.   My gosh, I can't even think,
of it without my left leg beginnin' to ache ! "

At this moment the street door was heard to open.
According to her usual custom Evarne had let herself in
with her latchkey.

" There she is," said Philia, and stepping out into the
passage she announced in somewhat triumphant tones
" There's a gentleman 'ere waitin' to see yer, dearie."

After an interval of somewhat unaccountable duration,
Evarne appeared in the doorway.   As she beheld Geoff her

whole expression changed, her lips parted into a smile, her eyes lit up.

"Oh, it is you! I am so very glad, so delighted!" she gasped.

"Well, I won't be hintrudin' no longer," declared Philia as she left the room.

But her absence or presence was unmarked at that moment. Evarne was in Geoff's arms, and each was gazing at the other as if years of separation had intervened between this moment and their last meeting.

"I am so very glad you have come," declared Evarne again. "You cannot tell how badly I have wanted you. I felt as if I should die if I couldn't see you! Do you know where I have been? No, how should you? I have been to your studio! I don't mean upstairs, but I walked past and looked up at the window. I hoped you might just happen to look out. I did want you so much; I wanted comforting so badly."

"Evarne, every time I see you, you make me love you even more devotedly than I did before. But how truly wicked to want to see me, and not send a message at once. I have been thinking about you every minute of the day. Dearest, tell me, are you worrying so sadly about anything Winborough said?"

"It is the whole thing—the whole business. Oh, why could you not have been poor? Why could not you have been just an ordinary person, so that we could have lived for one another, without anyone having either the wish or the right to interfere? I am so afraid of your cousin—and worse still, I know that everyone will be on his side I feel the force of the entire world against me, and it's crushing."

"But we can safely defy the whole world to weaken our love for one another, can't we, my best and dearest?"

She wrenched herself suddenly from his arms.

"Oh, I don't know!—I don't know! How can we be sure of anything?"

So saying, she flung herself down amid the cushions of the big velvet arm-chair. Geoff stood motionless for a moment, then seating himself on one of its wide arms, he leaned over, resting his hand upon the opposite side.

"Then know this henceforward, Evarne. You may with perfect confidence defy not only the world, headed by Winborough, but you may safely defy even yourself to destroy the love I have for you. You might wound me, and disappoint me, even forget me, yet while I live I shall love you, and after death also, if Heaven pleases. What more can I say than that?"

"Well, it's a very pretty sentiment, anyhow," was the lightly-spoken, almost mocking reply.

"Then truth is not always ugly," he answered quietly enough, but Evarne could see that he was not unmoved by her jeering tones. Impulsively she flung her arms around his neck, and drew his face down to hers.

"Geoffrey, I'm years and years—I'm centuries older than you in spirit. I have suffered so much in previous existences that my soul still retains its scars. Truth has always appeared to me so sad of countenance, that when I see it with a smiling face I dread deception. Yes, indeed. In my mind Truth is invariably so grim, so menacing, so destructive, that when anything appears in beautiful guise and calls itself Truth, I instinctively mistrust it."

"Then I suppose I can do nothing but wait, and let time prove my words."

A sudden impulse—a longing—seized Evarne to confess everything—there on the spot, without any preparation or delay. To take him at his word, to shatter his ideal, and see if the love he thought so invincible could really endure. What a triumphant answer to Morris—to meet him with Geoff by her side—Geoff knowing all, and unchanged by knowledge!

She sought for words with which to commence, but in the moment's hesitation she chanced to look full into his clear grey eyes. It was no use. A cold chill seized her, and a feeling almost of physical sickness. She was ashamed. It was impossible to find language for this task that her tongue could be brought to utter. She felt her cheeks flush red, and partly covered her face with her hand.

So much for this half-hearted attempt at confession. And as the impulse passed, a great thankfulness arose that she had not yielded to its wiles. That Geoff loved her now was as certain as that he lived, and at that very moment she could feel his warm breath upon her brow. But he spoke with untried confidence. Had he not once declared, practically in so many words, that he would rather see her dead than have aught destroy his love for her? He had, indeed, made an attempt to contradict himself a moment later; but she held those words to be the genuine offspring of truth—representative of his most usual frame of mind. No, her task was not to anticipate, but to strive to ward off the evil hour of disillusionment.

"My true lover," she murmured, "I know you are faithful and loyal and constant, and I believe you would be long-suffering. I trust you, depend upon you now, and rely upon you for the future without a single doubt or a moment's hesitation."

"And, dearest, am I to feel the same about you? Will you be always faithful and constant to me?"

"Oh, Geoff, always, always."

"Then all is well. I half feared that if Winborough got a chance to talk to you alone, and perhaps bullied and argued and persuaded and appealed to your affection for me, and all that sort of thing, you might perchance be led to imagine that you were really ensuring my ultimate happiness by going away and leaving no trace whereby I could discover you again. One hears of such things, you know."

"If I thought it would be really best for you, be sure I would——"

"Evarne, my dear—my dearest—remember——"

"Yes, Geoff, I do remember, whatever it might be you were going to remind me of, for I forget nothing. I do believe I can make you happy. You hear that? I firmly believe I can make your life happier than it could be without me. That belief is the foundation of all my actions. Will you always remember that? Please take it into your very heart of hearts, and let it fix itself there indelibly."

For some time they sat silent. With Geoff so very near to her, Evarne became conscious of a gentle calm, a certain sense of peace, a despondency that was mournful, but less desperate. It was with an effort that she finally roused herself sufficiently to take his watch out from his pocket and look at the time.

"Seven—seven o'clock and past!" she sighed, replacing it. "Ah me! You mustn't think, dear, that I'm dreadfully rude and inhospitable, but I'm afraid I must ask you not to stay any longer."

"Oh—h!"

"It's no use saying 'oh' in that dolorous manner," she declared, smiling. "You see—it's this way—old Philia has to leave here for the 'Poly' about seven. She will be going in a few minutes."

"But we don't mind, do we? We don't want the old lady."

Evarne cast down her eyes. The only excuse that had crossed her mind for getting Geoff out of the house struck her as being decidedly petty and unworthy.

"It is stupid, I know well; but people do talk so."

"Why, silly little Evarne, you are surely not bothering about Mrs. Grundy and the neighbours, are you?"

With a somewhat feeble and shamefaced smile she rose up from out the depths of the chair, and replied only by fetching his hat and offering it to him with a little curtsey.

"It's only till to-morrow. I shall come to the studio just as usual."

The young man took the proffered hat with undisguised reluctance.

"Of course, I cannot stay if my hostess turns me out thus firmly," he grumbled, "but I'm sure it is not necessary. I believe you're tired of me."

She shook her head confidently.

"I'm very sure you don't think that really."

His momentary ill-humour died away.

"Of course I don't, dear heart. I dare say you are in the right. Everything you do is perfect, only—I warn you—you will have to marry me sooner than ever for this. Can't you settle on a definite date by to-morrow? Do try."

She disregarded his question.

"I'm glad you're not vexed. You did frown at me, you did, and it made you look—oh, terribly ugly—just like a mediæval gargoyle."

"You and Mrs. Harbert have certainly entered into a conspiracy with a view to reducing me to a proper condition of self-depreciation," declared Geoff, smiling at the lofty expression of disdain with which his "Sweet Lady" was still surveying him. He shifted his hat from one hand to the other.

"Come out with me, Evarne. Let us go and have something to eat, and then on to a theatre or somewhere, eh?"

"I've still got the tiniest little headache; I would rather not," she declared. "Good-bye, dearest." Then, correcting herself somewhat wildly: "No, no. I didn't mean good-bye—only good-night! Don't speak ill-omened words, Geoff. Only say good-night."

At length he was gone. Evarne pressed her hand to her forehead. This unexpected visit had both weakened and strengthened her.

After a few minutes she went upstairs to change her dress. Hearing the approaching steps, Philia, who was in her own room tying on her bonnet, called out, and as the girl entered she inquired—

" Are yer any 'appier now, my pet ? Is it all right ? "

" You really are fond of me, aren't you, Philia ? " queried Evarne meditatively, without replying to the question she had been asked. Then, without waiting for any response to her own demand, she went on : " Would you mind doing a little errand for me ? The classes at the ' Poly ' end at ten, don't they ? Will you go afterwards to Edith Gordon's and ask her for the blouse pattern she promised to lend me ? It isn't very far out of your way, and you can stop and have a chat if she is in, can't you ? "

" Right yer are," assented Philia cordially, and five minutes later the door had closed behind her.

At length the coast was quite clear for Morris's visit.

Evarne carefully studied her three tea-gowns. It was an important point. The green one was a great favourite with everybody, but it was undeniably getting old. The crimson cashmere with the black lace suited her splendidly, but both colour and material looked rather heavy for such hot weather. The pale yellow was the most suitable, and she would wear a harmonising cluster of sweet-peas.

Although every nerve in her body seemed to be now on edge, she did not neglect the least detail of her toilette, and at its completion could not but realise that she was indeed fair to behold. She had quite got back her colour, and that peculiar sparkling brilliance that was her characteristic beauty. Her luxurious dark hair, faintly scented and piled high upon her head, was held in place by ornamental combs. Long enamel earrings, gleaming blue and green, served to emphasise the soft carnation bloom of the cheeks they hung against, while a brooch of the same iridescent tones held together the lace at the point of the V-shaped opening of her gown. Then she put her diamond engagement ring upon her finger, and, after a final critical gaze into the mirror, descended the stairs. There she drew the blinds and lit the lamp. It was five minutes past eight. She sat down and waited.

CHAPTER XXXVII

EVARNE FIGHTS FOR MORE THAN LIFE

THE silence was intense and oppressive; time dragged painfully; every minute was fraught with an entire round of mingled emotions. Fear and trembling apprehension alternated with eager impatience; stern determination, coupled with either forced or spontaneous hope, would be followed by a crushing sense of foregone failure and lack of self-confidence. After a while this ceaseless ebullition of feeling brought on actual physical fatigue, and Evarne leant back in her chair with a growing sense of exhaustion.

Suddenly a sharp, loud knock broke the silence. Although she had been expecting this—listening and waiting for it—the sound came finally as a blow dealt her highly-strung nerves. She gave a painful start, a gasp, and felt the hot blood surge to her head. She sprang to her feet at once, but then stood motionless. Now that Morris Kenyon was actually upon her doorstep, every moment that kept him from crossing the threshold seemed a priceless respite.

She believed that she remained as if spellbound for many minutes, but really only a brief time passed before she aroused herself and went to the front door. With apparent indifference she flung it half open, and at once returned to sink into her favourite big arm-chair, leaving Morris to enter, close the front door, and conduct himself along the hall.

The light streaming from out the one room into the darkness served as a guide, and in a minute she heard his advancing footsteps come to a standstill. She neither spoke nor looked up, but remained impassive, her eyes fixed on the beloved ring that sparkled upon her third finger.

Morris seemed well content to stand for a while in the doorway, surveying her with a keen scrutiny. Then he studied the surroundings, rapidly but with considerable interest; glanced over his shoulder into the dense blackness that enveloped the remainder of the house; listened a moment to the heavy stillness that held sway; then entered the room and closed the door, pausing calmly to admire the crimson velvet portière, on which was some of Evarne's exquisite embroidery. After laying down his stick and hat on a little table and leisurely removing his gloves, he drew up a chair close to his hostess, sat down, and waited silently until she should choose to speak.

He was in evening dress, and though in the abstract there was nothing to be surprised at in this sartorial detail, Evarne found it inexplicably disconcerting. Without raising her eyelids she contrived to study him through her long lashes. He was indeed dignified and imposing; he had lost none of his good looks; but the lines of his mouth seemed even sterner, more inflexible than of yore. Past memories rushed upon her mind. The leading events and many apparently trifling details that had gone towards making up nigh three years of her life passed now in rapid progression before her mind's eye.

Verily she had loved this man at one time—she shrank with self-loathing from recalling how devotedly. He it was had been the cause of all those wild storms of emotion that from time to time had convulsed her whole nature in the throes either of ecstasy or of anguish. Quite apart from the fact that he came at this crisis as the arbiter of her future fate, it would have been impossible for her to once more see him—to feel his near presence—and remain entirely unmoved.

Maybe some similar reflections passed through Morris's mind. At all events, when ultimately he broke the silence, his words referred, not directly to the business on hand, but to the days that were gone.

" The presiding spirits at our exciting and interesting farewell, five—six now, isn't it ?—six years ago, were not exactly those of Peace and Harmony, were they ? Where did the venturesome little birdie flutter when it left its gilded cage, and what did it do ? "

Considering the gravity of the circumstances to which he was alluding, this light mode of address aroused all Evarne's indignation. But she carefully concealed every trace of resentment. So far her behaviour towards him that evening had been decidedly cavalier ; but it was undoubtedly necessary, if she was to win her way with him, that he should be deferred to—conciliated, rendered as well disposed towards her as was possible. Thus she gently answered his question by a brief though absolutely frank recital of her short stage experience, her miseries at needlework and subsequent illness, and her ultimate success as an artist's model. She kept very much to generalities in this account of how the years had passed with her, and avoided the least mention of Geoffrey.

Morris listened with evident interest, and after a period of silence had shown that she did not intend to proceed to further details, he said carelessly—

" You've escaped monotony in life, at all events. But, indeed, some new experiences have come the way of nearly everybody you once knew. Tony Belmont married, and is now a respectable, sober citizen with two children. Lucinda is still in Paris, assailing hearts and banking accounts with undiminished success—not mine, though ! Little—whatever was her name ? Oh, Feronnier ! A man who once knew her told me he had seen her recently haunting the back streets with a face pitted by small-pox ! I, to my own vast surprise, find myself, *nolens volens*, an earl ! My lady-wife, the countess, grows more tenacious of life year by year. I should say also she has become more disagreeable and unpleasant daily, if she hasn't already arrived at an age when ugliness and unpleasantness in the fair sex are such that there's no distinguishing of degrees. Then Geoffrey Danvers finds himself my heir, with all the resultant privileges and drawbacks—amongst the latter being the dire necessity of marrying not merely to please his own fancy, but with a certain regard to the demands of his position."

At length this preamble had been manœuvred round to the main point.

Evarne leaned slightly forward in her anxiety, as she demanded, without any circumlocution—

" Morris, do you wish to prevent your cousin making me his wife ? "

Unconsciously she held her breath while awaiting his reply.

" Surely such a question needs no answer ? " he said, a certain sternness stealing into his voice. " My chief wonder is that you ever dared to think of marrying my cousin."

Explanation seemed but a waste of time, yet she found herself saying in a somewhat tremulous voice—

" But I didn't know. They all speak of you by your title, and I did not dream of connecting that name with you. I never saw anything about the matter in the papers. Five years ago I was doing needlework ; I read nothing and knew of nothing that happened outside my own four walls."

" Um ! I understand," rejoined Morris reflectively. Then with a sudden change of tone he continued—

" Now, see here. You must realise that, as things have turned out, this marriage is not to be thought of. While no one who has ever known you, *ma chérie*, can possibly connect Evarne and common sense together in their minds, you are experienced enough by now, I dare say, to be willing to admit that life has the drawback of being a serious affair, and not a pretty romance. Therefore you will surely see that the wisest thing you can do is to make the best of a bad job, to accept the inevitable, and—shall we say—travel a while ? Now, travelling costs money, and it is only fair that I, who am responsible for the necessity, should pay the piper. There's a cheque in my pocket-book, Evarne. If you will tell me what you think would be sufficient to—to settle up things comfortably—I will fill it in right away. Now, that's merely a business offer, to avoid trouble and annoyance for us both," he added hastily, noticing her changed expression. " I don't need any thanks, but at the same time I don't intend to put up with any of the abuse to which you treated me the last time I proposed concerning myself about your future. Now, what sum will satisfy you ? In any case you must realise that your marriage with Geoffrey is absolutely impossible."

Evarne lay back in the big chair and surveyed the speaker leisurely and critically. She was at a loss to decide on the best manner of refusing even to consider this suggestion. One variety of response after another flitted through her mind. She dared venture on none of them. She dreaded the effect her defiance would have upon him, declare it gently and meekly as she might. Finally words came, prompted by her protracted scrutiny of his cold, resolute face. A quivering sigh escaped her, and speaking half to herself she murmured—

" How much I have suffered at your hands ! "

For a moment his sympathy was aroused. He drew his chair a trifle closer, and laid his hand upon her knee.

" Evarne, why in Heaven's name do such things happen ? On my honour, I'm heartily grieved and worried over this imbroglio."

With hope flashing into her eyes she suddenly sat erect and caught at his arm.

" Then leave everything alone—dear, dear."

Her mellifluous voice was low and coaxing. Before he could reply she went on—

" Let all the cruel, hateful past be forgotten. I can—I will—be a good wife to Geoff. You should never, never have the least reason to regret having permitted our marriage—oh, I'm certain ! We are so strangely suited to one another—our natures are thoroughly harmonious. Oh, Morris, Morris, you don't know how much he cares for me, and I—I love him with my whole heart, with all my strength, with all that makes my life. We should be so happy together—do let it be."

Morris raised his hands, as if to request the opportunity of replying. But Evarne did not, perhaps could not, cease one instant in her impassioned appeal.

" You know better than almost anyone that I am not light-natured, or really indifferent to right and wrong. You did care for me once—I know it—and there was a time when I would have turned to you with perfect confidence in any trouble. By the memory of those days, I implore you not to drag me again into the lowest depths of misery. And Geoff too—pity him, and spare him. Let him live his own life, and love in peace, and marry as his heart dictates. You can't always go by hard and fast laws. I am sure, I am convinced, that the greatest good —that nothing but good—could ever come from your keeping silence upon the wrongs, the faults, the deceptions and miseries that have gone by. Only fresh harm, more widespread evil, immediate and life-long, irreparable and unnecessary—oh think, so unnecessary—can arise from your determination to oppose a marriage that would be— be . . . Oh, Morris, we do love each other so much ! "

She flung her whole soul into this plea. As so often happens, the actual words were by far the weakest part of the appeal. It was her voice, low-pitched in its earnest entreaty, and at times quivering and uncertain, that betrayed most clearly the depth of her agitation—the vital force of tortured feelings. And as these tremulous tones died away, her entire personality continued to give the impression that her very life hung upon Morris's response. She leaned towards him ; her fair face, so expressive, so appealing, was very close to his. Those eager brown eyes, now so full of passionate persuasion, seemed to burn to his innermost consciousness. Not for one moment could Morris doubt the reality of her deep affection for the man she desired to marry.

He admired total abandonment of any sort. Something of her old charm fell upon him, and for a passing moment he came near to envying his young cousin the possession of this all-dominating love that he himself had once so lightly flung aside and disregarded. Thus, besides the need of resisting the encroachment of sentiment upon his resolve, he felt a touch of jealousy—a decided though unacknowledged displeasure at finding the heart that was once his footstool now so entirely emancipated from his service. It was this sense of personal grievance that caused him to answer her with a dash of that brutality that came so easily to his lips.

" The saints protect me from the responsibility of disarranging any ideal union, but the one you suggest is in every way about as unsuitable as could possibly be imagined. Doubtless you are absolutely devoted to Geoffrey —thousands of girls could easily adore the heir to an earldom. But forget your charming romantic feelings and try to look at the matter from an impersonal point of view. You are an artist's model. It may be the most refined and elevating profession imaginable, but—well—we commonplace people who belong neither to the race of poets nor artists find it rather difficult to reconcile—well—you comprehend ? I won't press that point."

" That is nothing at all to Geoff ! " breathed Evarne.

" Then, if I understood rightly, you came very near to

including utter starvation in that intensely interesting re-
recital of your experiences," he went on. " Of course,
that's very sad—quite touching, in fact. But now, do
you suppose that a few years ahead we want troops of
American tourists trotting out to the slums to visit the
garret wherein the Countess of Winborough nearly starved ?
I can assure you that, although I shan't be here, I object
very strongly to the possibility. Oh, Geoffrey thinks he
wouldn't mind, I dare say. I only wonder he hasn't already painted a picture of you in rags and tatters gazing
into a cupboard like old Mother Hubbard and labelled it
' Suffering Virtue.' That's his belief about you, isn't it ? "

Evarne felt her whole body tingling with hot indignation. She rose impetuously from the arm-chair, and walked
rapidly to the farther end of the room. Such was the overwhelming hatred of this man that awoke again with renewed power within her breast, that his near presence was
not to be endured.

" And isn't it true ? " she demanded, speaking quickly
and with impassioned emphasis. " Is not the very phrase
that you are mean and base enough to fling at me in derision nothing more nor less than Heaven's truth ? Is it
not entirely because I did indeed prefer my own self-respect
to ill-gotten money that there is a showplace in London
such as you describe ? That squalid room, and the cruel
ordeals I underwent within its walls, are the very witnesses
that testify to my claim to be held a good woman and a fit
wife for any man. Not a day passed without my enduring
more than you can ever realise. I was entirely without
hope for the future, yet never once—never once, I tell
you—did I regret the choice I had made.

" That grinding poverty was no shame to me," she went
on, " but a glory ; and no one knows that better than you
—you, Morris Kenyon ! And I would go back to it—
live and die in it—rather than lose my own consciousness
of virtue. You despicable coward ! how dare you come here

and taunt me with humiliations for which you alone are responsible? Everything that is degrading and wretched in my life has been brought into it by you. You indeed did your best to turn me into a woman whom a man well might fear to entrust with his name and with his honour, but that garret cries out to you and to all the world the story of your failure. It is infamous—vile—to bring forward such an acceptance of poverty as a reason for opposing your cousin's choice of me as his wife. It is infamous, and you know it."

She paused, breathing hard, still struggling with a sense of outrage. Her words had not been devoid of a certain sting, and once or twice Morris had inwardly winced beneath the onslaught. But circumstances placed every advantage—every weapon of lasting keenness—into his hands. Thus it was with unruffled complacency that he declared—

"My dear Evarne, could you not contrive to conquer this tendency to wax melodramatic? You know I dislike it, and that it is always ineffective."

He waited a minute, half expecting her to answer. But obedient to his expressed will Evarne succeeded in stifling all retorts, and remained silent. Looking at her narrowly, he could see signs of the effort she made over herself, and smiled a little before he continued—

"You force me to speak more plainly than I had hoped would be necessary. Surely you must know that I do not really need to adduce any exterior or subsequent details of your career in support of my very natural objection to this marriage. The one fact of your having been my mistress is alone all-sufficient. Understand that, please! You calmly ask me to allow Geoffrey to walk blindly into the trap you have set for him, and hurl insults at my head when I refuse! I should like to know what you expected? Did you really believe I should become a party to this deceit?"

x

But again he received no answer. Evarne simply looked at him with eyes that had grown somewhat dilated.

" I know he is absolutely without any suspicion," Morris went on, " for only yesterday the poor fool spoke of you in a strain that almost caused me to laugh in his face."

It needed such words, uttered in tones of such supreme contempt, to bring home to Evarne the way in which others must view the position in which she had placed Geoffrey. The knowledge assailed her cruelly. A physical pain, keen as a knife, shot through her forehead from one temple to the other. Crossing to the sofa, she sat down, twisted her hands tightly together, shut her eyes, and waited while the sharp pang gradually passed away.

Without turning right round, Morris was no longer able to see her. Accordingly, he got up and sank into the arm-chair she had vacated. But a minute later Evarne was on her knees by his side. The new horror that his last words had aroused, goaded her into making yet another effort at persuasion. Leaning against the soft, wide arm of the chair, she cried somewhat wildly—

" No, I haven't told him, because somehow the occasion never seemed to come until he loved me so much that I couldn't endure to speak the cruel truth. And you mustn't tell him now, Morris—oh, you mustn't! If only you will keep silent, neither he nor anybody else will ever know."

" So you flatter yourself, but these things always leak out."

" This wouldn't—how could it ? We were abroad practically all the time—no one here knows. Besides, nobody at all can be really certain. There was always the veil of a plausible explanation of our being together. You didn't pick me up from nowhere. My father left me in your charge—everyone at Heatherington knew that. I worked steadily at Art all the time. There is scarcely the remotest possibility of anyone ever trying to make mischief ; but if they did, then you and I together could absolutely defy them. We could, couldn't we ? Morris, I beg of you—I implore your mercy—keep my secret. It can be done, and I am sure—— "

But Morris interposed.

" It is not a bit of use continuing, my dear. Such a proceeding on my part would be most dishonourable towards my cousin."

" It would be the truest kindness to him. And have I no claims upon your honour ? Will it allow you to betray me without scruple ? Do you owe me no consideration whatsoever ? "

" You view everything in a totally false light, Evarne. You don't seem to understand the difference—— "

" Of course I know Geoff is infinitely more important than I am ; but it is for his sake—that's what you won't see and believe. But—— "

" Now, *ma chérie*, it's no use arguing. There is really nothing more to be said on the matter, so don't let the morning milkman find us still wasting breath. It is absolutely impossible that I can stand by and watch my cousin run blindly into a marriage with—well—with you ! I think you really owe me some thanks for not enlightening him immediately. The fact is, I've always been ridiculously yielding and considerate where you are concerned, and the thought flashed across me yesterday that you might prefer to choose your own method of breaking with him. Now, what about—about that cheque, little girl ? There's no reason why you shouldn't make an excellent marriage yet. The world is wide. They say American men make good husbands, and I will give you my blessing in anticipation."

Evarne remained silently musing for several minutes. Morris augured well from this, and did not interrupt her train of thought. At length she asked, in tones not devoid of a slight tinge of bitterness—

"And am I expected to thank you for all your kindly consideration ? "

He merely shrugged his shoulders.

Somewhat to his surprise she answered quietly—

" Very well. I do thank you for keeping my secret so long, and for your offer of money, which I can well believe you mean simply as a kindness."

" Ah ! And you decide . . . ? What are you going to do now ? "

" I am going to marry Geoffrey Danvers."

" Evarne ! "

Morris was decidedly taken aback by this calm yet resolute response. Evarne rose from her knees, and sitting down continued—

" Yes, I am going to become his wife, and you shall never persuade me into telling him what I know well must cause him such profound sorrow. Not that it would make any lasting perceptible difference if you did betray me. You have no idea—for *you* can have no comprehension—of how deeply he and I love. I don't really think it lies within your power to realise the depth—such—such sincerity of affection. I am perfectly convinced that he would remain true to me, despite a far worse tale than you could tell."

" You don't really credit that romance. This attempt to marry him with a lie upon your lips proves you to be afraid of the effects of the truth."

" You're partly right, I admit ; but I do not fear that Geoff would cease to care for me. Love is not killed so easily—don't think it."

" I know differently."

" You know absolutely nothing at all about love ! Nothing ! "

" Well, I certainly cannot prophesy upon the delicate topic of my cousin's affections with anything approaching your delightful assurance. Probably he would suggest that he should occupy the same position towards you that I did once, but I'm quite convinced—— "

" Heaven save me from ever hearing such a proposition from Geoff's lips. But I know he never would."

" As I was about to say, I am perfectly convinced that he would never marry you—would never wish to ! Good gracious ! what do you take him for ? "

Evarne gave a little cry.

" And then—and then—what then ? Think of the struggle—the bitter anguish. Morris, Morris, do realise the cruel blow it would be to him. Oh, it must be warded off ! I cannot even think of it with anything like calmness."

And indeed, even as she spoke, the growing pallor upon her cheeks supported her assertion. She rose from her chair.

" I will not have this evil deed of so-called friendship done to him. Do you hear ? You are not to tell him. If you do, I shall deny it utterly. Do you hear ? "

" I'm afraid the loudest shouting must prove as impotent as the most persuasive of tones to drown the voice of my conscience in this matter," declared Morris, looking unmistakably self-righteous. Disregarding the scornful little laugh with which this sentiment was received, he went on—

" Really, Evarne, your morals are decidedly eccentric. But you require plain speaking, don't you ? Well, then, they are absolutely infamous. Everything you say only serves to confirm my original determination."

Both his voice and his look carried conviction. Waves of wild grief, of hopeless, crushing despair, swept over Evarne's spirit, followed by the most intense hatred and bitter indignation. Her caution demolished by a sense of utter failure, she placed no restriction upon the expression of her deep-rooted resentment against this man who had ever been her evil genius. She stood close to him, one hand spasmodically gripping the back of the chair from which

she had arisen, while her eyes, always brilliant, now fairly
blazed with anger and enmity.

"I shouldn't deny it—no, indeed. But from my lips
he should learn the whole truth—the entire shameful
story. He should know how my father on his very death-
bed gave me—still a child—into the keeping of his false
friend. Surely it will be easy to realise that, when in my
hour of loss and loneliness you came professedly to help
and comfort me, I unhesitatingly entrusted myself and the
guidance of my life into your hands. Was I blameworthy
so far ? But oh, what a cruel fate for any girl ! "

"You had a very good time, my dear," interposed
Morris testily.

"A good time ! " she echoed wildly. "Oh ! You
know, and Geoffrey shall know how, from the very
first, you systematically tricked and deceived me, lying
to me about your wife, and taking me alone with you
to Naples. Will it seem strange to him to learn that in
time you were able to make me care for you as blindly as I
trusted you ? I shall tell him how you worked upon all
that was best in my nature—how you appealed to my
sympathy—how you played upon my gratitude, my affection, to gain your own vile ends. I shall tell him all your
infamy. You cast me among absolutely depraved women—
meaning me to become as they were ; for finally you bade
me sell myself for money ! Yes, you would have deliberately started me on that path which is held to be the most
degrading—the most cruel—of all the tracks that lead
hellwards. That's what you did for me, an innocent child;
and that's what you would have done, could you have had
your entire will with me ! My God, how I hate you ! and
the man who loves me shall hate you too. But for me he
shall feel only a new, a different, a more desperate love.
Now, then—send for him this very hour—do you think
there is any trace of doubt or fear in my heart ? I defy
you absolutely—you most vile creature ! Tell him—tell

him all you can, and let him judge between us. What cause have I to fear you, or anything that such as you can say ? The life you lead, the evil you do, is repulsive in the eyes of every decent-thinking man. You to talk of honour—hypocrite, hypocrite ! Having ruined first my good name, then my every happiness, when both in turn were in your power, you come now, and under the pretence of immovable devotion to honour, calmly propose to sweep away everything that makes my life worth living. You offer me money, and think I'm going to creep away overwhelmed and silenced. I have promised Geoffrey to be ever true and loyal to him ; I shall keep my word ! Send for him immediately if you desire, and let him decide between us."

Morris likewise stood up before he answered. His brows were contracted in a steady frown, yet the first thing he did was to break into a little scornful laugh. Then he spoke, and his voice was tense with anger.

" Make out as touching a legend as your imagination can devise, yet your own lips will condemn you. Would you not be forced to admit that you belonged to me willingly enough until I grew tired of you ? Be very sure that after once acknowledging that single fact, the whole of your embroideries and explanations—all your heroics— would but fall on deaf ears. I know Geoffrey a great deal better than you can do ; you've only seen one side of his nature, and that, I can understand, may easily have given you an exaggerated idea of your sway over him. Haven't you found out yet that, honourable and straightforward himself, he is impatient of deceit and trickery and double-dealing ? "

She interposed with a little cry of anguish: " Oh ! Morris ! "

Unheedingly he went on.

" Truthful, Geoffrey is out of sympathy with liars ; good-natured and quiet though he be, it is only safe to impose on

him up to a certain point. You fondly hope you could melt
the anger and repulsion your confession would inevitably
create by means of easy tears and specious pleadings. I
very much doubt it. Do you think he is totally devoid
of pride and self-respect and firmness ? What leads you
to suppose that he would be satisfied with soiled goods ?
Do you really believe that the knowledge that he is not
first with you will merely give him a sort of sentimental
heartache—more or less violent—that will pass away once
he gets used to the notion? Do you think that he would ever
forget that every kiss of his wipes off one of mine ? Do you
dare hope you would not lose all value in his estimation
once he learnt that his own cousin, for one, knows exactly
the nature of the words you speak—the look that comes
into your eyes—all your pretty little ways when you are
most deeply lost in love ? Why should you think he is
devoid of the desire for exclusive possession ? For my
part, knowing him and his high-flown ideals, I fancy he
could no longer endure the sight of you once he realised
what you have been—that there is no mystery about you
upon which he cannot gain enlightment for the asking—
that however passionately he may hold you in his arms,
others have—— ”

" Stop, Morris ! stop ! "

The words, simple in themselves, rang out wildly in
mingled entreaty and command. They were fraught with
the arresting power of a great anguish, and left behind
them a trail of dead silence, in which nerves were thrilled
and hearts beat faster.

Evarne stood motionless for a minute, both hands
stretched out in mute appeal ; then, groping her way somewhat unsteadily to the sofa, she flung herself down, hiding
her distorted face in the cushions. But Morris had not
finished yet. He too crossed the room, and stood by the
side of the prostrate figure.

" You shall never marry my cousin—understand that

once for all. Never! Do you think I shall submit
to see him sacrificed to the plots of a designing woman?
I advise you not to venture on another bout with me.
I can assure you I've retained no pleasant recollections of
your temper and your impertinence.   Now, I'll give
you some money, and in twenty-four hours you must
go. Surely you can see the game is up? Do you
agree?"

He received no verbal answer, but the head buried in the
cushions was slightly shaken.

Morris found this obstinacy exasperating beyond endurance.

"What a fool you are, Evarne!" he cried roughly.
"What do you want to stop for? You can't surely think
you will pull off that marriage? Do you fancy you could
make yourself out to be merely a sort of martyr—an interesting victim? Absurd! Don't think Geoffrey would
be so dull as not to realise that in all probability I have
already had successors."

Evarne sprang to her feet and faced him, her eyes flashing, both her hands pressed against her breast.

"I thought you had said your very worst—you merciless monster! You, who know so well why I left Paris,
almost penniless, to starve. You do not believe your own
foul words—liar, slanderer!"

He put his hand firmly on her shoulder.

"Don't talk rubbish to me. Everyone knows 'it's
easy to take a slice from a cut loaf.' If Geoffrey had not
been so ridiculously strait-laced, he too could have got
all he wanted without any of this stupid talk about marriage. At last you've forced me to tell you exactly what
I think of you, and I hope you're satisfied! You know
now what I should have to tell that poor boy, so had you
not better come to terms with me?"

Evarne clenched her teeth ferociously, and, with a low
inarticulate cry, sharply struck Morris's hand from off her

shoulder. He made an angry gesture, but returning to the arm-chair, sat down quietly. Once more she felt that blind fury, that strange blackness and loss of consciousness, stealing over her mind to which she had succumbed six years ago. But now she resisted its domination with all her power. Had she not Geoff to remember? She pressed her lips with such desperate violence against the ring he had given her, that the sharp stones inflicted a tiny cut. It was merely trifling, yet the pain served to recall her to herself to some extent. But she neither could nor would make any effort to guard her speech as she turned upon her traducer. Her very voice sounded strange to her own ears, and she herself was totally unaware of what she was about to utter until the words had already rung out.

" It's none of it true—you know it's not true—you know it! You must never repeat to Geoffrey any of the abominable things you've said this evening. It would kill me— I mean it—I have been hardly able to endure it alone! I know well you have no pity. How earnestly have I appealed to that, again and again, always vainly? You never have mercy. But—listen! Are you not afraid of going too far at last, of driving me to desperation? I warn you now. You will tell such evil truth and such malicious lies at your peril. If you do thereby succeed in separating me and Geoff, I shall have nothing left to wish for but revenge."

" You're getting theatrical again. Now, Evarne, Evarne!"

" Don't trifle! I warn you, it will be wiser of you to stay your hand. If you do finally ruin my life—if you do thus remorselessly torture Geoff for our ill-deeds—you'll have done the worst for me that lies within the power of man. You will have destroyed all fear of any further suffering that Heaven or earth could inflict. I tell you I should be mad, and sooner or later you should be repaid. Yes, I warn you, Lord Winborough, it will be safer for you to avoid setting loose the devil that is in me. You guard

my secret—that's all I ask. I've hated you for years;
now my loathing of you is nigh as strong as is my love for
Geoff. I'm not the sort of woman to be defied with im-
punity. If you make me your active enemy I shall stop
at nothing. You can believe that, can't you? I would
shoot you like a dog, or stab you in the dark and glory in
it, caring less than nothing for consequences."

Morris was certainly no coward, yet he quailed before
the white, menacing face, in which two blazing eyes shone
like beacon-fires, sending forth their warning of danger.
He could well believe not only that Evarne at the moment
fully meant all she said, but that she might indeed act
upon her avowed intention in the future. Inwardly curs-
ing the bad luck that had led him ever to become entangled
with this resolute and determined little fury, he said,
without the least outward sign of apprehension—

"So you are actually threatening me! You must be
mad already!"

He crossed the room and took up his hat, but Evarne
barred his further progress. Flinging herself upon her
knees, she clung to the door-handle with a tenacious grip,
and made a final frantic appeal.

"You mustn't go—Morris, you mustn't go. I shall
keep you here. You're going to Geoffrey now—I know it.
You shall not. You can't drag me away from this door,
and I shall stay here until you promise not to go to him.
Oh, you can strike me, or anything you like—I don't care,
but I shan't move. Listen, Morris—do listen to me. I
implore you—spare me. Oh, I'm afraid—I'm afraid of
the future and what may come. I didn't realise before
how absolutely unendurable it would be for Geoff to know.
You mustn't tell him—I'd sooner die straight away—
now—and so keep my secret. Morris, Morris, think of all
I've endured, and spare me further—spare me this—spare
Geoff—spare yourself! What can I say—what can I do?
Oh, Heaven help me!"

A protracted silence ensued, in which Evarne made tremendous mental efforts to regain complete control over herself. She felt it to be necessary, and difficult though the task was in such a limited space of time, she practically succeeded. At all events she conquered outward and apparent calm, and rose from her knees, though still standing with her back pressed against the door. When she spoke next it was in strangely smooth and even tones, and with a look that was merely questioning.

"Tell me truly, Morris, do you dislike Geoff? Do you not feel resentful because he is so much younger than you are, and is to come after you in place of a son? No one can possibly realise more clearly than you do what it must mean to a man to learn about the woman he desired to marry such a story as you have to tell about me, yet you will not hold your peace. No law of right or justice can defend your thus forcing Geoff to share the misery consequent upon our past sin. You must surely have some reason for wishing him ill?"

"On the contrary, my chief object is to save him from the protracted miseries of an unhappy marriage, and incidentally to guard against his son—my future successor—being born of an unsuitable mother."

"I see. *Noblesse oblige.* Do you mean to say that if Geoff and I had been already married before you returned to England, you would not have remained silent?"

"It is scarcely worth discussing an imaginary case, is it?"

"But tell me."

"My dear girl, I don't know! Possibly. Indeed, I may even say probably. As a matter of fact, I'm really attached to the boy. If the evil had been beyond prevention I certainly might have seen fit to keep your secret. Even now, since my only aim is to prevent your marriage with him, if you prefer to go away without making any explanation, I give you my word that he shall never know details."

" Morris, Morris, must you tell him anyhow ? Is it quite inevitable ? "

" Yes, he must be told—that is to say, the engagement must be broken off. If you prefer to do the job yourself, by all means let it be so."

" You won't go to him to-night ? "

" I will say nothing until this time to-morrow. Perhaps you will have made up your mind to take the right course yourself before then. I'm sorry, but that's the limit of what I can do for you."

" No, no, give me longer," she implored.

Her lips quivered, causing Morris to fear that this period of calmness might not be long sustained.

" Well, I'll give you two days," he agreed. " But it cannot possibly be allowed to continue longer than that. That's forty-eight hours too long."

" Is that a promise ? "

" Yes, yes. Now stand aside from the door, there's a good girl."

As she obeyed silently, he stepped out into the passage.

" Go to bed, *ma chérie*," he advised. " Have a good night. You'll feel better in the morning."

Impatiently she signed to him to be gone, then flung herself into her favourite chair, rested her elbows on one of its arms, and supported her chin on her hands. Thus she sat motionless, gazing fixedly into vacancy with hard, dry eyes, forgetful or regardless of Morris's presence in the open doorway.

He lingered a few moments, looking with mingled feelings at her now expressionless but perfect-featured face and graceful form. But she neither spoke nor glanced in his direction, and very soon the street door had closed behind him with a final bang.

CHAPTER XXXVIII

CONFIDENCES

TIME passed, and still Evarne sat motionless—thinking, thinking. In the first dreadful minutes of solitude she had been conscious of very little save cruel, crushing despair, the most abject hopelessness. Her one other clearly defined idea had been that she must not, dare not, allow the wild paroxysm of anguish that was rending her brain, to get the mastery over her will-power. Fiercely resolved not to lose self-control even for a moment, she forced herself to sit calm and motionless, to drive back tears, to stifle sobs, groans, cries. And in time this resolutely simulated composure became very nearly genuine. Gradually she found herself growing able to think rationally, not desperately. Thus there was some chance for a practical idea—an inspiration—to evolve itself from out the rapid progression of her thoughts.

She was possessed of a quiet obstinacy that would not —that could not—acknowledge final defeat so long as the most shadowy possibility of ultimate success remained. The feeblest glimmer of hope was sufficient to support her courage, her energies. Now, although the end appeared to be so near, although she was faced by obstacles that certainly looked insurmountable, she could not bring herself to submit with meekness and resignation to what so surely seemed to be written in her fate.

Thus, still rebellious, she sat thinking, thinking. But no plan of possible action occurred to her mind. What could be done in two days to still a man's tongue, when prayers and entreaties and threats had all alike failed absolutely ? The only method yet untried was that of bribery, and there she was a bankrupt. She had nothing to offer—absolutely no inducement to hold out.

Slowly but surely the conviction forced itself upon her calmer reflection that she could indeed do no more ; that she was hopelessly in Morris's power. She felt herself enveloped by a fresh access of despair. What a dire misfortune—what a fearsome calamity—that he should have come upon the scene just at this crisis. He had declared almost with certainty that had he found her already his cousin's wife he would have held his peace. Why, oh why, had he not been kept out of her path for two short months longer—just until she was indeed safely married ?

Suddenly she started to her feet, her eyes glistening, her expression eager and alert. At length a light shone in the dense gloom—in the tangled jungle a path had been found.

At this moment Philia was heard opening the street door. The old woman made straight for the sitting-room, declaring as she came—

" Edie Gordon didn't know what pattern—— "

The words died on her lips as she beheld Evarne.

" My gosh, whatever made yer dress up pretty like that, to spend the evenin' alone ? " Then she added in a tone of sudden suspicion : " Seems to me there's somethin' goin' on in this 'ere 'ouse what I don't know of ! What 'ave I bin and done, to be kept in the dark about everythin' like this for ? "

" You shan't be any longer, Philia. After your supper I'm going to tell you everything."

" I'll buck up, then. ' A full stummick maketh a wise 'ead and a kind 'eart '—Shakespeare."

Ere long she had finished her meal, and was ensconced in the arm-chair. Evarne drew up a footstool and sat down, resting against the old woman's knee. But she remained without speaking. Once or twice she half started upon her task, but the words died on her lips.

Philia at length broke the silence.

" Dearie, I'm almost old enough to be your grandmother, but for all that we're jist real pals, ain't we ? Remember, pals can always trust each other, and nothin' ever makes any real difference between 'em."

Thus encouraged, Evarne took the plunge and told the story of her life. When she had finished, she asked pleadingly—

" You don't mind ? You're not very disappointed in me, are you, Philia ? I did care for him, really and truly I did."

Her eyes were downcast, the tone of her voice was full of anxiety. The old woman's response took the form of a query.

" What do yer expect me to say to yer ? "

Evarne shook her head somewhat hopelessly.

" I don't know," she murmured.

" Can't yer look me straight in the face ? I can't answer proper-like if yer won't."

Evarne's mind was far too entirely taken up with deeper thoughts, with future schemes, for her to be really overweighed with embarrassment before Philia. Without any effort she raised her head instantly. The necessity of an upturned face for an answer was then made clear. The old woman bent forward and kissed her straight on the lips —a noisy, unabashed kiss.

" I might think badly of some gals, Evarne, but you— why, no matter who was to tell me yer was a bad lot, I'd say ' Beggin' yer pardin', I knows 'er too well ! She's real good ! ' "

Evarne threw her arms impulsively around her old friend's neck, and murmured her thanks.

" But listen," she continued, settling herself down again

upon the footstool. " What I've told you is only the cause of my present trouble."

But almost in the same instant Philia had exclaimed—
" My gosh, what about Mr. Danvers ? "

" That's it—that's it ! I haven't told him, and I never mean to, never, never ! "

" And yer'd be a regular fool if yer did," declared this worldly-minded counsellor.

" But—oh, it's too dreadful ; it's too horrid ! "

" Hush, hush ! Don't git excited."

Evarne waited a minute, then went on quietly enough to relate the whole of her doubts and anxieties.

" At first I was in despair, as you may imagine," she concluded ; " but now I've got a fresh idea in my mind, and I want your help."

Philia rubbed her hands together with evident satisfaction. She had flung herself whole-heartedly on her pal's side in this affair.

" If we do succeed," went on Evarne, " I shall owe all my happiness to you, and so will Geoffrey, though he won't know it. I shall be grateful to you for ever and ever, and I shall look after you all your life, Philia. Now, listen carefully. Morris said that if he had found me already his cousin's wife—if our marriage had been an accomplished fact—then—very likely—he would of his own accord have remained silent forever concerning what he knows. He entirely repudiated the idea that his determination to betray me is prompted by any spite or hatred. As it is, he has promised to hold his peace until Wednesday evening. Very well, before that time I mean to be Geoffrey's wife."

" Goodness gracious to me, what a notion ! "

" It's absolutely my last resource. It's my one chance ; my only hope. I shall persuade Geoff to take me abroad immediately, so that Morris cannot straightway tell him my secret in a sudden outburst of rage. If he writes, I shall see that Geoff doesn't get the letter. Oh, I know it's leading me through vile deceitful tracks, but having started, I must go on. But I wish I'd never started, Philia. That's Heaven's truth. I wish I'd never started! Ah, well! Besides—once I am Geoffrey's wife, the keeping of this secret becomes a matter of life or death to me."

" But if the snake chose to tell after yer was safely married, 'e couldn't do no 'arm then, could 'e ? "

" No harm ? Oh, Philia ! If Geoffrey once reproached me for entrapping him—if I heard him regret his marriage— if he ever expressed half a wish that he could be free again, then, why then, there would be but one course open to me. I should kill myself."

Philia started.

" Don't talk of sich a thing," she almost wailed ; " don't plan it in cold blood like that. It's mad and wicked."

" Who says it's wicked ? "

" Why, everybody knows it is."

" ' There's nothing either good or bad, but thinking makes it so.' Did you ever hear that before ? ' Everybody knows,' forsooth ! Oh, Philia, how can you be so blind ! Surely it's perfectly obvious that it would be the one and only right course. As far as honour goes I should have no choice. Don't you believe it's necessarily wicked to kill one's self. Sometimes the weak—the cowardly—the really despicable thing to do is to cling to life. Oh, I'm beginning to hate myself—I'm being dragged through the mud and grimed almost beyond my own recognition. There, don't look at me like that. But you mustn't think I'm so infamous as to be planning to use Geoff's blind love— his noble, unquestioning trust in me—as the very means by which to fetter him in bonds that would remain unbreakable, even though they might suddenly become repulsive to him. It is because power lies in these hands of mine— soft and slender though they are—see them," and as she held them out and eyed them askance, they shook like aspen leaves. " It is because I can cut asunder all earthly ties between us, and set him free, that I dare expose him to the risk. It's no use, Philia. I can't love in a sane, temperate, moderate sort of manner—I can't do it, I tell you ! I love Geoff so much more than myself—so infinitely much more—that life or death for me seems scarcely worth a thought."

No words came to the old woman ; not even Shakespeare was able to suggest to her any comfort for this trembling girl, gliding so swiftly and surely into deceit and sin.

" I needn't have told you of what I intend to do in the event of Morris's betraying me after my marriage, though I shall tell him," Evarne went on ; " but I—I—couldn't bear that you should misjudge me, dear. It would be dreadful to me to think that you believed I was merely planning all this from an unscrupulous desire to make my own position secure at all costs."

" As if I'd think anything of the sort ! "

" Well, if you did, I for one couldn't blame you. I know it must look like it. Oh, Philia, I'm miserable at what I'm doing," Evarne cried, knitting her white brow. " If anyone had told me a week ago that I should sink to deliberate scheming to make Geoff marry me quickly, and that I was seriously proposing to watch his correspondence, I should—there, I am mad, perhaps ! I could almost wish to believe it. There is no truth, no honour in me ! Oh, Philia, Philia, how I hope my dead father cannot see what I am doing ! "

She shuddered, and buried her face convulsively in her friend's lap. The old woman, full of pity, passed her hand over the thick locks.

" Make up yer mind once and for all, my pet. Think about it well. Don't go and do what yer will be sorry for."

The head was lifted immediately, defiantly.

" Oh, I know what I am going to do. I have done with thinking. I am going to marry Geoff."

" But 'ow are yer goin' to work the trick, so sudden like, without 'im wonderin' what's in yer mind ? "

" That's where you've got to help me.　I don't see quite how to do it alone.　With your aid it will be wickedly easy for me to—to deceive him, because he trusts me so entirely.　Ah well !　Now listen to my plan　.　.　. "

Tired of her low seat, she drew up a chair close to Philia.

Long they sat into the night, arranging, discussing, even rehearsing what was to be done on the morrow.　At length they separated, but slumber was not for Evarne. No sooner had she laid her weary head upon the pillow than there came to her from the distance the steady throb, throb of machinery.

" What can that be ? " she mused fretfully.　" There's no factory about here, and if there were, why should it be working in the middle of the night ? "　She rose up on her elbow to listen ; the sound ceased.　Once more she sought repose ; the steady, distant beating recommenced.　" I couldn't sleep at the best of times through that persistent noise," she sighed.

Then she seemed to hear cautious footsteps within her room.　For a moment every muscle of her body contracted with terror, and the thud of the distant engines increased in volume tenfold.　Starting up, she struck a match.　The room was empty.　As she lay down once more she realised the meaning of all these strange, inexplicable sounds. Those steps, that dull, steady throbbing, all originated within her own tortured brain.

Repeatedly through that night of wakefulness she could have believed she heard movements, even whispers, within the room.　She lay on the borderland of slumber, against her will composing endless appeals to Geoff, begging for mercy, for forgiveness, for continued love, going over and over the pleas she might have uttered to Morris but had neglected.

" If I could sleep—oh, if I could only sleep ! " she cried wearily.

But the day broke without her having won oblivion for a single minute.

CHAPTER XXXIX

EVIL, THAT GOOD MAY COME

THE morning dawned radiantly clear, and hot to sultriness. Evarne dressed leisurely, and by nine o'clock, far from being at the studio, was still toying with her breakfast. Her magnificent health saved her from looking as exhausted as the sleepless night and the nerve-strain of the last few days would well have justified. Indeed, with a hectic flush upon her cheek, and eyes supernaturally brilliant, any untrained observer would have adjudged her a fit model for the goddess Hygeia herself.

" Do try and eat somethin'," persuaded Philia anxiously. " Goodness knows when you last 'ad a decent square meal."

" I don't feel that I can, and what's more, I can't stop looking at it any longer," declared the girl as she rose from the table. " Those poor young men will be thinking I'm not coming again."

And indeed at the studio everything did seem to be thoroughly disorganised.

" Well, we have done a fine lot of work these last few days," remarked Jack disconsolately.

But Pallister was in high spirits. He had seen Maudie Meridith on the previous evening, and, moved by his earnest reproaches, she had undertaken to do her level best to come this very morning to give him a first sitting for her portrait. Thus he answered Jack's complaining growl with light-hearted *insouciance*.

" Oh, well, we can't all keep our noses eternally to the

grindstone like you do, old chap. I think we're getting along splendidly."

But Jack was not to be thus pacified.

" I don't want to waste this morning. Do you think Miss Stornway will be coming, Geoff ? "

" Surely," rejoined that young man, turning from the open window from whence he had been watching the passers-by in the street below. " She would have sent a message, as she did yesterday, if she still felt too unwell."

And in a very few minutes his faith was justified ; Evarne appeared at the farther end of the street. He watched her as she drew near, noting how she showed graceful and dignified amid the crowd. Although the studio was on the third floor, the summer air was so clear that, as she drew nearer, he could see her features quite distinctly. Some attraction drew her gaze upwards, and she waved her hand in greeting, whereupon he ran downstairs and met her at the garden gate.

Her dress fitted exquisitely over her lovely figure ; it was of pink cambric, made according to her individual fancy in costume. Its rich hue emphasised her dark eyes and flawless complexion as none other could have done, while her simple straw hat was wreathed with blush roses. Geoff had never yet beheld her clad from head to foot in shades of pink, and thus arrayed, apart from all question of personal affection, she must have been a sheer delight to any artist's eye.

" I'm afraid I'm dreadfully late," she said apologetically to Jack and Pallister on gaining the studio. " Please forgive me, and you shall just see how quickly I can get into those Greek robes when I like."

" You must sit down first and have a rest after your walk," insisted Geoff, while Pallister declared gaily—

" Don't trouble about me. You're going to have a rival this morning."

" A rival ! This is very serious."

"Such a pretty one too."

"Really? Who is she?"

"Ha, ha! You'll see when she comes."

He jumped down from the studio flight of steps on which he had been perched, skipped gaily across the floor, and leant perilously far out of the low window.

"How excited that baby is," said Geoff, smiling indulgently. "He expects Miss Meridith to give him a sitting to-day. Now, come here, sit down by me and rest. Could you eat some of thòse cherries?"

Evarne consented to try, and took her seat on the divan beside Geoff, the plate on her lap. Pallister glanced at the little group.

"I say, Jack," declared the wise youth, "guess we're not exactly indispensable to the consumption of those cherries. Come down to the garden and let's have a smoke till Maudie arrives."

"I was thinking of sketching Geoff and Miss Stornway as they sat together there," said Jack simply. But since Pallister received this proposition with a hearty burst of laughter, he meekly wended his way downstairs, still complaining under his breath at the valuable hours he was losing.

"You're sure you feel quite well again?" demanded Geoff for about the fifth time, reading Evarne's face with an anxious, not over-satisfied glance. "You don't look quite the same as usual somehow, sweetest."

"You're fanciful," and the bright eyes were flashed upon him reassuringly. "I'm quite well and strong, and ready to face the world."

"That's good hearing. You'd laugh at me if you knew how I've been worrying about you. I vow I lay awake half the night thinking of you."

"Don't be so proud about it, for I did exactly the same thing for you. At least, to be exact, I sat up talking to old Philia about Geoff and all his faults and virtues. She really is a good old soul, and has taken quite a fancy to you."

"And since it seems that her presence in your little home is essential to my being allowed there, I have, perforce, taken quite a liking to her. Good thing it's a mutual affection, eh?"

"Isn't it indeed? Well, to-night sees the end of her sittings, so you will be able to come quite often if you care to. To start with, I herewith formally invite you to supper to-morrow night. Miss Evarne Stornway requests the pleasure of Mr. Geoffrey Danvers' company at supper to-morrow night, at seven-thirty. R.S.V.P."

"Mr. Danvers has much pleasure in accepting Miss Stornway's kind invitation for Tuesday evening," returned Geoff with mock solemnity.

"Right!" laughed Evarne, clapping her hands together gleefully. "You shall come out into the kitchen and help me make pancakes. I'm really quite adorable then. You will just love me when you see me making pancakes."

She tossed back her head and dangled a cherry into her open mouth. Geoff's reply was interrupted by the sound of stumbling footsteps mounting the stairs.

"Talking of angels," cried Evarne, as a panting figure leaned against the doorway. "Why, Philia, what do you want?"

"H'excuse my intrudin'," commenced the old woman. "Two young gentlemen sittin' in the garden told me to come right up, and I should find the studio at the top of the stairs, and the door standin' open. I couldn't lose me way if I tried, they said; and sure enough I'm 'ere."

"Then come in and sit down, Mrs. Harbert," said Geoff. "I hope nothing's the matter?"

"I'm quite well, thankin' you, sir, and the same to you. I wanted to consult Evarne on a matter of great himportance. I've got to decide in a 'urry, or I wouldn't 'ave hintruded."

"Well, here is Evarne. I'll leave you for a while."

"Don't go, Geoff," said the girl, laying her hand on his arm. "I don't suppose it's any great and wondrous secret, is it, Philia?"

"Not a bit of it. Jist after you'd gorn comes a letter for me from that very nice gentleman, Mr. Topham—the same as I sat for six months ago as the Countess o' Suffolk, saying as 'ow she wouldn't 'ave 'er 'ead cut off."

"I remember."

"Well, now—well. What do you think? You'd never guess! 'E wants me to go to Scotland for two 'ole months to pose for 'im out of doors all among the gorse and 'eather and 'eath! It's a bit o' kindness on Mr. Topham's part, for I s'pose there's elderly ladies in Scotland 'e could paint, but 'e allus was good to me. I'm to telegraph me answer and go on Thursday mornin'. I'd like to go ever so much—wouldn't I jist, my gosh!—but I'm worryin' about 'ow you'd git on without me, Evarne."

"Oh, you ought not to miss such a splendid offer. Let me see the letter, may I?"

After glancing through its contents the girl handed it back.

"She really ought to go, Geoff, oughtn't she? Mr. Topham offers very generous terms, including the fare both ways. She needs a change. Don't you, Philia? It will be splendid for you to get out of London this hot weather. I only wish a holiday could be managed for poor little Evarne. Yes, I decide for you—you must accept."

"That's all very fine for me," demurred the old woman : "but what about you, left all alone in the 'ouse?"

"Ah, indeed!" demanded Geoff. "What will you do?"

"That's jist what I was wonderin' as I came along 'ere," declared Philia. "Comin' 'ome tired as she does, 'ardly able to stand sometimes—pore child—and not a soul there to say a word to 'er, or git 'er so much as a cup o' tea!

I'm afraid I ought to tell Mr. Topham as 'ow I can't come."

Evarne did not answer for a few seconds.

" It does sound a touching picture, certainly. You make me quite sorry for myself," she confessed. Then with a sudden forced renewal of brightness : " But there, it can't be helped. Any number of models live alone always. Of course Philia must go to Scotland, and I mustn't be selfish and lazy."

" It ain't a question of bein' jist selfish and lazy," rejoined the old woman rather testily. " I ain't sure it would be right of me to go gallawantin' jist now. 'Twould be different if yer was quite well and strong. But I ask yer to answer honest. Ain't this 'ot weather upsettin' yer ? Ain't yer bein' overworked or somethin' ? She 'arf fainted again last night, sir. She ain't so strong by 'alf as she likes to make out. I didn't ought to go, I knows it, though I do want to."

" Evarne, you told me you felt better," cried Geoff in mingled reproach and alarm.

" So I am this morning," she rejoined, smiling at him. " Now, you run off home, Philia, and think about packing."

But the old woman shook her head, lingered and looked at Geoff with eyes full of doubt and anxiety.

" Do you think I ought to leave 'er lonely, sir ? "

He was decidedly uneasy at the idea.

" I don't like the notion—really I don't. Look here, can't you get a servant ? "

Evarne smiled again, this time somewhat ruefully.

" He does think we're rich, doesn't he, Philia ? Dear Geoff, to speak frankly, I can't afford it."

He put his hand on her arm.

" Darling, surely you will let me see to that for you ? "

She shook her head with unhesitating decision.

" I couldn't possibly let you ever give me money."

At length Philia saw an opening, and no alert lawyer could have darted at it more promptly.

"Until 'e is yer 'usband, yer mean. Then he'll 'ave a
right to, won't 'e ? "

"Of course, everything will be different then," she assented, with a swift, shy glance at her lover.

"But, you dear little silly," he rejoined tenderly, "it's
only a question of two or three weeks at the very outside.
What real difference can it possibly make ? "

"It does—I feel it does. Please don't press the point.
Now, Geoff, remember I'm always right. You owned that
yesterday evening."

"Yes, and what did I tell you ? Have you forgotten ?
That you would have to marry me all the sooner on account
of this terrible correctness. Now, then, how much sooner
does this fresh example bring it ? "

Here Mrs. Harbert chipped in again, desperately seizing
the bull by the horns.

"It's a real pity yer 'aven't bin engaged a week or two
longer, both of yer. Then I'd say, git married at once—
to-morrow—to-day, and let Evarne 'ave a 'usband to look
after 'er 'enceforward."

Geoff's eyes brightened.

"I say—— " he was commencing, but Evarne interrupted in tones of obvious annoyance.

"You ought not to say things like that, Philia. It's
very inconsiderate."

But the culprit was in no ways disconcerted.

"Lor, she's a regular babby," she declared laughing.
"The very idea o' really gettin' spliced makes 'er that
bashful."

And sure enough the colour on Evarne's cheeks had
perceptibly deepened.

"Jist look if she ain't gorn as red as a radish," continued Mrs. Harbert. "And all along o' the idea of a
weddin' ! "

"It's not that," declared Evarne with energy; "it
was your silly suggestion of getting married at once—

without any delay—that vexed me. You oughtn't to say things of that sort. You're excited about this Scotch tour, you stupid old Philia. As if people ever rushed off and got married at twenty-four hours' notice ! And for no better reason than that I run the risk of feeling lonely and unhappy in an empty house. Bless the darling, she shan't have any of the hardships of life—no, she shan't ! You've got no right to mortify me so ; it's horrid of you, I'm really vexed with you."

She moved away, and sat down with her back to Philia, tapping the floor angrily with the tip of her pretty pink shoe. The old woman shrugged her shoulders and appealed to Geoff in decidedly nettled tones.

" Mr. Danvers, sir, am I a fool or is she ? One of us is, that's certain, and though I asks yer which it is, I knows without bein' told. Maybe I 'ave taken liberties. I was only jokin'. Still, it's unkind o' Evarne to talk to me like that, ain't it ? I'd better make up me mind not to go away, and 'ave done with all talk. ' Lonely and un'appy ! ' Why, it might be the death of 'er—that's what it might be. Yes, my beauty, you've chucked yerself downstairs in a faint once in yer life. You'll be doin' it again."

Evarne glanced over her shoulder.

" Rubbish ! I was ill then."

" So yer are now ; what's the good o' denyin' it ? You'll take a header over the banisters one fine evenin' and cut yer 'ead open on the floor, and it will bleed and bleed and bleed, and no one will know. You'll lie there all night, and in the mornin' you'll be dead—a corpse— d'you hear ?—cold and stiff—and all the howlin' in the world won't make yer alive agin."

Evarne laughed at this lurid visionary tableau, and recovered her temper.

" Why, what a very vivid imagination—— " she was commencing.

But Geoff interrupted. He had been rapidly turning

over in his mind this startling idea of an immediate wedding,
and found it rose-coloured. Not only did he long for the
day that should give him the woman he loved, but he fore-
saw that, by his marriage being once put beyond the pale
of argument, he would probably avoid a great deal of useless discussion and consequent ill-feeling between himself
and his cousin. Except Winborough, he had no relations
sufficiently near to feel themselves aggrieved at not having
been confided in about the matter—and indeed when
were aunts or cousins ever seriously considered in such a
case ? The one objection to this unconventional suddenness was that it might be more pleasant for Evarne not to
have had her wedding in any way apparently hurried
or peculiar. But now other circumstances seemed to
counter-balance this really very small and indefinite
objection.

Thus his meditations were not long protracted, and he
interrupted Evarne's sentence upon sudden impulse.

" Mrs. Harbert is quite right. It would not be at all safe
for you to be living absolutely alone while you're liable to
these horrible fainting attacks. Dearest—dearest—marry
me to-morrow and give me the right to really look after
you and care for you. Please don't shake your head.
Obviously it is in every way best and advisable. Why do
you hesitate ? We don't want a smart wedding or anything alarming of that sort, do we ? You do care for me,
really and truly, don't you, and you believe that you will
be safe and happy with me ? Mrs. Harbert, you've had
a really brilliant idea—— "

" Lor, sir, I only spoke in fun. I never thought of your
takin' it serious-like."

" But you see now, don't you—don't you, Evarne—
that to procure a special licence and get married to-morrow
morning, without any unnecessary preparation, will save a
world of annoyance and anxiety ? My dear one, do think
how I should worry about you. Besides—besides—the

truth is, I want to feel that you are mine beyond the possibility of your changing your mind."

" You think I might, then ? "

" Well, I don't mean that exactly. There, I don't want to have to think about it at all ; I want to make our marriage a fact. I want to be secure of you. Our circumstances are somewhat peculiar. We have neither of us got any relations we need to think of ; we've only got each other in the whole world, Evarne. Why should we run any risks ? Dear one, dear love, be persuaded. Say ' yes,' and you shall never, never regret it."

He spoke in tones soft and coaxing enough to melt a heart of stone, yet he received no answer, either by word or look. Somewhat puzzled, Philia broke the protracted silence.

" Yer can't love 'im as much as yer told me, or you'd be 'appy at the idea of callin' 'im 'usband."

But Evarne heeded her not. She was overwhelmed with shame at the ease with which her own plot had succeeded. Where she was concerned, Geoff was absolutely devoid of the faintest suspicions of any description. The bare possibility of trickery, of prearrangement or of falsehood having any part in Philia's unexpected visit to the studio, obviously never entered his mind. It was enough to him to be made to see that his ' Sweet Lady's ' material well-being would be benefited by her becoming his wife at once, and immediately his whole desire was to persuade her to this course of action. Knowing that practically every word she had spoken that morning had been uttered with the full intention of deceiving—as part of a deliberate scheme—the perfect confidence he had in her integrity and honour, his loyal, generous, and complete trust, were to her a bitter reproach. It stabbed her conscience, and she stood silent and abashed before him.

But far was it from her thoughts to waver in her purpose at this eleventh hour. Raising her head, she looked for a

minute full into Geoff's earnest grey eyes, and within her
heart she again registered a vow to put his happiness, his
welfare, first and foremost now and in the future.   These
minutes of apparent hesitation were sacred, and her expression was intense and solemn as she replied in a slightly
quivering voice—

"My own beloved, I am yours, absolutely and without
restriction.   You are to decide my life, my actions; to
guide my very thoughts as is most pleasing to you.   Everything shall be done exactly as you desire."

Entirely oblivious of Mrs. Harbert's presence he thanked
her by kisses.

"I'll telegraph to Mr. Topham, then," interposed the
overlooked Philia after a minute.   "I'll tell 'im I'm comin'
right enough.   Now, 'owever will I find out what train
to git or what station to go from, or anything else?"

Evarne came back to earth.

"Ask Geoff to look it up in the time-table for you," she
suggested.

"Certainly.   Where is it you want to go to?"

"Saint—Saint—it's Saint somewhere," and Philia again
peered into her letter.   "St. Andrews."

As the young man left the studio to find the time-table,
she came close to Evarne, a broad smile of triumph on her
genial countenance.

"Well, now, ain't I bin and gorn and done well?   Ain't I
a fine hactress?   Didn't the stage lose a shinin' light when
I took up Hart as a profession?   Ain't I got a fine inven-
tion too?   Didn't I ought to 'ave written books?   Ain't
I been wonderful sharp?   Pity I ain't a beastly lawyer."

Evarne seized both the old woman's hands in a somewhat
frantic grip.

"Oh, my dear, I shall never forget what you've done for
me.   I'm saved.   Thank God—thank God!"

"Keep quiet, duckie.   It's not quite done yet.   You've
got to prevent 'im from tellin' the snake till after it's over."

" I know, but Heaven is on my side."

In a few moments Geoff returned with a slip of paper in his hand.

" See here, I've written down times and station, so you'll have no difficulty. We must go away for a honeymoon, mustn't we, Evarne ? "

" Of course. I shouldn't feel that I'd been legally married without that," she declared promptly and gladly.

" You'll help her pack, then, and look after her generally, won't you, Mrs. Harbert ? Do you know of anything she wants ? If so, tell me."

" There's nothin' as I knows of as won't wait until Thursday, when yer can git it for 'er yerself," declared Philia.

" Please don't talk about me as if I wasn't present," remonstrated Evarne. " You run away now, Philia. By the way, Geoff, you must come to supper with me to-night. It will be the last real opportunity I shall have of playing genuine hostess to you. Think of that ! "

He naturally agreed, whereupon Evarne and Philia indulged in a brief whispered debate concerning the *menu* for the evening meal. At length the old dame took her departure, thoroughly well satisfied with her own hitherto unsuspected cleverness.

CHAPTER XL

A FRESH COMPLICATION

IMMEDIATELY they were alone Geoff seized Evarne by both hands, and holding her at arm's length, surveyed her from head to foot, as if for the first time.

" Evarne, Evarne ! to think that by to-morrow evening you will be my wife ! Can you realise it ? I hardly can."

" I'm not going to try," she asserted. " It doesn't do to make too certain of anything in this world. Perhaps we shan't be able to get a special licence."

" Oh, it's quite simple. A friend of mine was married by that means. We have to make solemn affidavits that there is no legal impediment. Then it is essential that the ceremony shall take place in the parish where one of us has lived for a certain length of time. You won't mind being married in church ? "

" Oh no."

" Besides getting the licence, then, all we have to do is to arrange with a clergyman, and there need not be an hour's delay. It's not even necessary to heed the canonical hours. I'd better go down to Doctors Commons almost immediately and see about it."

Just then a girl's bright laugh fell upon their ears, footsteps were heard mounting the stairs, and in a minute Maudie Meridith, Jack and Pallister entered the studio. The little lady, though somewhat breathless, was in high spirits. She evidently looked upon this visit quite in the light of an adventure.

" Only fancy my getting here safe and sound, Mr. Danvers ! " she exclaimed in her gay voice. " It's just like a novelette, isn't it ? "

Pallister speedily introduced the two young women to one another. Although it was tacitly recognised that Geoff's engagement was not to be made public knowledge just yet, Pallister had not been able to resist the temptation of relating to Maudie the events that had arisen from Winborough's visit to the studio on Monday afternoon. She therefore gazed with the keenest interest upon the beautiful model who was one day to become a countess, and greeted her with the utmost cordiality and sweetness.

" Did you find it awfully difficult to escape by yourself ? " inquired Pallister, stumbling over the stand of his easel as he rushed about making final preparations.

" It was fairly simple. I was so frightened at breakfast, for auntie suddenly announced she was going out somewhere or other—anyhow, she suggested that I should go with her. I was dreadfully upset, for I couldn't think of any reasonable excuse for refusing."

" But an idea came at last ? "

" Fortunately there was no need. Auntie, who was opening her letters, came to one from Madame Constantia, her dressmaker, saying she should call this morning. So I was able to slip away easily—lucky, wasn't it ? "

" Rather ! Now let's pose you for this wondrous picture."

After many different attempts, he turned to his friends with a satisfied air : " I think that's perfect. What do you say, you others ? "

Public opinion decided that the model's left arm had better be placed negligently over the arm of the chair.

" Ah, that's a great improvement," confessed the artist.

" It can't possibly be altered for the better, I'm sure."

" How am I to pose my eyes ? " inquired the docile model.

"That doesn't matter at present. Now, keep quite still."

Holding a stick of charcoal at arm's-length, Pallister unconsciously put on a stern and impressive frown as he commenced to put leading lines upon his big new canvas.

Geoff and Evarne once again sat down side by side on the divan, and in low tones proceeded to discuss the prosaic business arrangements for the eventful morrow. Evarne did not disguise her anxiety to leave England immediately on the completion of the wedding ceremony, and thus Geoff had now to make arrangements for the journey, find out times of trains and boats, take tickets and telegraph to hotels, as well as procure the licence and arrange with a clergyman.

The discussion of the many details that had to be considered occupied some time, and at length the silence of the room, broken only by the indistinct murmurs of this inaudible conversation, became boring in the extreme to Miss Maudie.

"I wish I could see you working as I sit, Frankie; but of course that isn't possible," she said somewhat plaintively.

"I'm afraid not," agreed Pallister. "But you must have plenty of rests, and then you can see how I'm getting on, though you know it's never very pleasant to show work in its early stages to any but a fellow-artist."

"But won't you do better than ever, knowing that I'm going to look at it? Am I not an inspiration?"

"Of course you are, but you'll see yourself looking like a nightmare, with black eyes and yellow cheeks and so on. But don't worry about that. It's only at first. I feel that in the end I'm going to make this a veritable masterpiece."

After a very few more minutes' silence she spoke again.

"What fun this is! I'm not really tired yet, and I've been sitting a long time already, haven't I?"

" Oh Maudie, hardly that."

" What, haven't I ? Dear me, I thought I had."

" Don't wriggle your head, there's an angel."

" Was I wriggling ? " inquired the victim. " I'm so sorry ; my neck felt stiff."

" You must have a rest, then."

" Oh no, thank you. It doesn't matter. I can bear it."

But the tones of resignation were too touching. Pallister laid down his brushes.

" Come along. Don't let yourself get thoroughly tired, or you'll not want to come again. Besides, models sometimes faint if they have to go on posing after they are tired out. You ask Miss Stornway if you don't believe me."

Evarne corroborated Pallister's assertion, though in her heart she did not think there was much danger of Maudie collapsing yet awhile. Nevertheless the girl gladly descended from the throne, and almost instantly her glance fell upon the diamond ring sparkling upon Evarne's hand.

There seems something particularly attractive to " Sweet Seventeen " about engagement rings.

" Oh, Miss Stornway," she cried, " do let me look at your ring. What a perfect beauty ! "

Evarne was pleased by this admiration.

" You ought to see it in the sunshine," she declared. " It is too lovely for words then."

She rose from the divan, and crossed over towards the window. Standing in the full flood of golden August sunlight, she held out her hand for Maudie's continued inspection. For a time she too revelled in the rainbow-hued scintillations of the diamonds, but after a few moments her glance strayed casually down the street. Immediately she broke in upon the girl's rapturous comments with a strangled little cry of mingled dismay and surprise.

" What is it ? " demanded Geoff, rising quickly to his feet.

Maudie gazed wonderingly out of the window. Suddenly

she too uttered an exclamation, then drew sharply back
behind the curtains as she announced in excited tones—

" Why, there's Lord Winborough coming down the road.
He's making straight for here. I know he's coming up.
Oh, my word, now what shall I do ? "

Jack was on the alert in a moment.

" Lord Winborough coming here ? "

" Yes, yes. Whatever am I to do ? "

" Why should you do anything ? Does it matter ? "
queried Jack, considerably puzzled.

" Matter ! " retorted the girl somewhat tartly. " Of
course it does. He knows my father quite well, and he
would be sure to tell him he had met me here. Oh, I shall
get into dad's black books, and so will auntie. What can
I do ? "

" Ask him not to say anything about it," suggested Jack
promptly.

Maudie waxed impatient.

" One can't do that sort of thing. It would only make
it seem worse. Can't I hide somewhere ? Frankie, I do
think you might have told me he was coming."

" But he wasn't expected till this afternoon. You can't
blame me," declared Pallister in expostulation.

In the midst of this fluster Evarne stood for a minute as
if stunned. Here was an entirely unforeseen *contretemps*
to be dealt with. Quite heedless of Maudie's infinitesimal
troubles, she bent all her thoughts on safeguarding her own
situation. What would be the result of this visit ? Morris
would most assuredly hold himself released from his
promise of forty-eight hours' silence if he learnt from Geoff
that the forbidden marriage was to be actually celebrated
within that time. Did Geoff intend taking his cousin into
his confidence ? She must know that. Concealing every
sign of undue anxiety she whispered—

" Are we going to tell him about to-morrow ? "

She breathed a sigh of relief at the answer.

" Not unless it becomes inevitable."

" Isn't there another way out, Mr. Danvers ? " cried the distracted Maudie.

Geoff came to the rescue.

" Why not take Miss Meridith out by the back entrance, Pallister ?   You know—out into Langthorne Place."

" He mustn't come with me," declared the girl emphatically.   " I mustn't have any of you with me.   Somebody would be certain to see us.   People one knows always are about when one doesn't want them to be."

" But you can go this way by yourself if you like," said Geoff ; and getting the necessary key, he hastened down the little passage between the plaster-room and the model's dressing-room, and unlocked and unbolted the door at the end.   Then returning he explained—

" Go down those stairs, and you'll find yourself in a corridor.   Turn to the left and go straight ahead ; take the second turning on the left again, and on the right you'll see another flight of stairs.   That is the Langthorne Place' entrance to this block of flats.   When you get into the street, turn to the right, and then the first to the right again brings you—— "

Maudie interposed plaintively.

" I forget already what you said first. I'm sure to get lost."

At this moment the electric bell rang out.

" Shall I come with you, and put you safely into a taxi ? " suggested Evarne suddenly.

This offer was accepted with alacrity.

" Oh, that is kind of you, Miss Stornway. You must think I'm a silly little baby, but—— "

Evarne did not listen.   She picked up her hat.

" I wish he had not come," she said softly to Geoff as she inserted hatpins.   " Don't let him talk about me, will you, or you may quarrel, and I should be so worried about that ? "

Here the bell rang out again—a long insistent strain.
Evarne stepped hurriedly with Maudie into the little corridor, closing the studio door after her. Geoff waited a
minute or two to allow them time to get clear away, then
admitted his cousin.

The course Evarne had thus adopted was indeed prompted
by cowardice, but it was also upheld by policy. At the
sound of Winborough's first ring, a terrible shudder of
repulsion had thrilled through her every nerve. The
necessity of again beholding that man who stood without
seemed absolutely overwhelming. She clenched her hands
violently at the remembrance of his brutal and gratuitous
insults of the previous evening. Had she the strength, the
fortitude to meet him once more and remain impassive?
She mistrusted herself. Ah, if she only dared flee before
him as Maudie was doing.

And from this desire had sprung the thought that she
would probably really safeguard her own cause by being
absent at this moment—that her presence in the studio, far
from being necessary, would be a decided additional menace
to her safety. At the present moment Morris was under a
pledge of silence concerning her; Geoff, too, had a secret
he was not anxious to divulge. Unless provoked by some
exterior event, it was more than probable that her name
would be deliberately avoided by both men. Moreover,
the presence of Jack and Pallister would further suffice to
prevent the cousins willingly introducing a subject that
was likely to lead to contention.

But were she actually in the room with them, who could
tell what might not result from so painful and awkward
a situation? A hundred unforeseen complications might
easily ensue, leading to defiance, loss of self-control, disregard of promises, betrayal! No, this precious chance
so innocently offered her by Maudie of getting out of the
place for a time was not to be neglected.

Yet no sooner had she taken the decisive step than she

half regretted her choice. After all, there had been but scant time for consideration. Was she indeed acting wisely? Sudden suspicion clamoured loudly.   Was Morris's promise to be relied on? Why had he come that morning? She hesitated, and stood still. A cold fear seized her, causing her heart to throb still more painfully. Then, regardless of what her companion might think, she very softly turned the handle of the studio door, pushed it an inch or two ajar, and stood listening.

Winborough was apparently in an amiable frame of mind. He greeted the three young men with the utmost friendliness, and after a few desultory remarks concerning the weather, proceeded to explain the reason of his unexpected arrival.

"It is not convenient for me to spare any time this afternoon, Mr. Hardy. I should prefer that you perform your operations upon me immediately, if possible."

Jack remained speechless, quite disconcerted by this unexpected demand.

"The life-mask?" queried Pallister.

"Yes. What do you say, Geoffrey?"

"Certainly. Just as you choose. Jack has got all the materials ready and waiting for this afternoon, haven't you?"

"Oh yes, indeed I have. I can do it just as well at once," assented that young man, finding his tongue.

Evarne waited to hear no more. It was with the most cordial thanksgivings that she listened to the very simple explanation of this visit that a moment ago had seemed so sinister. She sped before the sound of Jack's approaching footsteps, locking the outer door very gently with the key that Geoff had left in the lock.

The wondering and decidedly shocked Maudie was waiting patiently outside. Concealing the sick anxiety that she must feel so long as those two men were together, Evarne said cheerily—

" Just fancy, Lord Winborough is going to have his life-mask taken immediately. Mr. Pallister will be interested. He is so clever at modelling, isn't he ? I should think he would be very successful some day."

Maudie swallowed the bait, and forbearing to ask awkward questions, commenced to chatter brightly about Frankie's marvellous talents.

Thus they wended their way downstairs, and gained the street.

CHAPTER XLI

HOW "LA BELLE DAME" LED JACK ASTRAY

JACK set to work with somewhat feverish ardour to collect the necessary materials for his task. In a minute or two Pallister entered the little room.

"Can I help in any way?" he inquired.

Jack glanced up.

"Yes. You might go and get one of my clean painting-blouses from the box, and give it to Lord Winborough. He must put it on, or he will get smothered with this messy stuff."

Pallister obeyed. Shaking out the laundress's folds, he laid the clean garment insinuatingly over a chair. Then noticing that Winborough was standing surveying the charcoal outline of Maudie, he whistled softly to himself, made a grimace, and skipped rapidly back to the safety of the plaster-room. For the nonce Geoff and his cousin were left alone.

Oft-times who can tell precisely how it was, or why or whence a quarrel sprang to life? Geoff was resolved not to mention Evarne; Winborough was practically bound by honour to the same course. Yet certain it is that this one subject—religiously tabooed, yet all the time uppermost in both minds—somehow came to the front. Then a word taken amiss, a tone of the voice, a glance of the eye, and hot anger sapped the resolutions of cooler moments. In the main, both cousins held firm to their original determinations. Geoff made no mention of the imminence of his marriage; Winborough guarded his fatal secret loyally.

But despite this, their voices, raised loud in wrath, penetrated to the ears of Jack and Pallister in the plaster-room.

"Good gracious, what's up?" queried Pallister, with a startled expression. "Do you suppose Lord Winborough has found out that Maudie has been here?"

"Of course not. Can't you guess? I'll bet anything you like they're quarrelling over Geoff's engagement."

"They jolly well are quarrelling, aren't they?"

"I should just think so. I wonder what we had better do."

"Is everything ready? How very awkward. We can hardly intrude in the middle of a family debate, can we?"

They remained in doubt, listening with growing concern to the storm that was raging in the next room. In a few minutes the question of the course they were to take was settled for them. The door of the studio opening on to the little corridor was flung wide, and Winborough's voice was heard calling in curt, imperative tones—

"Mr. Hardy! Mr. Hardy!"

With a bound Jack appeared at the door of the plaster-room. Winborough's face was flushed with anger, his words were brief and final.

"Possibly I may write to you about this bust. I'll consider the matter. Good-day."

Waiting for no response, he turned and strode across the studio to the other door. There he spun round suddenly on his heel and flung a final threat at Geoff.

"As to you—well—you'll be convinced of your folly very shortly. On Thursday morning you will receive a packet of papers from my lawyer that may serve to bring you to your senses. After that, I wash my hands of you."

So saying, he left the room, and in another moment the front door had banged behind him.

"What's up," inquired Pallister with assumed innocence, entering the studio. "Where's his lordship gone to, running off just when we are ready for him?"

Geoff made no answer. He sat moodily by the table, his chin resting upon his clenched hand. He murmured a few words beneath his breath, but bestowed not the least attention upon his two companions.

Jack spoke despondently.

" I'm afraid Lord Winborough isn't going to let me do that bust after all. Didn't you hear what he said ? That possibly he would write to me. Only ' possibly.' I know those ' possiblies.' "

Pallister's countenance assumed an expression of incredulous disgust.

" Oh, I say—lost our lord ! What's the matter with him ? "

Jack remained silent, unable to answer his query. Geoff pulled himself together.

" It can't be helped," he said briefly. " Winborough and I have been expressing our candid opinion of one another, and one of the results is, as Jack surmises, that the sittings for the bust are indefinitely postponed. Where is Evarne ? Hasn't she returned yet ? "

" No, I expect she went a little way with Maudie."

" I'm glad she didn't see that brute," announced Geoff, going to the window and looking frowningly after the motorcar that was bearing his cousin swiftly down the road.

" What a fine old row," murmured Pallister. Then keen regret for the abandoned life-mask swept across his mind, and he cried impulsively : " Oh, I say, though ! What a beastly disappointment it all is. Don't you think you're a jolly nuisance, Geoff, spoiling all our arrangements so calmly ? "

Geoff turned sharply round at this piece of impertinence, but ere the angry retort had passed his lips, his eye fell upon Jack, who was sitting silently apart, both his attitude and expression betraying the uttermost dejection. Geoff crossed over and stood before his friend.

" I am sorry, Jack," he said simply.

"Don't trouble about me," was the somewhat sullen answer. "Luck is always against me—always has been—always will be, I suppose. He won't write. He was only doing it to oblige you. Of course I knew that well enough. Now I shall stick in the mud forever, I suppose. I never seem to get a chance like other fellows. Well—never mind! Don't let's talk about it any more."

Here Pallister laid his hand somewhat timidly on Geoff's arm.

"I didn't mean to vex you," he said in a very small voice.

Geoff turned his gaze from Jack for a moment. Pallister's troubled countenance touched him.

"That's all right," he said with a fleeting smile, at the same time giving a reassuring pat to the hand that lay on his arm. Then he forgot all about that youth again, and looked with worried eyes at his friend once more.

Jack was dismally wiping his fingers free from plaster. This task completed, he stood up.

"I may just as well go home," he said. "there's nothing for me to do here. I—I shall have to think about what new piece of work I can commence."

"What rubbish!" cried Geoff encouragingly, putting his hands on Jack's shoulders and giving them an affectionate squeeze. Then pushing him back into the vacated seat: "Whatever should you go home for? You can think quite as well here, you dear old duffer, and we can help you. I'm awfully sorry about Winborough, though I know that does no good, does it? But look here, Jack. I know a few other people of public interest. We'll find someone else quite as good for our purpose to fill the breach. I'll see to it for you. Now, who shall it be? What about—— "

But before he could make any suggestion Pallister interposed eagerly.

"I say, what about himself, Jackie, my boy? Since he

is going to do such a romantic story-bookish thing as marry
the most beautiful model alive, it will make him a far more
interesting person than old Winborough has been for many
a year. If you could sculpt a bust of Miss Stornway also,
so that you could exhibit the two together at the Academy
or somewhere—why, everybody would be planking down
their shilling just to see your work ; your name would be in
everybody's mouth ; orders would come rolling in ; you'd
make your reputation in a day. Now, isn't that a brilliant
idea of mine ? We're always forgetting the little fact that
Geoff really is an important person. But he is, you know,
both as the rising great artist and as a future peer."

Jack hardly waited for the conclusion of this speech
before he interposed. There was already a fresh note of
hope in his voice.

"It's perfectly true—it is indeed. Not all that talk
about orders rolling in and reputations made in a day. I
know that sort of thing doesn't happen. But what he said
about you, Geoff, was true. If you would only sit for me,
it would be every whit as helpful as if Lord Winborough
had done so. As you say, Pallister, even more valuable,
as this marriage with Miss Stornway is quite certain to
arouse interest. Will you consent ? "

The proposed victim laughed.

"I didn't bargain for this," he declared. "Perhaps,
after all, you had better go home, Jack, and do your thinking there, away from this young man and his brilliant
ideas ! "

"So even you can't deny it is a splendid solution of the
difficulty ! " declared Pallister gleefully.

Evidently Jack was of the same way of thinking. The
sullen unhappy expression had entirely vanished from his
features.

"Please do, Geoff," he said very earnestly ; and this
proved all-sufficient. His friend gave the required promise
without further hesitation.

"But I must warn you," he went on, " that I am going away—out of England—very soon indeed. It may be several months before I can sit for you. Hadn't you better choose someone else, after all ? "

But Jack was adamant.

" No indeed. But I can take a mask now, can't I ? Then with its aid I can get well forward without you. You'll let me do it at once, won't you ? Everything is ready."

" Well, I don't know, I can't stop long. I've got to get down to the City."

" But a mask is quite a short job. It can easily be finished before lunch."

This was not to be gainsaid, and the afternoon gave more than sufficient time for Geoff's other still more urgent affairs. Thus he gave in with the brief remark—

" Set to work, then."

Pallister indulged in a leap of delight.

" Now, Jack ! How do we start ? What can I do ? "

" First of all, hand Geoff that blouse, while I bring in the materials."

Pallister seized the clean holland overall, and while Geoff removed his coat and obediently arrayed himself therein, the youth sped away to lend his indispensable assistance in the plaster-room.

Soon all was ready. The long divan was drawn forward. Geoff lay down, moving his head restlessly until it was endurably at ease amid the protecting towels. Jack wrapped further cloths carefully over the fair hair, tucked yet another round his subject's neck, then set to work with cold-cream, quills and cotton wool.

" Don't forget that when you raise your left hand it means ' yes,' and your right means ' no,' " he said, as he proceeded to mix the plaster with warm water. After a moment he announced, " It's all ready now."

" Forge ahead, then," said Geoff cheerfully, as he noisily

and ostentatiously sucked in a last draught of fresh air. Then he smiled, but seeing the first spoonful of liquid plaster approaching his face, he shut his eyes quickly, composed his features, and resigned himself to fate.

After the first layer was safely on, the two strings that were required for cutting up the mask were laid in place and pressed down firmly. Then the remainder of the plaster was used. Pallister watched every stage with eager interest.

"Can you hear anything now?" he queried.

"Our voices even don't reach him unless we shout very loudly, but all the time he is hearing his own heart thud, thud, thudding. I know!"

They waited in silence until the moment should be reached when the plaster was in a fit condition for Jack to draw up the two strings and thus divide the mask. As they sat there a slight tumult was heard in the street without. It was merely a couple of dogs fighting, yet under any circumstances Pallister found it impossible to remain impervious to external excitements. In an instant he was at the window.

"Pooh! I hoped it was a mad dog, but it's only a silly fight, and now even that's over," he remarked in disgusted tones.

He was turning away, when suddenly he stopped short, bent forward, then beckoned excitedly to Jack.

"I say, Do come here! Hurry up and look. Don't you dare grumble at your luck again, for I'll eat my hat if here isn't your long-sought 'Belle Dame'! Isn't that just the red hair and pale little face you want?"

In a second Jack was by his side. His glance followed Pallister's directing finger, and he positively gasped.

"Good heavens!" he cried excitedly, staring down into the street. "It's exactly what I've been looking for! Pallister, it's like a dream!"

Undeniably the girl was uncommon—beautiful in her own curious style—individual—almost peculiar.

" But do you think she would pose for you ? It's wildly unlikely that she should just happen to be a model."

Some magnetic wave had apparently drawn the passing damsel's attention upwards towards Pallister. She saw him beckon ; saw another masculine figure appear by his side in response to the summons. She had cast down her eyes demurely enough and walked on, but at this moment she looked back, flashing a quick glance upwards over her shoulder. Seeing the two men gazing as if spellbound at her retreating figure, she smiled at them. It was a fleeting smile, wicked and subtle, narrowing her eyes and bringing alluring dimples into either cheek. Then she passed on her way.

" I'm positive she would sit for you, if you paid her enough," commented Pallister sagely. " Hi, there ! Hi !— Miss ! "

But the girl did not hear his voice.

And then Jack fell away from grace. The hand of ambition beckoned, and the faint whisperings of duty proved impotent to stay his following steps.

" I must go ; I must get her ! " he declared hoarsely, shaken from his habitual calm. " My luck will indeed turn now. I shall win everything from that picture. It will drive me mad never to paint it. Pallister, you can keep an eye on Geoff, can't you ? He's all right ; he wants nothing whatsoever but to be left alone. The mask is very nearly ready to come off now, but that's a slow job. I can't stop, can I ? Geoff won't be scared by the waiting. He's been through it before, you know. You just sit quietly by him."

" Trust me ; I'll nurse him," assented Pallister gaily. " Buck up, old chap, or she'll be gone."

But the remainder of his sentence was wasted upon the atmosphere. Jack was already bounding downstairs, every other thought excluded from his mind by the mental picture of a pale-faced girl smiling upwards over her shoulder.

" I shall succeed now ! I shall succeed ! I know it—if I can get this girl to sit ! "

Thus his innermost conviction spoke loudly as he hurried along the busy street ; yet every second the tiny voice of conscience grew more clamorous and insistent. Under such urgent stress of circumstances, surely any artist would have maintained that it was forgivable enough to have thus left Geoffrey for several minutes longer than was necessary, in what was certainly an unpleasant and possibly a dangerous situation ! But knowing Frank Pallister, would not one and all have asserted that under any pretext it was infamous that Jack should abandon his friend to so unreliable and careless—let alone totally inexperienced—an assistant ?

" I must go back. Soon—almost immediately," Jack declared within himself ; and with his mind torn in two directions, he hurried on with yet more frantic haste in pursuit of this long-desired and widely-sought model.

Meanwhile, heedless of the instructions to sit by Geoff and watch him, Pallister adopted the more interesting occupation of following the pursuit from his post of vantage at the window. He gave Jack an encouraging cheer as that young man appeared from out the house, rushed through the garden and along the road. Suddenly the watcher beheld a state of affairs that filled him with dismay. The quarry turned out of the main road and continued her journey down a side-street, while Jack, still hurrying along the crowded thoroughfare, ran straight over this crossing without so much as thinking to glance down it in his haste. He passed it by heedlessly, continuing his now vain journey onwards.

Pallister literally danced with distress.

" He will lose her—oh, the idiot ! Hi, Jack ! Jack ! Round that corner."

But Jack was much too far off to hear this shout. In an instant Pallister's mind was made up. He alone could save the situation. He made a dash towards the door.

Suddenly he remembered Geoff, and stopped his hurried rush so abruptly that he slid several yards on the polished boards. But Frank Pallister, Esq., that youth of energy and enterprise, was not easily to be baulked when one of his brilliant ideas was on hand. He sped hastily back to the couch.

" Hullo, Geoff ! I say, Geoff ! You all right ? "

The left hand of the prostrate figure was immediately raised in token of assent. With his mind now perfectly at ease, Pallister darted downstairs. He was in a glow of self-appreciation. What resource he showed in all emergencies ! What a truly valuable all-round friend he was, to be sure !

CHAPTER XLII

THE *Coup de Grâce*

THEN for a brief space of time the studio remained deserted, save for the prostrate figure lying motionless upon the couch. A big blue-bottle fly buzzed around the open window, flinging itself at intervals noisily against the glass. From the street without arose the low hum of passing traffic. Otherwise a dull, peaceful silence held sway.

But in the adjoining chamber sat one from whom all peace was far remote. Even as Pallister had darted down the front stairs, Evarne had entered from Langthorne Place and gained the plaster-room. An irresistible force had drawn her back to the vicinity of her lover and her enemy ; but still unwilling to make her presence known to them, she had crept softly into the one little room to which access was possible without entering the studio.

As she sat there waiting—waiting for she knew not what —every nerve in her body thrilled painfully. Restless nights and lack of food had rendered her unfitted to cope with the continuous train of cruel, tearing emotions that had fallen to her lot that morning. The gnawing anxiety of the last half-hour had been nigh unendurable. A very few seconds of this further suspense, this acute nerve-strain, and she uttered an audible groan, forced from her lips by both mental and physical distress.

Startled by the sound, she tried to turn her thoughts from the present to all that was most bright in the future.

" So—we are to be married to-morrow. Oh, Geoff, Geoff, my darling ! "

But anxiety and apprehension beset her too closely to be avoided. Close upon this blissful reflection followed another.

" Then—after that—not only my dear one's happiness, but my life—my very life—depend upon that vile creature here, to whom nothing is sacred. Am I doing right by Geoff ? Oh, if I could only rid myself of these doubts ! "

She sighed and twisted her hands together. Then composed herself to thought once more.

" But my mind was fully convinced, my conscience upheld me surely enough until Morris came. Would to Heaven the vessel that brought him to England had sunk to the bottom of the sea, and that he lay silenced forever beneath the waters."

Again she sighed. Again she thought.

" Ah me ! If these were but the times when witches reigned, gladly would I sell my very soul to the powers of evil in return for a charm—a spell—to ensure that man's eternal silence."

Under the stress of such desperate desires, she found it impossible to remain quietly seated. Rising, she moved restlessly and without object to and fro from end to end of the little room. Suddenly she noticed that her dress had brushed against the table, and become slightly soiled with plaster. It was but a trifling matter, but as she shook and brushed it clean again, a sudden hot anger burned in her veins.

" It is outrageous ! " she said fiercely within herself— " outrageous, that I should be thus forced to hide, with fear and trembling, in back rooms ! Oh, how I hate that man ! How he degrades me ! How he has cursed my life ! From the very first hour we met he has dragged me steadily downwards, and now—now—he is going to use his own sin to damn all the remainder of my life !

" Promises—what does that word mean to Morris Kenyon ? Did he not promise my father to watch over me—to guard me—and how did he keep his word ? And what promises did he not make to me—oh, again and again !—in what tender, earnest tones ; and then—liar, liar ! Morris talking morality to me ! What right has he to do that ? What about himself ? What injustice, what evil, equals that of a man—middle-aged, wise in the world, strong, clever—using every advantage to win a young girl, and then—then—pretending that, even in his eyes, his own success renders the girl, not himself, infamous for ever ? "

She clenched her hands violently. The bright colour that had flooded her cheeks mounted to her temples.

" I hate him—I loathe him ! But, Heaven, how I fear him ! If he should—oh, if he dares ! If he only dares, I'll—I'll . . ."

In the heat of this sudden but enduring paroxysm of anger she lost the power of further thought. Her throat swelled, and before she could control herself she had given utterance to a series of half-sobbing, half-moaning cries of misery and baffled rage. Frantically she pressed both hands with desperate energy across her lips. She had but little self-control left ; only by physical force could she possibly stay those cries of fear and anguish.

Then she stood motionless, glued to the spot by apprehension. Surely the men in the next room must have heard that wild lamentation ? She strained her ears for the sound of footsteps. Her breast shook with the convulsive pantings of rage that is forced to subdue itself. Every throb of her heart came as a sharp pang.

No sound—no sound whatsoever. Suddenly she reeled against the table, clutching it at for support. A terrible idea—a conviction—had now assailed her. Morris was doubtless even at this moment telling her secret to his cousin. Ah—she knew ! A whispered conversation was going on in that strangely silent studio. Once again she was being cruelly betrayed by that man. This was surely more than flesh and blood could be called upon to endure.

In an instant all the tigress in her nature sprang eager and palpitating to the fore. Without a moment's hesitation she rushed wildly into the passage, and flung open the door of the studio.

On the threshold she stopped short in amazement. Solitude, save for the prostrate form upon the couch.

"Wherever are Geoff and Mr. Hardy and Pallister? Where can they have gone, to leave Morris alone in this manner?"

Even in the midst of her excitement, a plausible reason for the absence of at least one of the trio suggested itself.

"Oh, of course, Geoff had doubtless gone down to Doctors Commons to get that licence."

Then, shaken by a fresh access of indignation:

"And because of this vile creature here it may prove futile—a mere piece of waste paper! Or it may turn out to be really my death-warrant. Oh, my God, I cannot endure to look at him—to be beneath the same roof!"

And then, such are the powers of imagination, that, believing the man who lay before her to be him whom she had such ample cause to fear and hate, she instinctively knit her brows and drew a sharp breath audibly between her teeth, huddling her hands together on her chest with an actual shudder of repulsion.

And verily, even Love's penetration could scarce be blamed for not here discerning the truth. Even had Evarne been told to distinguish between her lover and her enemy under such conditions, the task would have bordered upon the impossible. With face and head completely covered, with hands strangely identical, with height and build so similar, and yet further disguised by an all-concealing painting-blouse, the most loving eye might easily have blundered.

But Evarne did not doubt—did not question. The very last words she had heard spoken in that studio were to the effect that Morris had come on purpose to submit himself to this operation. What room, then, was there for suspicion regarding the identity of this man whose face was concealed with the plaster mask? Upon the first glance she averted her eyes, standing trembling. After a minute of enduring this agony of repulsion she spoke aloud—unconsciously aloud—quite softly to herself. Her voice, though low, was curiously discordant and hoarse, pulsating with the powerful emotions that were so rapidly proving more than she could bear.

"Oh, it's wicked—it's cruel—it's unjust! He will tell everything after I'm married. He will glory in it. I know him. He is a devil incarnate! What have we done, Geoff and I, that we should be tortured here on earth? Oh, what can I do to save us both—what can I do? To be so helpless—to be driven utterly helpless into a corner like this—oh, I can't—I can't endure it! What am I to do? Tell me—tell me! I want help—help of any kind. Is there nothing Here or There can hear and help me?"

Her voice faded away. She stood, turning her head from side to side, looking around wildly. Her brow contracted itself into deeper furrows. In the silence she unconsciously bit at her finger-nails, tearing one down to the quick—yet she felt no pain.

Quite suddenly there awoke in her memory an almost obliterated recollection. Loudly and wrathfully she cried—

"Sekhet—you have failed me—you have forsaken me! I prayed to you once. Now you must answer my prayer, for I invoke you. You are great now as ever. I demand your help—demand it! How can I ensure that man's eternal silence? Tell me—tell me!"

She stood for a moment with trembling forefinger outstretched, indicating the motionless form upon the divan. Did she expect some mystic voice to respond to her appeal?

No sound broke the silence, save the fly which hummed and buzzed and flung itself with blind unavailing endeavour against the window-panes.

But into her brain—that poor brain so tortured and goaded by cruel anxiety, by a bitter insult, by a great, passionate love threatened with destruction—sprang the instinctive thought of that primæval resource :

"Death ! Death ! Only death can bring eternal silence ! "

Swiftly, yet very surely, a strange, unfamiliar influence had enwrapped this rebel against Fate. Who can declare authoritatively what supreme Power behind the Veil she had not summoned in that moment's distraught and reckless invocation ? Be that as it may, she became obsessed by one of those all-mighty, dominating impulses that conquer the will, the judgment, even the desire ; that crush down previously accepted ideas of right and wrong, forcing a fresh, oft-times dreaded, idea masterfully into a shrinking heart and mind.

And the message that had come to Evarne was terrible—terrific !

" Call Death to your aid ! Kill your enemy ! Kill him while there is yet time ! "

Even through the passion of rage that shook her, she felt a momentary subduing chill of horror. She pressed her hands to either cheek, and with strained features, parted lips and staring, dilated eyes, gazed wildly into vacancy.

But this horrible inspiration was as a white light suddenly illuminating the dense dark path along which she had been groping. She laughed—a low laugh—terrible, for there was no ring of mirth therein.

" It is only justice—justice—justice—justice ! " she cried, her voice rising upon every word. " He is the devil's emissary. The world will be well rid of him. It is justice—justice—justice ! ' '

She had no more consecutive thoughts, no more reflection, no more hesitation. But one word rang in her mind. Justice! Justice! Justice! She rushed across the room with wild haste, and seized upon Andromache's golden fetter that lay upon a chair. With anger, fiery indignation and hatred, terror and mad love raging within her brain, all other emotions were effectively excluded. Pity, caution, lawfulness, fear of consequences—none of these found any place within her spirit in that dreadful hour. If the souls of the dead can verily watch over those they loved in life, broken indeed must be their heavenly peace and happiness. Rather they must be oft-times in hell.

Softly she fastened one fetter around a strong portion of the openwork carved wooden back of the couch; then, without a moment's warning, the handcuff at the other end of the chain was snapped round the nearest wrist of the prostrate figure. Futile was the immediate startled effort of the death-doomed man to rise. In an instant Evarne had dragged away those two quills through which was drawn the breath of life, and had pressed the still slightly unset plaster over the tiny holes. Then sinking on her knees, she seized her victim's remaining arm, clutching it to her breast with a desperate vigour.

Her eyes were convulsively shut, her lips parted over clenched teeth, as for what seemed an interminable period she was flung to and fro by the frenzied struggles of the strong arm she held captive. But gradually her task grew easier. Very soon that dire deed had taken its place amid the record of things done.

Cautiously she slackened her grasp. The arm, released, drooped heavily downwards from its shoulder, the hand resting inertly upon the floor. Evarne rose to her feet. Unfastening both ends of the golden fetter, she flung it back upon the chair, then left the studio without another glance at the twisted, distorted form of that dead man whose lips would speak no more words, either of devotion or of malice.

Deliberately she washed the plaster from her fingers. Her glance was firm and high, her bearing resolute and undaunted. Yet, as she dried her hands, she suddenly paused, and, leaning heavily on the edge of the little sink, uttered a long, trembling sigh such as can well up only from a cruelly over-burdened heart—a low, piteous moan—a stifled wail of despair.

"Oh, Geoff, Geoff! What am I? What have I become for your sake?"

She went out again into Langthorne Place and walked away. Only about five minutes had passed since she trod that pavement before, yet now . . . ? Her pulses throbbed wildly, but she was assailed by no regret, no trace of self-reproach. She was appalled by, yet exalted in, her desperate deed. She was triumphant. She had conquered!

.   .   .   .

Jack, hastily returning, almost collided with Pallister, who issued from the side-street.

"So we've lost your unique 'Belle Dame,' worse luck to us! And a precious couple we must look out here, with no hats, and smeared painting-blouses and . . . "

But the remaining words died away at the sight of Jack's expression of undisguised alarm.

"Pallister! You surely haven't left Geoff alone! How infamous! Oh, how could you?"

Without waiting for any answer he darted across the road and ran with all speed for the studio.

"It doesn't matter," declared Pallister, somewhat subdued, hurrying after him. "He's all right. What's the trouble?"

"Oh, don't speak to me! How could you leave him?" was the sole response.

"Well, you seem to forget you did it yourself, if it's such a crime," Pallister replied tartly.

' More blame to me! But I left him in your charge;

you left him alone—surely that makes all the difference.
Good gracious, though—whatever possessed me? You're
as irresponsible as a child, and I knew it—I knew
it!"

He turned into the garden, and in a minute was bounding
upstairs, closely followed by the indignant Pallister.

.   .   .   .

A quarter of an hour later, Evarne, pale yet supremely
beautiful in her blush-rose gown, in her turn mounted the
stairs. As she came in sight of the front door of the flat
she saw that it stood wide open. From it was wafted
faintly a piteous sound of sobbing and wailing.

"I suppose some will mourn Morris. I did not remember that," she reflected, as she entered and closed the front
door behind her. Then, making her way across the hall to
the studio, she went in, inquiring in splendidly feigned
surprise and alarm, "What is the matter? What has
happened?"

Poor Pallister was lying prostrate on the floor near the
window, his hands, flung over his head, convulsively grasping great masses of fur that he had torn from the bear-
skin rug by which he lay. His whole body was writhing
beneath choking, rending sobs. From him, Evarne slowly
turned her gaze on Jack, who was seated near the couch.
He, too, was shaking violently from head to foot; but as
regards fixity of expression, hue and voluntary action, he
might have been a figure of despair cut from marble.

A sudden pain darted through Evarne's brow. Un-
nerved by the display of such unexpected and unrestrained
emotion, she was forced to lean against the side of the
doorway for support, while her white face grew paler still.

"What—oh, I—what?"

None responded to her incoherent words. A cold chill
encircled her. In the hot studio she shivered as in wintry
weather.

"What has happened to Lord Winborough? Oh—

where's Geoff? I want him quickly. I must see him, I tell you. Where is he?"

Jack rose from his chair.

"Go away—go away!" he breathed. "I—I can't—you mustn't know. Go away!"

Evarne was fast losing her forced calmness. She was assailed by a desperate longing to gain new courage from the ever-tender eyes of the man who loved her.

"I will go! I want to! I'm frightened here! But where is Geoff? Tell me, Jack—tell me! Send for him!"

"Geoff! Geoff!" wailed Pallister.

Evarne gave a violent start, and without moving from the doorway against which she was leaning, she bent her body forward in Pallister's direction.

"Why do you also call for him?" she queried.

The only response was a farther lament.

"Geoff, come back! Oh, Geoff, how could I leave you?"

Still bending forward, she swayed round towards Jack. Then her reluctant glance wandered from him to the form upon the couch. The mask had been removed, exposing a terrible face beneath, distorted somewhat, disfigured with fearsome livid patches and blue swollen lips. Around the mouth and nose clung mucus froth.

Evarne choked, struggling with sickness; but suddenly she sprang forward and seized Jack by the shoulders with unnatural strength.

"If you don't tell me where Geoff is, I'll—I'll——"

The menacing tones ceased abruptly, as Jack put out his shaking hands and grasped her wrists.

"I see you must be told. Well, then—this is it! He took his cousin's place, Evarne, and we—we left him alone —and—and something happened!"

For one long minute absolute silence reigned within the room. Pallister ceased sobbing and held his breath. Evarne did not speak, but stared at Jack with unwinking

gaze. He saw a fearsome change steal over her face.
Every feature seemed to alter, to be transformed under his
very eyes, becoming unrecognisable—horrible! Without
warning, she pushed him violently away, and with a few
rapid steps was by the side of the dead man. She laid her
hand upon the fair hair.

" So it is you I have killed, Geoff ! " she said, quietly
enough.

" God in Heaven, what ? " shouted Jack at the top of
his voice.

Evarne did not speak, but suddenly plunging her hands
through her damp hair she began to scream—wild, piercing
shrieks that chilled the blood of those who heard. Nothing could stay her—until her voice gave way. Still she
screamed on spasmodically, producing merely horrible and
discordant sounds.

Loud shouts arose from the street. A policeman's
shrill whistle blew frantically again and again.

And then Evarne commenced to laugh, a hoarse, de-
risive gurgle.

" Do you hear that laughter ? " she cried huskily. " It
is Morris Kenyon. It is funny for him, isn't it ? And
it's—yes—I see—that cat-faced goddess—Sekhet ! So you
all think the game is played out, do you ? We'll see."

She clasped her arms around the dead form, pressing it
tightly to her breast. She laid her cheek to Geoff's, and
so rose with her white, distorted face besmeared and sullied.

Now loud continuous blows were resounding on the outer
door. The electric bell rang forth unintermittently.

With swaying steps Evarne crossed the room. Pallister
instinctively shrank back as the terrible spectacle advanced in his direction. At this a pair of bloodshot eyes
were turned upon him, while a strained voice whispered
calmly enough—

" Avoid Sekhet—tell everyone what I said. Never,
never love too much. It is always dreadful in some way—

always! Sooner or later—always! I must go now and tell Geoff everything myself."

Then, ere they could realise what was next to happen, she had put one knee on the window-sill and flung up her arms wildly. Instinctively both men rushed forward, but, happily, too late!

In another instant a broken mass lay peacefully unconscious forever upon the green bosom of Earth—our Mother.